Preparing for the Certified OpenStack Administrator Exam

A complete guide for developers taking tests conducted by the OpenStack Foundation

Matt Dorn

BIRMINGHAM - MUMBAI

Preparing for the Certified OpenStack Administrator Exam

First published: August 2017

Production reference: 1220817

Published by Packt Publishing Ltd.
Livery Place
35 Livery Street
Birmingham
B3 2PB, UK.

ISBN 978-1-78728-841-6

www.packtpub.com

Credits

Author
Matt Dorn

Reviewer
James Denton

Commissioning Editor
Kartikey Pandey

Acquisition Editor
Prateek Bharadwaj

Content Development Editor
Sharon Raj

Technical Editor
Mohit Hassija

Copy Editor
Stuti Srivastava

Project Coordinator
Virginia Dias

Proofreader
Safis Editing

Indexer
Aishwarya Gangawane

Graphics
Kirk D'Penha

Production Coordinator
Aparna Bhagat

About the Author

Matt Dorn is a senior technical instructor who has previously served in IT leadership roles and has helped hundreds of teams around the world build private clouds with OpenStack. He understands that many feel a great deal of intimidation when approaching open source projects and is fanatical about providing an easy-to-understand learning path that makes OpenStack accessible and fun.

Special thanks to the OpenStack community for becoming an incredible testament to the power of the well-organized. Thanks to Oliver from Flaticon for the icons used in many of the images in this book.

About the Reviewer

James Denton has more than 17 years of experience in systems administration and networking and has been deploying, operating, and maintaining OpenStack clouds since late 2012. He is a principal architect at Rackspace, and prior to joining the Rackspace Private Cloud team, he spent 5 years as an enterprise network security engineer. James has a bachelor's degree of business administration and management with a focus on computer information systems from Texas State University in San Marcos, Texas. He is the author of *Learning OpenStack Networking* by *Packt*, first and second editions, as well as *OpenStack Networking Essentials* by *Packt*, and can be found on Twitter at `@jimmdenton`.

> *I'd like to thank Matt Dorn for providing me the opportunity to review this book and to everyone at Rackspace, NASA, and the OpenStack community for building such a great platform.*

www.PacktPub.com

For support files and downloads related to your book, please visit www.PacktPub.com. Did you know that Packt offers eBook versions of every book published, with PDF and ePub files available? You can upgrade to the eBook version at www.PacktPub.com and as a print book customer, you are entitled to a discount on the eBook copy. Get in touch with us at service@packtpub.com for more details. At www.PacktPub.com, you can also read a collection of free technical articles, sign up for a range of free newsletters and receive exclusive discounts and offers on Packt books and eBooks.

https://www.packtpub.com/mapt

Get the most in-demand software skills with Mapt. Mapt gives you full access to all Packt books and video courses, as well as industry-leading tools to help you plan your personal development and advance your career.

Why subscribe?

- Fully searchable across every book published by Packt
- Copy and paste, print, and bookmark content
- On demand and accessible via a web browser

Customer Feedback

Thanks for purchasing this Packt book. At Packt, quality is at the heart of our editorial process. To help us improve, please leave us an honest review on this book's Amazon page at `https://www.amazon.com/dp/1787288412`.

If you'd like to join our team of regular reviewers, you can email us at `customerreviews@packtpub.com`. We award our regular reviewers with free eBooks and videos in exchange for their valuable feedback. Help us be relentless in improving our products!

Table of Contents

Preface

Preparing for the Certified OpenStack Administrator Exam provides you with a specific strategy to pass the OpenStack Foundation's first professional certification: the Certified OpenStack Administrator. In a recent survey, 78 percent of respondents said the shortage of OpenStack skills had deterred them from adopting an OpenStack cloud. Consider this an opportunity to increase employer and customer confidence by proving you have the skills required to administrate real-world OpenStack clouds.

What this book covers

Chapter 1, *Introducing OpenStack and the Certified OpenStack Administrator Exam*, takes you through a journey of the history of cloud computing and provides an introduction to OpenStack. You'll also learn about the exam and explore the seven steps to becoming an official Certified OpenStack Administrator.

Chapter 2, *Setting Up Your Practice Exam Environment*, provides instructions on setting up the virtual appliance included with this book. The appliance gives you a working OpenStack environment that can easily be deployed on your laptop or desktop and is great for working through exam objectives.

Chapter 3, *Keystone Identity Service*, introduces Keystone and all Keystone-related exam objectives, including creating and modifying domains, groups, projects, users, roles, services, endpoints, and quotas.

Chapter 4, *Glance Image Service*, defines cloud images and Glance exam objectives, including uploading and downloading cloud images, sharing images with specific projects, and utilizing metadata definitions.

Chapter 5, *Nova Compute Service*, explores Nova compute and covers exam objectives, including launching Nova instances, getting console access to booted instances, defining flavors, managing key pairs, and creating instance snapshots.

Chapter 6, *Neutron Networking Service*, dives into the world of OpenStack networking by providing an overview of Neutron and covers exam objectives including managing tenant and provider networks, subnets, security groups, routers, and floating IPs.

Chapter 7, *Cinder Block-Storage Service*, explains Cinder persistent block storage and exam objectives including creating volumes, attach/detaching volumes, volume snapshots, and creating volume types.

Chapter 8, *Swift Object-Storage Service*, discusses the birth of AWS S3, Swift object storage, and exam objectives, including setting Access Control Lists (ACLs) on containers and setting objectives to expire at specific times.

Chapter 9, *Heat Orchestration Service*, explains OpenStack Heat and exam objectives including creating and updating stacks.

Chapter 10, *Troubleshooting*, shows you how to perform debugging on the OpenStack CLI, manage OpenStack daemons, analyze OpenStack log files, and perform basic operations on an OpenStack database.

Chapter 11, *Final Tips and Tricks*, gives you some useful tips and tricks to keep in mind before taking the COA exam.

Chapter 12, *Practice Exam*, is a mock COA exam that you can use to put your OpenStack skills to test!

What you need for this book

Please download all materials from the official book repository at `https://github.com/PacktPublishing/Preparing-for-the-Certified-OpenStack-Administrator-Exam`. The repository also contains an OpenStack virtual appliance that can be imported into VirtualBox to perform all exam objective exercises.

Who this book is for

This book targets IT professionals, system administrators, DevOps engineers, and software developers with basic Linux command line and networking knowledge.

Conventions

In this book, you will find a number of text styles that distinguish between different kinds of information. Here are some examples of these styles and an explanation of their meaning.

Code words in text, database table names, Linux programs, folder names, filenames, file extensions, pathnames, dummy URLs, user input, and Twitter handles are shown as follows: "You can fulfill majority of the exam objectives with `python-openstackclient`."

A block of code is set as follows:

```
export OS_AUTH_URL=http://192.168.56.56:5000/v3
export OS_REGION_NAME=RegionOne
export OS_PROJECT_DOMAIN_NAME=default
export OS_USER_DOMAIN_NAME=default
export OS_USERNAME=admin
export OS_PASSWORD=admin
export OS_PROJECT_NAME=logistics
export OS_TENANT_NAME=logistics
```

Any command-line input or output is written as follows:

```
$ openstack help
```

New terms and **important words** are shown in bold. Words that you see on the screen, for example, in menus or dialog boxes, appear in the text like this: "From the VirtualBox menu bar, select **Preferences.**"

Warnings or important notes appear in a box like this.

Tips and tricks appear like this.

Reader feedback

Feedback from our readers is always welcome. Let us know what you think about this book-what you liked or disliked. Reader feedback is important for us as it helps us develop titles that you will really get the most out of.

To send us general feedback, simply e-mail `feedback@packtpub.com`, and mention the book's title in the subject of your message.

If there is a topic that you have expertise in and you are interested in either writing or contributing to a book, see our author guide at `www.packtpub.com/authors`.

Customer support

Now that you are the proud owner of a Packt book, we have a number of things to help you to get the most from your purchase.

Downloading the color images of this book

We also provide you with a PDF file that has color images of the screenshots/diagrams used in this book. The color images will help you better understand the changes in the output. You can download this file from `https://www.packtpub.com/sites/default/files/downloads/PreparingfortheCertifiedOpenStackAdministratorExam_ColorImages.pdf`.

Errata

Although we have taken every care to ensure the accuracy of our content, mistakes do happen. If you find a mistake in one of our books-maybe a mistake in the text or the code-we would be grateful if you could report this to us. By doing so, you can save other readers from frustration and help us improve subsequent versions of this book. If you find any errata, please report them by visiting `http://www.packtpub.com/submit-errata`, selecting your book, clicking on the **Errata Submission Form** link, and entering the details of your errata. Once your errata are verified, your submission will be accepted and the errata will be uploaded to our website or added to any list of existing errata under the Errata section of that title.

To view the previously submitted errata, go to `https://www.packtpub.com/books/content/support` and enter the name of the book in the search field. The required information will appear under the **Errata** section.

Piracy

Piracy of copyrighted material on the Internet is an ongoing problem across all media. At Packt, we take the protection of our copyright and licenses very seriously. If you come across any illegal copies of our works in any form on the Internet, please provide us with the location address or website name immediately so that we can pursue a remedy.

Please contact us at copyright@packtpub.com with a link to the suspected pirated material.

We appreciate your help in protecting our authors and our ability to bring you valuable content.

Questions

If you have a problem with any aspect of this book, you can contact us at questions@packtpub.com, and we will do our best to address the problem.

1
Introducing OpenStack and the Certified OpenStack Administrator Exam

> ## World Wide Web
>
> The WorldWideWeb (W3) is a wide-area hypermedia information retrieval initiative aiming to give universal access to a large universe of documents.

The snippet above is from a web page. It appears unremarkable upon first glance. It contains no graphics, sound, JavaScript, or CSS. A plain, stark white background, some simple text, and a few hyperlinks.

The page existed as a single HTML file, hosted on a 25 MHz NeXTcube workstation. The machine boasted 8 MB of memory and a 17-inch monochrome monitor. The 1-foot-on-all-sides metal cube-shaped system sat on the floor of a small office, the colorful NeXT logo affixed near its metal power button.

This computer was not hosted in a data center, but in a small office at the European Organization for Nuclear Research, a.k.a. CERN. Straddling the French-Swiss border. CERN's expansive campus is currently home to the Large Hadron Collider, the world's largest particle accelerator. But in 1991, something much larger than the collider lurked in Tim Berners-Lee's Building 31 office.

This web page was the first *Hello World* of the internet. The birthplace of modern communication. And although in 1991 it would have been unlikely to find anyone with internet access (let alone a computer that could support it), it's difficult to believe how far we've come. Little did Berners-Lee know that a fundamental shift in human communication would rapidly evolve over the next 25 years.

Today's business environment moves faster than ever. Online companies such as Amazon, Netflix, and Uber have completely changed the way the world does business. To stay competitive, enterprises must be able to provide desktop and mobile applications that deliver cutting-edge, secure, and self-service capabilities directly to the customer. Although we need skillful software developers to provide these applications, it's extremely difficult to be agile in corporate environments with overly bureaucratic IT policies and outdated software.

OpenStack is the answer to this lack of agility. It is an open source cloud operating system that has revolutionized computing and provides true power to developers. The Certified OpenStack Administrator Exam is your opportunity to learn the skills required to operate OpenStack clouds, and like Berner-Lee's first website, spark a transformation—one that will facilitate the development, deployment, and management of today's most critical applications.

In this chapter, we will cover the following topics:

- A brief history of the cloud
- An overview of OpenStack
- The Certified OpenStack Administrator exam
- Seven steps to becoming a Certified OpenStack Administrator

After this chapter, you will be ready to set up your very own OpenStack testing environment and begin working through the objectives covered in the following chapters.

A brief history of the cloud

It's impossible to go anywhere these days without hearing about cloud computing. If you currently work in the technology world, I'm sure you've been at a gathering with family or friends when someone finally asks you, "so... what IS the cloud?" Even to the most technically savvy, it is a difficult question to answer. "Cloud" is often used as a buzzword, describing computing or storage infrastructure that can be accessed by many users from any location. To provide the right context, let's take a moment to dive into a brief history of the cloud. If you've heard this story before, feel free to skip ahead!

The plight of the software developer

The application. Whether we are swiping through colorful icons on our smartphone home screens or logging on to our laptop's operating system, the app is everywhere. In fact, the term is used so frequently that it's difficult to give *app* a proper definition.

So, rather than attempt to define what apps are, we can surely define what they do: solve problems. Apps can provide solutions to some of our most critical business headaches, saving and making money for organizations (and individuals). But more importantly, they often present users with unrealized needs. Think about how many people consider Twitter, Facebook, and LinkedIn on their smartphone to be a necessity to their daily lives.

We typically call the minds behind applications **software developers**. But life for the software developer wasn't so easy 20 years ago. A developer would hack away on their home or office desktop, perfecting and testing their code into the late hours of the night. When the time for them to share their work with the world, they would need a physical computing device with CPU, disk, and memory. The computer would likely require internet access so it could reach a greater population. And in order to make that happen, a software developer would typically rely on a group of system engineers to call up a hardware vendor and get this machine shipped to the office or data center.

After going through the grueling process of getting the machine unboxed, racked, stacked, and wired up, system engineers would then need to configure the operating system, install the necessary programs and frameworks, and ensure the software developer could connect to the machine from their desktop. Consider some of the technical practices at this time: high availability and fault tolerance, although widely discussed, were not commonly enforced.

Once the servers were ready to go, the software developer would share their masterpiece, placing it on the provided infrastructure. As users accessed the application, all would be great... until the app was no longer accessible. Suddenly, the software developer's phone would ring in the middle of the night. System engineers would struggle to fix hardware failures, thus bringing down the application and facing many angry end users. This required trips to the data center—which itself needed disaster recovery plans in case of a fire, flood, or storm. And how about if the application had a spike of major success? If tons of users rushed to type the URL into their browsers and navigate to the site, resources on existing hardware could be overloaded. The system engineers would need to purchase and install additional servers, firewalls, and load balancers to provide more resources for the additional traffic. All of these potential hazards could be a headache for everyone involved—especially a software developer whose focus should stay on the application itself.

The birth of enterprise virtualization

November 10, 2003: A group of IT executives in dresses, business suits, and blazers stood around a boardroom, watching a screen projecting a video clip of *Terminator II: Judgement Day*. "Are you ready?" said one of the men standing at a podium. On the bottom right of the screen, a small box of a few Microsoft Windows control panels displayed icons representing running servers.

These servers were virtual machines, and the video clip the room was watching was being played from a file server on one of these virtual machines. Suddenly, the host clicked on a few context menus on the virtual machine and a progress bar appeared. The video continued to play as the T-1000 Advanced Prototype morphed from liquid metal into human form, chasing John Connor in a burning police car. The room exploded with hoots, hollers, and cheers—and it wasn't because of the Terminator. This was a demo of a technology called VMotion, which would revolutionize the IT operations world for years to come.

Although virtualization had been around out since the 1960s, VMware can certainly be credited for bringing it to the masses in their official release of *VMware VirtualCenter featuring VMotion*. VMotion allowed system engineers to convert their existing physical machines to hypervisors, enabling the running of virtual machines. It also kept those virtual machines up by live-migrating them to another hypervisor in the event of an underlying hardware problem. This was done by transferring the virtual machine's active memory and execution state over the network.

Software developers and system engineers alike were overjoyed with the technology, knowing they would now sleep quite well while their application hummed along regardless of hardware headaches. The software developers continued to develop their incredible applications, but their development methodology remained the same. They were still developing their application as if they were on traditional physical machines!

Gartner, the information technology research and advisor company, has labeled this type of environment Mode 1, otherwise known as **enterprise virtualization**. In fact, enterprise virtualization still exists today and is the most adopted type of the cloud by enterprises around the world. See *Figure 1.1*.

Enterprise Virtualization (Mode 1)	Elastic Cloud (Mode 2)
GUI-emphasized	API-emphasized
Expensive Hardware	Standard Hardware
Vertical Scaling	Horizontal Scaling
Proprietary	Open Source
Traditional Software Development	Cloudy Development

Figure 1.1: Enterprise Virtualization (Mode 1) versus Elastic Cloud (Mode 2)

Here are some common characteristics of the enterprise virtualization cloud:

- **GUI-emphasized**: When one creates a new virtual machine in this model, they typically do so via a **Graphical User Interface (GUI)**. This may be something like vSphere Web Client or Hyper-V Manager. Command-line tools may exist but are less popular with a majority of its operators.
- **Expensive hardware**: Enterprises that buy into enterprise cloud also buy into expensive blade servers, SANs, network/fabric switches, component redundancy, and high-cost, boutique super microcomputers—specialized hardware with a high price tag.
- **Vertical scaling**: If your application begins getting more traffic, the ability to scale will be necessary. In the enterprise virtualization world, this means assigning more resources to virtual machines powering the application. When one scales up or vertically, they go about this by adding more CPU, RAM, or disk space to the individual virtual machines. This is the opposite philosophy to scaling horizontally.

- **Proprietary**: The infrastructure code in this model is closed source. This includes software such as *VMware VCenter* powered by Microsoft Windows Server. If a bug is discovered while working with the software, it must be filed with the vendor. Because one monolithic organization controls access to the code, bug fixes can take weeks or months to be patched.
- **Traditional software development**: In an Enterprise Virtualization cloud, the software developer continues to develop the applications in the same manner they developed applications on physical machines. This is sometimes referred to as the *monolithic* approach. Although the web server or database may reside on different virtual machines, the application's functions are combined into a single program from a single platform. This differs drastically from the cloudy development approach explained in the next section.

Amazon - not just a place for books

In March of 2006, Michael Arrington—founder of Silicon Valley news blog *TechCrunch*—had an exciting announcement:

Amazon Web Service is launching a new web service tonight called S3 – which stands for "Simple Storage Service". It is a storage service backend for developers that offers "a highly scalable, reliable, and low-latency data storage infrastructure at very low costs... This is game changing."

Arrington was right. At this time, Amazon Web Services had yet to release the catalog of services we all know today. **Simple Storage Service (S3)** provided users with the ability to create an account, enter their credit card number, and have access to upload files to AWS's hosted infrastructure within seconds. One benefit stood out above all: unlimited storage space.

At the time, hosting companies offered **virtual private servers (VPS),** allowing one to rent a server and use it for backup or file storage. The problems with these solutions was the space limitation on a particular server, not to mention the responsibility of the customer to maintain the health and security of the operating system. While a VPS may have charged users with monthly or yearly flat rates, S3 billed the user for what they used, much like a household electricity bill. The software developer now had the power to avoid the purchase of additional physical servers and storage arrays.

In 2006, there was one surprise left from AWS. On August 25, 2006, Jeff Bar, Chief Evangelist at AWS, announced the launch of **Elastic Compute Cloud (EC2)**:

"Amazon EC2 gives you access to a virtual computing environment. Your applications run on a "virtual CPU", the equivalent of a 1.7 GHz Xeon processor, 1.75 GB of RAM, 160 GB of local disk and 250 Mb/second of network bandwidth. You pay just 10 cents per clock hour (billed to your Amazon Web Services account), and you can get as many virtual CPUs as you need."

This post was the shot heard 'round the IT operations world. Not only could the software developer have access to unlimited storage space with S3, but create as many virtual machines as they wanted. A college student in their dorm now had access to the data centers, bandwidth, and computing power of large-scale enterprises. It was the competitive advantage they needed. This truly provided power to developers. They would quickly scale their application during times of success (with a few clicks of a button) and quickly handle failure elegantly if anything went wrong.

Gartner labeled this type of cloud Mode 2, otherwise known as **elastic cloud**. See *Figure 1.1*.

Here are some common characteristics of the elastic cloud:

- **API emphasized**: Both AWS S3 and EC2 offered **Simple Object Access Protocol (SOAP)** and **Representational State Transfer (REST)** APIs at the time of launch. The power of the API is the ability for a developer to easily incorporate these web services into their web application software logic. Visualize a website allowing users to upload and share photos. The developers creating the web application could make API calls to S3 whenever a user uploads or downloads a photo, thus ensuring all the users' uploaded photos were stored in AWS's S3 infrastructure. Although the SOAP API was deprecated by AWS in December 2015, the much more elegant REST API allows browsers to easily communicate with GET, PUT, POST, HEAD, and DELETE methods over the protocol that powers the web: HTTP.
- **Standard hardware**: Werner Vogels, Vice President and CTO of Amazon, once said *everything fails all the time*. The inevitability of hardware failures means that redundancy and high availability are going to be a fundamental part of the application running on top of the underlying hardware. If hardware fails, it shouldn't be a problem because the developer has ensured that their application follows the cloudy development style (see final bullet point).
- **Horizontal scaling**: When one needs more computing power, they rarely bother with resizing existing instances. They instead choose the unlimited nature of elastic cloud by creating more virtual machines and do work in parallel. This is also known as scaling horizontally.

- **Open source**: Although AWS's overall design and infrastructure are considered proprietary information, the release of its core services sparked a revolution in the tech startup world. Startups with a little cash and a few tech-savvy individuals could use and deploy open source tools, adopt a continuous deployment model, and focus on delivering minimum viable products to customers.
- **Cloudy development**: Perhaps the most important difference with elastic cloud is cloudy development. As AWS continued to release more services and features throughout the late 2000's, its users began to develop new methodologies for deployment and continuous integration. Many of the users embraced the "fail fast" motto by shipping application code into production as soon as possible to enhance the customer experience. These developers also began embracing a new cloudy methodology, moving from *monolithic* applications to *microservices*—utilizing message queues to avoid tightly coupled services, and embracing cloud automation and instance personalization via tools such as Puppet and Chef.

Amazon gripes

Although Amazon was beginning to gain traction as an incredible way to deploy applications, there were many concerns:

- **Security**: Amazon has significantly improved its security offerings over the years, but at the time of its release, Amazon only offered shared hosted infrastructure. The physical machine hosting your virtual machine most likely served other customers, including competitors! Companies with strict security compliance requirements found this unacceptable.
- **Cost**: There's no doubt that Amazon is much cheaper than choosing to purchase, deploy, manage, and support the infrastructure yourself. But what about all that AWS cloud spending over time? This is a subject of much debate. But in some scenarios, hiring a company to manage your cloud may be cheaper over time.
- **Vendor lock-in**: As companies began to place more and more of their production workloads on AWS, this required employees investing hours and days of their time learning the ins and outs of the unique AWS ecosystem. This included digging through official AWS documentation so that one could learn how to code to their APIs. As a single organization in charge of all aspects of the offering, AWS could easily choose to change their API syntax or even raise their resource usage prices. Imagine the hassle involved in attempting to migrate workloads on AWS to another cloud provider.

NASA and Rackspace open source the cloud!

In 2008, NASA was interested in utilizing AWS EC2 to perform scientific computation, but had some concerns about security. As a result, they decided to build their own open-source cloud platform called Nebula. Nebula was a scalable compute-provisioning engine that was loosely based on the EC2 offering.

Around the same time, Rackspace, a managed hosting company from San Antonio, Texas, was working on an open source project called Swift. Swift was (and still is) a distributed object storage system similar to AWS S3, which became a part of Rackspace's Cloud Files offering.

It wasn't until July of 2010 that NASA and Rackspace officially announced the plan to actively combine the Nebula and Swift projects, inviting the world to begin contributing code to a new open source cloud project known as OpenStack. Discussions about the direction of OpenStack began immediately, as more than 100 architects and developers from more than 25 companies traveled to Austin for the first OpenStack conference. Just as quickly, hundreds of developers, hardware manufacturers, and IT software companies began contributing code, inspired by the OpenStack mission:

"To produce the ubiquitous Open Source Cloud Computing platform that will meet the needs of public and private clouds regardless of size, by being simple to implement and massively scalable."

This mission statement appeared on the wiki on May 24th, 2010 and still captures the long-term goal of the OpenStack community today.

 OpenStack wasn't the only open source cloud in town—it was in an open source cloud war with Eucalyptus, OpenNebula, and Apache CloudStack. Although these clouds were quite popular between 2008 and 2010, they could not compete with the number of large IT vendors (such as IBM, Ubuntu, and Red Hat) officially announcing their support for OpenStack. Suddenly, more and more people dedicated their precious coding time to OpenStack, and the other cloud projects fell by the wayside.

About OpenStack

Now that we understand a bit about enterprise virtualization, elastic cloud computing, and the origin of OpenStack, let's discuss some details about the OpenStack project.

The OpenStack Foundation

The OpenStack Foundation was created in 2012 with the simple mission to protect, empower, and promote OpenStack software and the community around it.

Since the Foundation's initial formation, there have been more than fifteen OpenStack Summits. The OpenStack Summit is an incredible gathering of more than 5,000 software developers, CIOs, systems engineers, and technical writers from all over the world. Membership of the foundation is free and accessible to anyone; everyone from individual contributors to large enterprises are members, including companies like AT&T, Red Hat, Rackspace, Ubuntu, SUSE, Google, and IBM.

Even if you haven't used OpenStack yet, join the OpenStack Foundation! It's fast, free, and fun. `https://www.openstack.org/join/` .

The four opens

The OpenStack Foundation is committed to ensuring that OpenStack follows "the four opens":

1. **Open source**: The OpenStack source code is licensed under the Apache License Version 2.0 (APLv2). OpenStack is committed to creating truly open source software that is usable and scalable.
2. **Open design**: OpenStack is also committed to an open design process. Every six months, the development community meets for a Project Team Gathering (PTG) to create the roadmap for the next release. This includes brainstorming ideas, gathering requirements, and writing blueprints for upcoming releases. The PTGs are always open to the public.
3. **Open development**: OpenStack keeps its source code publicly available through the entire development process (`https://github.com/openstack`). Everything is open, including code reviews, release roadmaps, and technical discussions.
4. **Open community:** All processes are documented, open, and transparent. The technical governance of the project is democratic, with a community of contributors electing technical leads and members of technical committees. Project meetings are held in public IRC channels, and technical communication is primarily done through public mailing lists.

OpenStack types

Wandering the exhibition floor of an OpenStack Summit can be extremely daunting to the OpenStack newcomer. Every major IT company appears to have some sort of OpenStack solution, and it's often difficult to decipher what is actually being offered. The best way to explain these various OpenStack offerings is by breaking them down into four distinct types. See *Figure 1.2*.

- **Project**: The OpenStack project can be found at http://github.com/openstack. This contains the publicly available source code that thousands of developers are actively committing to throughout the day. It's free to download and install yourself.

- **Distributions/appliances**: OpenStack is incredibly complex due to its many moving parts, and therefore difficult to deploy, manage, and support. To reduce complexity, companies and communities alike create OpenStack distributions or "appliances." These are easy, turnkey approaches to deploying OpenStack. They typically provide opinionated methods for deployment by using popular configuration management tools such as Ansible, Puppet, or Chef. They may install OpenStack directly from the project source code on GitHub, or via packages that have been developed by popular operating system communities like Ubuntu and Red Hat.

- **Hosted private clouds**: Customers looking for the security and reliability of a private OpenStack cloud without the need to manage it themselves should consider a hosted private cloud solution. These solutions typically use an existing OpenStack distribution and also include 24/7 customer support, with guaranteed uptime via an SLA (Service Level Agreement).

- **Public clouds**: There are quite a few public clouds built on OpenStack software. These include Rackspace and OVH Public Cloud. Similar to Amazon Web Services, Azure, or Google Cloud Platform, an OpenStack Public Cloud solution resides in the provider's data centers. The provider is responsible for the management of the environment, which is used by multiple customers on shared hardware.

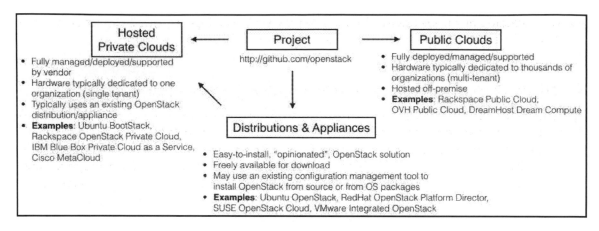

Figure 1.2: Different types of OpenStack

OpenStack jobs

As you can see from *Figure 1.3*, the need for those with OpenStack skills has been increasing over the years:

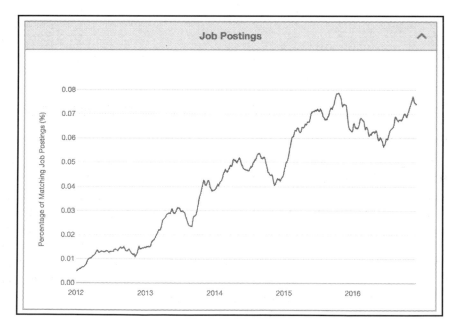

Figure 1.3: An increase in OpenStack Job postings since 2012

But what specific positions are available to those who know OpenStack? Let's break down a few of the different roles an individual with OpenStack skills may possess.

Application developer - developing on OpenStack

The application developer who understands OpenStack uses it to create virtual resources so they can deploy their applications on top of OpenStack. They typically have a background in Amazon Web Services, Azure, or Google Cloud Platform, and treat OpenStack as an **Infrastructure as a Service (IaaS)** platform. They are most likely full-stack developers, well-versed in all layers of web applications. They love the speed and agility of OpenStack. It allows them to instantly deploy an application when inspiration strikes and ship applications to their customers quickly and efficiently.

OpenStack administrator/operator - administrating the cloud

The OpenStack administrator or operator is the target audience for the Certified OpenStack Administrator exam. This individual typically has some years of experience as a Linux System Administrator, and is comfortable acting as the go-to individual for all OpenStack-related questions. They are responsible for managing new users, domains, and projects. They must also know how to interact with OpenStack, as well as how to train others to create virtual resources using the services installed in the environment.

OpenStack engineer/infrastructure engineer - doing the DevOps thing

An OpenStack engineer may spend a lot of their time in the datacenter working with automation tools like Puppet, Chef, and Ansible. When OpenStack needs more capacity, the OpenStack engineer is responsible for racking, stacking, and wiring up the servers, ensuring the operating systems have the latest patches, and seeing that all proper OpenStack components get the proper configuration file values, permissions, and settings. Although the Certified OpenStack Administrator exam doesn't require test takers to understand specific values for configuration files (or how to upgrade existing services), OpenStack engineers most likely know how to do this inside and out—often finding themselves working on automation scripts to ease their daily responsibilities.

OpenStack product developer - simplifying OpenStack deployment/management

The OpenStack product developer works on developing an OpenStack distribution or appliance. They understand the difficulty of building clouds; in turn, they create opinionated distributions to ease the OpenStack deployment and management process. Examples include Red Hat OpenStack Platform Director, SUSE OpenStack Cloud, and Rackspace Private Cloud. These companies may also offer professional service or support in addition to the product.

Upstream OpenStack developer - making OpenStack better!

Those eager to contribute to the actual OpenStack project are known as OpenStack upstream developers. These developers develop for OpenStack—building blueprints, chatting with other OpenStack developers on IRC, attending the PTG meet-ups, and contributing code—as they to make OpenStack the ubiquitous cloud operating system. Upstream developers have an impact on the OpenStack roadmap and are part of a healthy community that strengthens enterprise adoption.

OpenStack services overview

OpenStack is made up of a variety of services that are all written in the Python programming language and serve a specific function. OpenStack's modular nature facilitates the modern cloudy application design philosophy and also allows easy expandability; any person, community, or company can develop an OpenStack service that can easily integrate into its ecosystem.

The OpenStack Foundation has successfully identified nine key services they consider part of the core of OpenStack, which we'll explore in detail.

Keystone - identity service

Keystone handles authentication. It acts as a common authentication system across all core services in an OpenStack environment. Both human users and services must authenticate to Keystone to retrieve a token before interacting with other services in the environment.

Visualize the process of logging on to a website with your username and password. When a user does this on the Horizon dashboard, they authenticate against Keystone to successfully login and begin creating virtual resources. Keystone also stores the service catalog, users, domains, projects, groups, roles, and quotas—exam objective concepts you'll examine in `Chapter 3`, *Keystone Identity Service*.

Glance - image service

Glance provides discovery, registration, and delivery services for disk images.

When one boots a virtual machine (also known as an *instance*), it is typically required to provide a disk image. These typically contain an operating system (such as Ubuntu or Red Hat Enterprise Linux), and are best described as a snapshot of a disk's contents. Examples of disk image types include QCOW2, VMDK, VHDX, ISO, and RAW. The disk image has usually been previously created by a person or script who has gone through the initial installation procedure and has installed specific configuration files to ensure it is cloud-aware. Glance can store images in a variety of data stores, including the local filesystem or OpenStack Swift.

Nova - compute service

Inspired by Amazon EC2, Nova is the compute service and the core of the OpenStack cloud. It is designed to manage and automate pools of compute resources, and can work with widely available virtualization technologies as well as bare metal servers.

It's important to note that Nova is not a hypervisor. It's a system of services that sit above the hypervisor, orchestrating availability of compute resources. Some examples of hypervisors include Hyper-V, VMware ESXi, Xen, and the most popular, KVM (Kernel-based Virtual Machine). Nova also supports the ability to utilize Linux container technology such as LXC and Docker.

In OpenStack, the term *booting* is used to refer to the creation of a virtual machine. A virtual machine booted with Nova is often called an **instance**.

Neutron - networking service

Neutron is a service that allows users to manage virtual network resources and IP addresses.

If one wants to boot an instance, they typically need to provide a virtual network on which to boot that instance so that it has network connectivity. With Neutron, users can view their own networks, subnets, firewall rules, and routers—all through the Horizon dashboard, CLI, or API. One's ability to create and manage network resources depends on the specific role they have been assigned.

Neutron also contains a modular framework powered by a variety of plugins, agents, and drivers, including Linux bridge and Open vSwitch.

Cinder - block storage service

Inspired by Amazon's Elastic Block Storage (EBS) offering, Cinder allows users to create volumes that can be mounted as devices by Nova instances.

Cinder volumes behave as if they were raw unformatted hard drives. Once data is written to these volumes, the data persists even after terminating the instance or an instance failure. This is because the written data is stored on a dedicated Cinder storage server, not the compute nodes where the instances reside. Cinder also supports snapshots which capture the current state of a volume. These are useful for providing backup protection, and they can also be used to instantiate new volumes that contain the exact data of the snapshot. You can also write images to a block storage devices for compute to use as a bootable persistent instance.

Swift - object storage service

Inspired by Amazon S3, Swift is a redundant storage system that provides developers and IT teams with secure, durable, and highly scalable cloud storage. A user creates a container and stores static files, also known as objects, in the container. These objects can be anything from pictures or movies to spreadsheets and HTML files. From the end user's perspective, storage is limitless, inexpensive, and accessible via a REST API. Features can also be turned on via the Swift API. These include hosting a static website, versioning, setting specific objects to expire, and even setting Access Control Lists (ACLs) allowing public access to the objects inside the container.

On the backend of Swift, static files (also known as objects) are written to multiple disk drives spread throughout servers in a data center. The Swift software is responsible for ensuring data replication and integrity across the cluster. Should a server or hard drive fail, Swift replicates its contents from other active nodes to a new location in the cluster.

Heat - orchestration service

Inspired by Amazon's CloudFormation service, Heat helps operators model and set up OpenStack resources so that they can spend less time managing these resources and more time focusing on the applications that run on OpenStack.

You begin with a blueprint or Heat Orchestration Template (HOT) that describes all the OpenStack resources to be provisioned. Heat then takes care of provisioning and configuring, with no need to worry about dependencies or order of execution—a template describes all the resources and their parameters. After the stack has been created, your resources are up and running.

Templates are extremely convenient because they allow operators to check them into a version control system to easily track changes to the infrastructure. If problems occur after deploying a Heat template, you simply restore to a previous version of the template. If you want to make a change to the stack, you can easily update it by providing a modified template with new parameters.

OpenStack services in action

Let's take a high-level look at these OpenStack services in the wild, from the perspective of the Horizon dashboard home screen. See *Figure 1.4.*

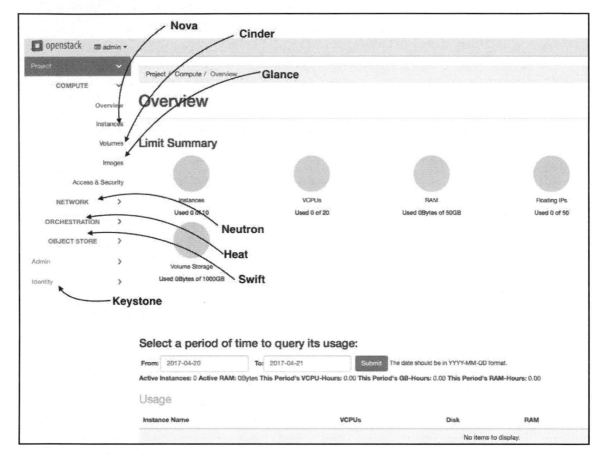

Figure 1.4: OpenStack services on the Horizon dashboard

Let's start from the top:

- **Instances**: The **Nova** instances section is where you can manage your virtual machines. You can start, stop, pause, lock, and suspend instances—as well as create snapshots, view console logs, and log in into the instances via an interactive console. Learn more about this section in `Chapter 5`, *Nova Compute Service.*

- **Volumes**: In this section, you can create **Cinder** block volumes, snapshots, and backups. You can also attach your volumes to instances. Learn more about this section in Chapter 7, *Cinder Block Storage Service*.

- **Images**: The **Glance** images section is where you can see your currently available images as well as upload images and edit metadata associated with the images. Learn more about this section in Chapter 4, *Glance Image Service*.

- **Access & Security**: This section is a mix of a few services and contains four primary sections: Neutron Security Groups, Nova Keypairs, a list of Service Catalog public endpoints, and a place to download a pre-populated credential file for interacting with OpenStack with a command-line interface with the currently logged-in user. Learn more about this section in Chapter 3, *Keystone Identity Service*, Chapter 5, *Nova Compute Service*, and Chapter 6, *Neutron Networking Service*.

- **NETWORK**: In this section, you can utilize Neutron by creating tenant networks, tenant subnets, routers, and floating IPs. Learn more about this section in Chapter 6, *Neutron Networking Service*.

- **ORCHESTRATION**: Here, you can create Heat stacks by either uploading a Heat orchestration template or pasting it into the dashboard. You can also list and update existing stacks in this area. Learn more about this section in Chapter 9, *Heat—Orchestration Service*.

- **OBJECT STORE**: Create Swift containers and upload static objects such as photos, movies, and HTML files. Learn more about this section in Chapter 8, *Swift—Object Storage Service*.

- **Admin**: This admin panel only appears when the user logging in has the admin role. It features an admin-only look at all virtual resources across all domains and projects in the environment.

- **Identity**: This is where Keystone domains, projects, users, roles, and quotas are listed. If one has the admin role, they can do a variety of things in here, including creating new projects, adding new users to those projects, assigning roles, and modifying quotas. Learn more about this section in Chapter 3, *Keystone Identity Service*.

Interacting with OpenStack

The power of OpenStack is in the REST API of each core service. These APIs can be publicly exposed and thus accessible from anywhere in the world with public internet access: a smartphone, a laptop on the coffee shop WiFi network, or remote office.

There are a variety of ways in which one can interact with OpenStack to create virtual resources from anywhere. As we work our way down these various methods, the amount of automation increases, allowing a software developer to easily create virtual resources and deploy applications on top of those resources with minimal user interaction. See *Figure 1.5*.

- **Horizon dashboard (GUI)**: If you are new to OpenStack, this is the best place to begin your journey. You simply navigate to the Horizon URL via the web browser, enter your username and password, verify you are scoped to the proper project, and then proceed—creating instances, networks, and volumes with the click of a button. See *Figure 1.4* for where the services are located upon first logging in. Because not all OpenStack service features are available via the Horizon dashboard, you will need to also interact with OpenStack services via the command-line interface to utilize additional functionality.

 A majority of the exam objectives can be completed via the Horizon dashboard. Each chapter will break down completing objectives via the command-line interface and Horizon dashboard (when available).

- **Command-line interface (CLI)**: The OpenStack command line interface will unlock a majority of the OpenStack service features and can easily be installed on Windows, Mac, and Linux systems. For Linux gurus with Bash shell experience, the CLI is the tool of choice.
- **Software development kit (SDK)**: Although the bash shell and OpenStack CLI combination are extremely powerful, SDKs provide more expressiveness. One example scenario: a developer hosting their popular application on OpenStack virtual infrastructure so that additional resources can be automatically provisioned when specific thresholds are met. Or, imagine an Android application that allows an organization's employees to create OpenStack resources with a few simple clicks of a button. Simply put, OpenStack SDKs allow you to programmatically interact with OpenStack services in the comfort of your favorite language. OpenStack SDKs are currently available in the following languages: C, C++, Closure, Erlang, Go, Java, JavaScript, .NET, Node.js, Perl, PHP, Python, and Ruby.

- **Heat orchestration template (HOT)**: You can deploy Heat templates (similar to Amazon Web Service CloudFormation Blueprints) that utilize the OpenStack service APIs—creating OpenStack resources with the simple click of a button. The user defines their application by describing OpenStack resources in the template. The Heat templates provide maximum automation to the cloud user, deploying an entire application without manual creation of individual resources or dependencies. One can even check these into a version control system such as Git to easily track changes to the infrastructure.

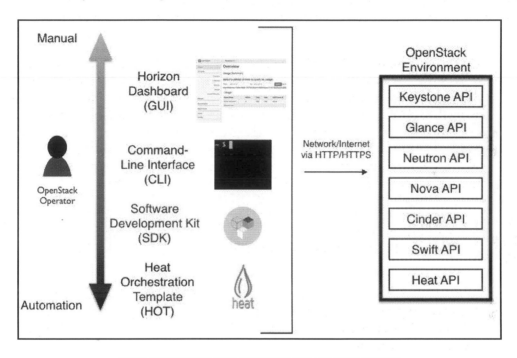

Figure 1.5: The various methods one can use to interact with an OpenStack environment

The OpenStack clients

Although the majority of the COA exam can be completed on the Horizon dashboard, understanding how to use the OpenStack CLI is critical if you want to pass! Although it can appear a bit unsettling to those with minimal experience, over time you'll notice that the CLI will reveal the true fun of OpenStack.

Service-based clients - traditional clients

Every core OpenStack service has an associated command-line client. Like the OpenStack services, the command-line clients are written in the Python programming language (available at `http://github.com/openstack`). The clients also contain the service API bindings for developing Python code that can talk directly to a specific service without requiring long-winded API requests. For years, the most popular clients used by OpenStack administrators were the following:

- `python-keystoneclient`
- `python-glanceclient`
- `python-neutronclient`
- `python-novaclient`
- `python-cinderclient`
- `python-swiftclint`
- `python-heatclient`

Python-openstackclient - the unified client

Because it was quite frustrating to remember commands for each separate client, the OpenStack community created a new OpenStack client called **OSC (OpenStack Client)** in 2013. The actual program is named `python-openstackclient` and available at `http://github.com/openstack/python-openstackclient`.

See *Figure 1.6*. `python-openstackclient` is a CLI client for OpenStack that brings all the traditional service-based clients into a single shell with a uniform command structure. It has a consistent and predictable format for all of its commands and takes the following form:

openstack [<global-options>] <object-1> <action> [<object-2>] [<command-arguments>]

For example, if you wanted to create a brand new Nova virtual machine instance, you could simply run:

```
$ openstack server create demo-instance1 --flavor m1.tiny --image cirros
MyFirstInstance
```

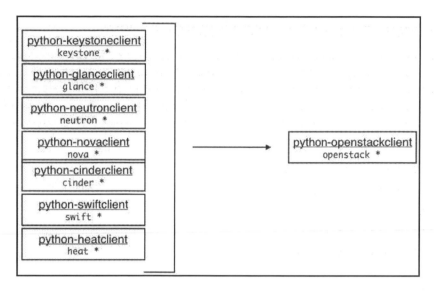

Figure 1.6: python-openstackclient brings the traditional service-based clients into a single shell with a uniform command structure

You can also view help commands by running the following:

```
$ openstack help
```

The OpenStack clients will be discussed in more detail in upcoming chapters. As of September 2017, the COA exam tests on the Newton version of OpenStack. The exam will provide access to `python-openstackclient` and all service-based clients. A majority of the exam objectives can be completed with `python-openstackclient`, except where noted in this book.

OpenStack daemon communication

Now that we've discussed the various ways in which an OpenStack operator interacts with OpenStack via the API, let's discuss internal communication among the core OpenStack services. In *Figure 1.7*, you can see the color code in the top left that shows the service and daemon. The service is simply the name of the OpenStack service, while the daemon represents the program that is actually running to bring the service to life.

To avoid tight coupling, communication amongst the daemons within a specific service is achieved via an **Advanced Message Queueing Protocol** (**AMQP**). In a typical OpenStack environment, this can be software such as RabbitMQ or Qpid.

Recall the cloudy development methodology that we discussed in the history portion of this chapter. While OpenStack encourages its software developers to follow this methodology when deploying applications on it, the actual OpenStack infrastructure follows the exact same principles: highly available, scalable, and loosely coupled.

For example, when a user sends a request to `nova-api` to boot a server, `nova-api` will publish this message on the AMQP bus. This message will then be read by `nova-scheduler`. Now let's visualize an OpenStack cloud that often receives hundreds of requests to boot instances. To solve this problem you would deploy more servers in the infrastructure, install more `nova-scheduler` daemons, and simply point them to the OpenStack environment's AMQP server. That's Horizontal scaling in action!

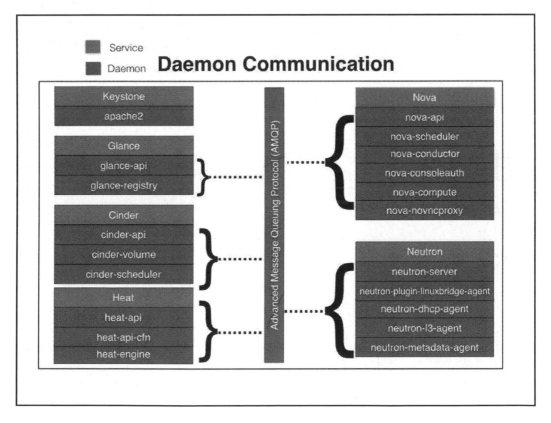

Figure 1.7: OpenStack daemons within a specific service use the AMQP bus to communicate among themselves

OpenStack API communication

While the OpenStack service daemons rely on AMQP for communication among daemons within their specific service, the APIs are used both by OpenStack users wishing to create virtual resources *and* for **service-to-service** communication.

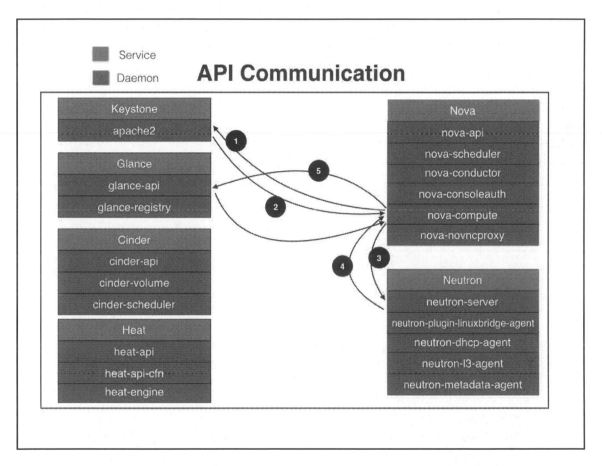

Figure 1.8: An example of API communication amongst OpenStack services

Envision a user sending a request to `nova-api` to boot an instance. In order to boot that server, quite a few internal API calls would need to take place. Let's look at an example sequence of API calls that would take place when booting a virtual machine instance.

An OpenStack user would first send a POST API call to the `nova-api` daemon with details about what sort of virtual machine they'd like. That message would get put on the AMQP message bus and consumed by the `nova-scheduler` daemon. The `nova-scheduler` daemon would then choose the best fit for the virtual machine using its scheduling algorithm. The `nova-compute` daemon residing on the compute node consumes this message. Before the server can be boot, the following must occur (see *Figure 1.8*):

- **(1):** The `nova-compute` daemon sends an API request to Keystone to retrieve a scoped token.
- **(2):** `nova-compute` gets back a 200 HTTP response along with a scoped token. Now `nova-compute` has a scoped token and can freely communicate with other OpenStack services.
- **(3):** `nova-compute` now sends a request to `neutron-server` to verify whether the specified virtual network on which to boot the instance is available.
- **(4):** `nova-compute` receives a response that the network is available and capable of attaching to the instance.
- **(5):** `nova-compute` must then send an API call to `glance-api` to retrieve the operating system image.
- **(6):** The `glance-api` responds back with the image that will reside on the compute node.

Now our instance will be booted! That was a lot of work!

 Don't worry! You don't need to understand all the magic occurring behind the scenes in OpenStack to be successful on the exam. This is for educational purposes only!

About the Certified OpenStack Administrator exam

Now that you've learned a bit about OpenStack, let's get down to why you're really here:

To pass the Certified OpenStack Administrator exam!

Benefits of passing the exam

Ask anyone about getting started in the IT world and they may suggest looking into industry-recognized technical certifications. IT certifications measure competency in a number of areas and are a great way to open doors to opportunities. While they certainly should not be the only determining factor in the hiring process, achieving them can be a measure of your competence and commitment to facing challenges.

If you pass...

Upon achieving a passing grade, you will receive your certificate (see *Figure 1.9*). Laminate, frame, or pin it to your home office wall or work cubicle—it's proof that you have met all the requirements to become an official OpenStack administrator. The certification is valid for three years from the pass date, so don't forget to renew.

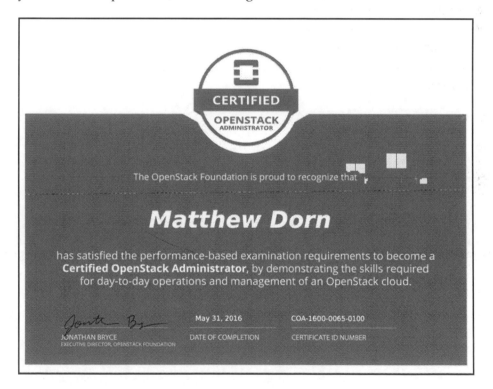

Figure 1.9: A certificate you receive when you pass the Certified OpenStack Administrator exam

In addition to the certification, a COA badge will appear next to your name in the official OpenStack Community Directory, available at `https://www.openstack.org/community/members/`.

Figure 1.10: Upon passing the exam, you will also receive an official COA badge next to your name in the OpenStack Foundation Member Directory

 The OpenStack Foundation has put together a great tool for helping employers verify the validity of COA certifications. Check out the Certified OpenStack Administrator Verification Tool (`https://www.openstack.org/coa/coa-verify/`).

Seven steps to becoming a Certified OpenStack Administrator

Let's begin by walking through some steps to become a Certified OpenStack administrator.

Step 1 - study!

Practice. Practice. Practice. Use this book and the included OpenStack All-in-One Virtual Appliance as a resource as you begin your Certified OpenStack Administrator journey. If you still find yourself struggling with the concepts and objectives in this book, you can always refer to the official OpenStack documentation—or even seek out a live training class at https://www.openstack.org/marketplace/training/.

Step 2 - purchase

Once you feel that you're ready to conquer the exam, head to https://www.openstack.org/coa/ and click on **Get Started**. After signing in, you will be directed to checkout to purchase your exam. The OpenStack Foundation accepts all major credit cards, and costs $300.00 USD as of September 2017 (subject to change, so keep an eye on the website). You can also get a *free* retake within 12 months of the original exam purchase date if you do not pass on the first attempt.

 To encourage students in academia to get their feet wet with OpenStack technologies, the OpenStack Foundation is offering the exam for $150.00 (50% off the retail price) with a valid student ID. Check out https://www.openstack.org/coa/student/ for more info.

Step 3 - COA portal page

Once your order is processed, you will receive an email with access to the COA portal. Think of the portal as your personal COA website, where you can download your exam receipt and keep track of your certification efforts. Once you take the exam, you can come back to the COA portal to check your exam status and score, and even download certificates and badges for your website or business cards.

Step 4 - hardware compatibility check

The COA exam can be taken from your personal laptop or desktop, but you must ensure that your system meets the exam's minimum system requirements. A link on the COA portal page will present you with the compatibility check tool, which will run a series of tests to ensure you meet the requirements. It will also assist you in downloading a Chrome plugin for taking the exam. At this time, you must use the Chrome or Chromium browser and have access to reliable internet, a webcam, and microphone.

Figure 1.11 shows a current list of minimum requirements.

Component	Minimum Requirement
Operating System	- Windows XP, Vista, 7, 8 - Mac OS X and above - Linux - Chrome OS
Web Browser	Google Chrome or Chromium version 32 and above
Browser Settings	Your browser must accept 3rd party cookies for the duration of the exam ONLY.
Webcam/Microphone	- Minimum VGA 640 x 480 resolution - Enabled built in or external microphone
Google Chrome Extension	Install Innovative Exams Google Chrome Extension
Ports	**TCP:** port 80 and 443
Bandwidth	Minimum 500kb/s download and 256kb/s upload
Hardware Requirements	- 1GB RAM & 2GHz dual core processor - Minimum 1280 x 800 resolution
Testing Environment	- Room must be quiet, private and well lit. Public spaces such as coffee shops, stores, etc. are not allowed. - Desk must clear of all notes and electronics. - Examinee should reside in the center of the camera frame - No bright lights or windows behind the examinee

Figure 1.11: A list of minimum requirements for the COA exam

Step 5 - identification

You must be at least 18 years old and have proper identification to take the exam. Any of the following pieces of identification are acceptable:

- Passport
- Government-issued driver's license or permit
- National identity card
- State or province-issued identity card

Step 6 - schedule the exam

I recommend scheduling your exam a few months ahead of time to give yourself a realistic goal. Click on the **Schedule Exam** link on the COA portal to be directed and automatically logged in to the exam proctor partner website. Once logged in to the site, type `OpenStack Foundation` in the search box and select **COA exam**. You can then choose from available dates and times. The latest possible exam date you can schedule will be 30 days out from the current date. Once you have scheduled it, you can cancel or reschedule up to 24 hours before the start time of the exam.

Step 7 - take the exam!

The day has arrived! You've used this book and have practiced day and night to master all of the covered objectives. It's finally time to take the exam!

One of the most important factors determining your exam success is the location. You cannot be in a crowded place. This means no coffee shops, work desks, or football games. The testing location policy is very strict, so consider taking the exam from home or a private room in the office.

Log in to the COA portal 15 minutes before your scheduled exam time. You should now see a **Take Exam** link which will connect to the exam proctor partner website so you can connect to the testing environment.

Once in the exam environment, an exam proctor chat window will appear and assist you with starting your exam. You must allow sharing of your entire operating system screen (including all applications), webcam, and microphone. Once it's time to begin, you have two and a half hours to complete all exam objectives. You're almost on your way to becoming a Certified OpenStack Administrator!

About the exam environment

The exam expects its test takers to be proficient in interacting with OpenStack via the Horizon dashboard and command-line interface. *Figure 1.12* shows is a visual representation of the exam console as outlined in `https://www.openstack.org/assets/coa/COA-Candidate-Handbook-V1.4.14.pdf`:

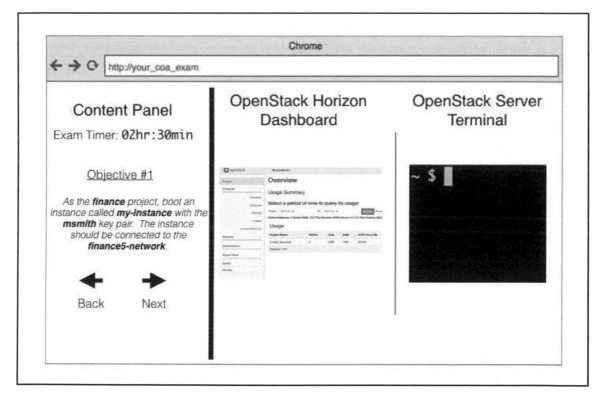

Figure 1.12: A visual representation of the COA exam console

The exam console is embedded into the browser. It is composed of two primary parts:

- **Content Panel**
- **Dashboard/Terminal Panel**

The Content Panel is the section that displays the exam timer and objectives. As per the COA handbook, exam objectives can only be navigated linearly. You can use the next and back button to move to each objective.

The Dashboard/Terminal Panel gives you full access to an OpenStack environment. `Chapter 2`, *Setting Up Your Practice Exam Environment*, will assist you with getting your practice OpenStack environment environment up and running so you can work through all the objectives.

The exam console terminal is embedded in a browser, and you cannot SCP (secure copy) to it from your local system. Within the terminal environment, you are permitted to install a multiplexor such as `screen`, `tmux`, or `byobu` if you think these will assist you, but they are **not necessary** for successful completion of the objectives.

You are not permitted to browse websites, email, or notes during the exam, but you are free to access `https://docs.openstack.org/`. However, this can be a major waste of exam time; it shouldn't be necessary after working through the exam objectives in this book. You can also easily copy and paste from the objective window into the Horizon dashboard or terminal.

If you struggle with a question, move on! Hit the **Next** button and try the next objective. You can always come back and tackle it before time is up.

The exam is scored automatically within 24 hours, and you should receive the results via email within 72 hours after exam completion. At this time, the results will be made available on the COA portal. Be sure to also review the Professional Code of Conduct on the OpenStack Foundation Certification Handbook.

The exam objectives

Let's now take a look at the objectives you will be responsible for performing on the exam. As of June 2017, these are all the exam objectives published on the official COA website. These objectives will test your competence and proficiency in the domains listed. These domains cover multiple core OpenStack services as well as general OpenStack troubleshooting. Together, they make up 100% of the exam.

Because many of the objectives on this official COA requirements list overlap, this book utilizes a customized convenient strategy to ensure you can fulfill all objectives within all content areas.

Getting to know OpenStack (3%) - Chapter 1

- Understand the components that make up the cloud
- Use the OpenStack API/CLI

Keystone: identity management (12%) - Chapter 3

- Manage Keystone catalog services and endpoints
- Manage/create domains, groups, projects, users, and roles
- Create roles for the environment
- Manage the identity service
- Verify operation of the identity service

Glance: image management (10%) - Chapter 4

- Deploy a new image to an OpenStack instance
- Manage image types and backends
- Manage images (for example: add, update, or remove)
- Verify operation of the Image Service

Nova: compute (15%) - Chapter 5

- Manage flavors
- Manage compute instance actions (such as launch, shutdown, or terminate)
- Manage Nova user keypairs
- Launch a new instance
- Shut down an instance
- Terminate an instance
- Configure an instance with a floating IP address

- Manage project security group rules
- Assign security groups to an instance
- Assign floating IP address to an instance
- Detach floating IP address from an instance
- Manage Nova host consoles (rdp, spice, tty)
- Access an instance using a keypair
- Manage instance snapshots
- Manage Nova compute servers
- Manage quotas
- Get Nova stats (hosts, services, and tenants)
- Verify operation of the compute service

Neutron: networking (16%) - Chapter 6

- Manage network resources (such as routers and subnets)
- Create external networks
- Create project networks
- Create project routers
- Manage network services for a virtual environment
- Manage project security group rules
- Manage quotas
- Verify operation of network service
- Manage network interfaces on compute instances
- Troubleshoot network issues for a tenant network (enter namespace, run tcpdump, and so on)

Cinder: block storage (10%) - Chapter 7

- Manage a volume
- Create volume group for block storage
- Create a new block storage volume and mount it to a Nova instance
- Manage quotas
- Manage volume quotas
- Manage volume backups

- Back up and restore volumes
- Manage volume snapshots (such as take, list, and recover)
- Verify that block storage can perform snapshotting function
- Snapshot volume
- Manage volume encryption
- Set up storage pools
- Monitor reserve capacity of block storage devices
- Analyze discrepancies in reported volume sizes

Swift: object storage (10%) - Chapter 8

- Manage access to object storage
- Manage expiring objects
- Manage storage policies
- Monitor space available for object store
- Verify operation of object storage
- Manage permissions on a container in object storage

Heat: orchestration (8%) - Chapter 9

- Launch a stack using a Heat/Orchestration template (for example, storage, network, and compute)
- Use Heat/Orchestration CLI and dashboard
- Verify Heat/Orchestration stack is working
- Verify operation of Heat/Orchestration
- Create a Heat/Orchestration template that matches a specific scenario
- Update a stack
- Obtain detailed information about a stack

Horizon: dashboard (3%) - Chapters 3 through 9

- Verify operation of the dashboard

Troubleshooting (13%) - Chapter 10

- Analyze log files
- Backup the database(s) used by an OpenStack instance
- Centralize and analyze logs (such as /var/log/COMPONENT_NAME, database server, messaging server, web server, and syslog)
- Analyze database servers
- Analyze host/guest OS and instance status
- Analyze messaging servers
- Analyze metadata servers
- Analyze network status (physical and virtual)
- Analyze storage status (local, block, and object)
- Manage OpenStack services
- Diagnose service incidents
- Digest OpenStack environment (Controller, Compute, Storage, and Network nodes)
- Direct logging of files through centralized logging system
- Back up and restore an OpenStack instance
- Troubleshoot network performance

Summary

OpenStack is an open source cloud software that provides an Infrastructure as a Service environment, allowing its users to quickly deploy applications by creating virtual resources such as virtual servers, networks, and block storage volumes. The IT industry's demand for individuals with OpenStack skills is continuing to grow, and one of the best ways to prove you have those skills is by taking the Certified OpenStack Administrator exam.

In the next chapter, we will import an All-in-One Virtual Appliance based off the Newton version of OpenStack. This appliance is an incredible learning aid, allowing us to interact with OpenStack anytime and anywhere, while working though all the exam objectives explained in this book. Get ready to become an official Certified OpenStack Administrator!

2
Setting up Your Practice Exam Environment

In the previous chapter, we took a look at the origin of OpenStack as well as some details on the Certified OpenStack Administrator exam. We will now focus on installing the OpenStack Newton virtual appliance included with this book. This virtual appliance will give you a working OpenStack environment that can be accessed on your local laptop or desktop! It is recommended that you have this environment up and running before working through the chapters in this book.

As you read through each objective, follow along by performing the actions in your environment. If you already have access to an OpenStack environment, you can certainly use it—but be aware that the appliance has been previously populated with users, projects, instances, networks, and templates to replicate a real-world OpenStack environment. For a script to create the resources, please see check out the official book Git repository at `https:/ /github.com/PacktPublishing/Preparing-for-the-Certified-OpenStack- Administrator-Exam`. As of June 2017, the COA exam tests on the Newton version of OpenStack.

In this chapter, we will cover the following topics:

- VirtualBox and OVA files
- Traditional OpenStack environments
- The all-in-one OpenStack Virtual Appliance (included with this book)
- Installing the OpenStack Virtual Appliance on Mac/Linux and Windows

OpenStack can be installed on a variety of operating system environments, including Ubuntu, CentOS, Fedora, Red Hat Enterprise Linux, SUSE Linux Enterprise Server, and OpenSUSE. As of June 2017, a test taker can choose between taking the exam on Ubuntu or SUSE Linux Enterprise Server when scheduling the exam. This book will focus on Ubuntu 16.04.

After this chapter, you will have a working OpenStack environment on your local machine and will be ready to begin working through the objectives required to pass the Certified OpenStack exam.

About VirtualBox

VirtualBox is a popular hypervisor available for download for Windows, Mac, Linux, and Solaris. Unlike VMware Workstation Pro for Windows and VMware Fusion for Mac, VirtualBox is free and open source. It's ideal for testing or developing, and allows you to set up multiple operating systems on one system. VirtualBox is considered to be a **Type-2 hypervisor,** which is intended to run on a host operating system. **Type-1 hypervisors**, also known as native or bare-metal hypervisors, run directly on a host's hardware.

Open Virtual Appliance (OVA)

To make deployment of your practice COA exam environment simple and easy, this book provides you with an OVA or Open Virtual Appliance to easily import into VirtualBox. An OVA is a compressed .tar file containing the following:

- **Virtual Machine Disk File (VMDK)**: A snapshot of a disk's contents. The particular VMDK included in your OVA contains a previously configured OpenStack Newton environment.
- **Open Virtualization Format (OVF)**: An XML file that describes how the VMDK should be run. It includes information on the number of virtual CPUs, memory size, network configuration, and virtual devices.
- **Manifest (MF)**: This contains a hash of each file to validate the authenticity and integrity of the package.

A traditional OpenStack cloud

A typical production OpenStack cloud consists of the following:

- **Controller**: The controller is the backbone of the OpenStack cloud. It usually contains:
  - **MariaDB database**: A community-developed fork of the MySQL relational database. Most OpenStack services use a SQL database for storing data in tables of columns and rows. For example, imagine viewing all the tables inside a Nova database. You would see names of the instances, their **unique identifiers** (**UUIDs**), the projects that own those instances, and other Nova-related metadata.
  - **RabbitMQ**: A popular message queue service that provides messaging services via the AMQP protocol. RabbitMQ allows the daemons within a specific service to communicate status information and coordinate fulfillment of specific actions. Although OpenStack supports a variety of message queue programs, RabbitMQ is most commonly used because most Linux distributions support it.
  - **API daemons**: All the API daemons associated with OpenStack-related services run on the controller. Think of these APIs as the primary gateway to each service. When users want to interact with a service, they send API calls to the API daemon that resides on the controller.
  - **Horizon dashboard**: The Horizon dashboard runs under the popular Apache web server and also resides on the controller.
- **Network nodes**: The network node contains the Neutron daemons, which provide DHCP services so instances can automatically obtain IP addresses. Network nodes also contain Layer-3 services, which allow users to create routers that connect Neutron networks to each other. There are also network plugin agents to assist in connecting instances to these networks, as well as the Neutron metadata daemon (inspired by Amazon Web Service's popular EC2 Metadata Service).

- **Compute nodes**: If the controller is considered the brain of the OpenStack cloud, then the compute nodes are the muscle. Compute nodes provide disk, CPU, and memory resources that are consumed by the instances. Each node contains a Type-1 hypervisor, as well as the Nova-compute daemon for talking directly to that hypervisor. There is also a Neutron plugin agent on these servers to assist the instances in getting plugged into the virtual network infrastructure.
- **Block storage nodes**: The block storage nodes provide Cinder block volumes to instances running in OpenStack. They typically run **Logical Volume Manager (LVM)**, a popular Linux program for managing storage, as well as an iSCSI target daemon. When a user wants to attach a volume to an instance, an iSCSI connection is initiated from the instance's compute node to the block storage server where the volume resides.
- **Object storage nodes**: The object storage nodes make up the Swift object storage system. These nodes consist of commodity servers with cheap, high-capacity storage. The Swift daemons running on these servers are responsible for ensuring data replication and integrity across the entire object storage cluster.

The all-in-one Newton environment

The provided virtual appliance contains all core OpenStack services on a single virtual machine. To download the appliance, please go to the official book repository at `https://github.com/PacktPublishing/Preparing-for-the-Certified-OpenStack-Administrator-Exam`.

See *Figure 2.1*. The appliance runs inside VirtualBox which runs on your host operating system. *Figure 2.2* provides some additional information about the virtual appliance details. We will talk more about this as we progress through the chapters.

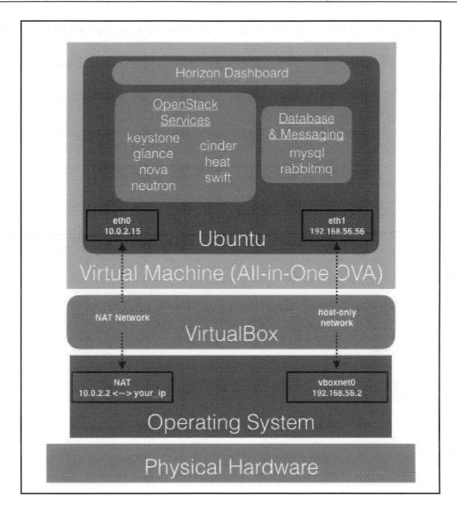

Figure 2.1: The virtual appliance contains all core OpenStack services featured on the COA exam

The Ceilometer Telemetry service is not a required learning objective on the exam and is not installed on the virtual appliance.

Operating System	Ubuntu 16.04
Operating System User Credentials	username: openstack pasword: openstack
VCPU	1VCPU
Memory	6GB RAM
Disk	80GB (dynamic)
Hostname	coa-aio-newton
VirtualBox Networking	Adapter1: NAT Adapter2: Host-Only (vboxnet0)
Operating System Networking	eth0: 10.0.2.15 eth1: 192.168.56.56
Database	MariaDB
AMQP	RabbitMQ
OpenStack Services	Keystone, Glance, Neutron, Nova, Cinder, Heat, Swift
Install Method / OpenStack Version	Ubuntu Cloud Archive - Newton
Horizon Dashboard URL	http://192.168.56.56/horizon
OpenStack User Credentials	username: admin password: admin
Horizon Multi-Domain Support	Disabled

Figure 2.2: Information about the virtual appliance included with this book

Minimum hardware requirements

Although VirtualBox has minimal system requirements, the included all-in-one OpenStack Newton Virtual Appliance requires:

- 2 GHz or faster 64-bit (x64) processor with Intel VTx or AMD-V support
- 6 GB available RAM
- 10 GB available hard disk space

Most modern CPUs contain a hardware-assisted virtualization feature to help accelerate Type-1 and Type-2 hypervisors. Before importing the OVA, ensure that your system's virtualization extensions are turned on in the BIOS or UEFI. Access your BIOS or UEFI firmware by entering the setup screen. Once inside, look for any of the following options and make sure they are turned on: Intel Virtualization Technology, Intel VT-X, AMD-V, Virtual Extensions, and so on. Save your settings and reboot the system.

Downloading and installing VirtualBox

Once you are on a system that meets the minimum system requirements, proceed with the following steps:

1. Navigate to the VirtualBox downloads page at `https://www.virtualbox.org/wiki/Downloads`.
2. Download and install the latest version of VirtualBox for your host operating system.

Configuring VirtualBox networking

1. Launch the VirtualBox application.
2. From the VirtualBox menu bar, select **Preferences**.
3. From the VirtualBox Preferences menu, select the **Network** icon.
4. Verify that **Host-only Networks** is highlighted.

Mac/Linux

1. If you can see **vboxnet0** on the list, highlight and click on the tool icon.
2. If you do not see **vboxnet0**, click on the + icon. Next, highlight and click on the tool icon. Click on **OK** to save your settings. See *Figure 2.3*.

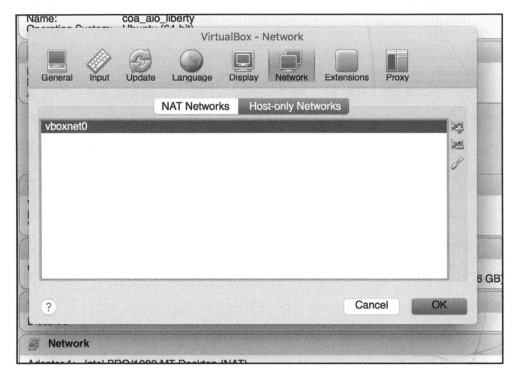

Figure 2.3: Adding the vboxnet0 host-only network to VirtualBox on Mac or Linux

Windows

1. If you can see **VirtualBox Host-Only Ethernet Adapter** on the list, highlight and click on the tool icon.
2. If you do not see **VirtualBox Host-Only Ethernet Adapter** on the list, click on the **+** icon. See *Figure 2.4*.

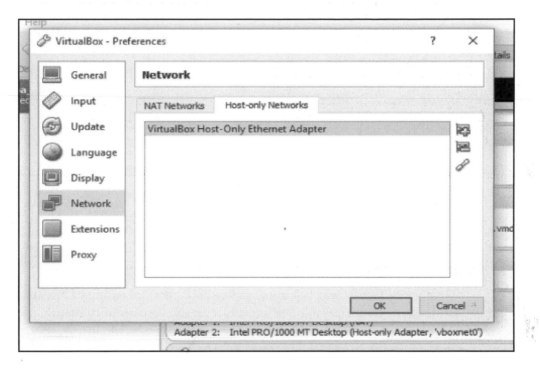

Figure 2.4: Adding the VirtualBox Host-Only Ethernet Adapter to VirtualBox on Windows

Confirming a host-only network IP address

Verify that your **vboxnet0** or **VirtualBox Host-Only Ethernet Adapter** looks like *Figure 2.5*.

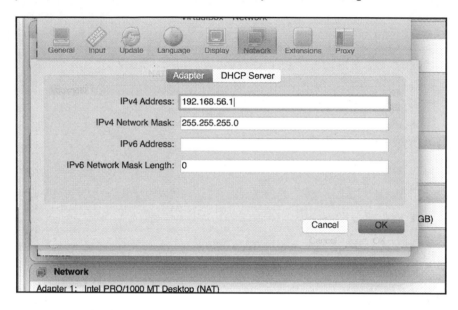

Figure 2.5: vboxnet0 or VirtualBox Host-Only Ethernet Adapter should have 192.168.56.1

If you are currently using your host-only networks for other virtual machines in VirtualBox, you can create a new host-only adapter. Verify that the new host-only adapter looks like *Figure 2.5*. After importing the virtual appliance, right-click on the appliance and select **Settings**. Navigate to the **Network** section and select this host-only network for **Adapter 2**.

Importing the appliance

1. From the VirtualBox menu bar, select **Import Appliance**. This will be under the **File** menu in Windows.
2. Click on the folder icon to browse your local drive.
3. Select **coa-aio-newton.ova** and click on **Import** or **Open**.
4. Click on **Continue** to proceed with installation.

5. Click on **Import**.
6. Once importing has completed, verify that the virtual machine has the proper network settings. See *Figure 2.6*.

Figure 2.6: The virtual appliance should automatically have two adapters assigned

7. Start up the virtual machine by highlighting the appliance and clicking on **Start**. See *Figure 2.7*.

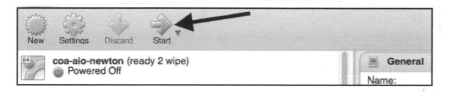

Figure 2.7: Select start to power on the virtual appliance

 If you receive an error when attempting to start the virtual machine, verify you meet the aforementioned minimum system requirements. Also verify that virtualization extensions are turned on in the BIOS or UEFI.

8. Give the appliance time to boot. You will know it's up and running once you see the Ubuntu login prompt. See *Figure 2.8*.

Figure 2.8: The virtual appliance is up and running once you see the login prompt

Although you are free to use the VirtualBox console for interacting with your newly imported OpenStack environment, you should SSH into the appliance from a terminal client on your host operating system.

SSH into the appliance

Using a terminal client to SSH into the virtual machine appliance is the best way to work through the objectives in this book. Once connected, you can easily copy and paste commands from this book into the terminal client window.

 If you are not able to SSH directly to the instance, you may be connected to a corporate or school VPN that is rerouting LAN traffic. Disconnect from the VPN and attempt to reconnect. Custom SSH proxy configurations can also cause problems connecting and should be disabled or configured to ignore LAN traffic.

Mac/Linux

1. Open up your built-in terminal.
2. Run the following:

   ```
   $ ssh openstack@192.168.56.56
   ```

3. When prompted for a password, enter openstack.

Windows

1. If you do not already have a terminal client installed, download Putty at http:// putty.org.

2. Once Putty is running, fill in the username, **IP address**, and **Port**. See *Figure 2.9*.

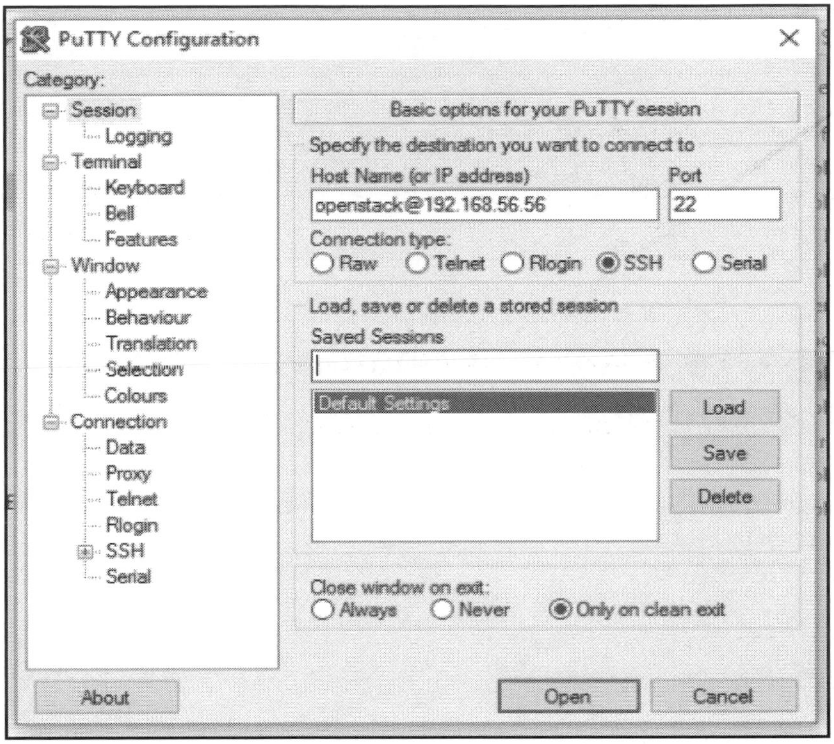

Figure 2.9: Use Putty for SSH'ing into the virtual appliance on Windows

3. When prompted for a password, enter `openstack`.

Verifying OpenStack service connectivity with the CLI

1. Once connected to the virtual appliance, source the openrc file:

   ```
   $ source openrc
   ```

2. Use `python-openstackclient` to confirm you can successfully retrieve a token:

   ```
   $ openstack token issue
   ```

3. You should receive a response similar to *Figure 2.10*.

Figure 2.10: Output from the 'openstack token issue' command

Verifying OpenStack connectivity with the Horizon dashboard

The Horizon dashboard is compatible with the latest versions of Mozilla Firefox, Google Chrome, Chromium, Microsoft Edge, and Opera. To confirm you can reach the dashboard, perform the following steps:

1. Open up your system web browser and navigate to `http://192.168.56.56/horizon`.
2. It may take some time for the page to load. It will eventually show the Horizon login screen. See *Figure 2.11*.

Figure 2.11: Horizon dashboard login screen

3. Put in the following credentials and click on **Connect**:

- **User Name**: `admin`
- **Password**: `admin`

4. You should then be presented with the Horizon overview screen. See *Figure 2.12*.

Figure 2.12: Horizon dashboard overview screen

In a production OpenStack cloud, you would connect to the Horizon dashboard and API endpoints via HTTPS (SSL/TLS).

Summary

You should now have your very own working OpenStack environment, fully deployed and running on your laptop or desktop! This chapter discussed VirtualBox and the convenience of the OVA format, as well as the components that make up a traditional OpenStack environment.

At this point, you should be able to connect to the virtual appliance via the Horizon dashboard and terminal client on your system. You are certainly free to use your own OpenStack environment, but the exercises and practice exam in this book will require resources previously created in the provided virtual appliance.

In the next chapter, we will discuss the Keystone identity service and work through all Keystone exam objectives via the CLI and Horizon dashboard. Let's get started!

3
Keystone Identity Service

Let's begin our preparation of the Certified OpenStack Administrator exam objectives by discussing Keystone, the OpenStack identity service. Understanding Keystone is one of the primary building blocks of passing the COA exam.

In this chapter, we will cover the following topics:

- Authentication and authorization?
- Keystone architecture
- Keystone concepts
- Authentication in action
- Project scope on the Horizon dashboard and CLI
- Exam objective - managing quotas
- Exam objective - managing users, roles, groups, projects, and domains
- Exam objective - managing the service catalog - services and endpoints

After this chapter, you should have a solid understanding of Keystone and the skills necessary to successfully fulfill all Keystone-related objectives on the exam.

About Keystone

All users and services rely on Keystone. Without Keystone, users would not have the ability to properly authenticate and create virtual machines, networks, and other resources. OpenStack services would not be able to properly authenticate in order to successfully fulfill user requests, or to make requests to other OpenStack services.

Authentication or authorization?

Before we begin to dive into the details of Keystone, let's take a moment to think about the concepts of **authentication** and **authorization**. These two words are sometimes misused, so let's provide a proper definition.

Authentication is the act of confirming the identity of a specific user—in other words, proving that a user is whom she or he claims to be.

Authorization is the function of determining access rights for that specific user.

Keystone has a variety of functions, but first and foremost, it provides **authentication**. All OpenStack users are required to authenticate to Keystone via the **Horizon dashboard**, **command-line interface (CLI)**, **SDK**, or directly to the **API**.

Once a user is authenticated, Keystone is not involved in determining the user's access rights. Access rights include things such as whether a user can create a Neutron virtual router or perhaps create Glance images that are publicly accessible. This **authorization** is handled by a file called `policy.json`, and it lives in each installed OpenStack service's configuration directory. The exam does not require you to understand how to modify authorization via this file, but understanding the difference between authentication and authorization is fundamental before we proceed.

Keystone architecture

Let's take a brief look at the Keystone architecture. Keystone is the common authentication system across the entire cloud, receiving more requests than any other OpenStack service. Since the Liberty version of OpenStack, the Keystone development team moved over to using Apache as the API frontend to Keystone. See *Figure 3.1*. The Apache daemon is bound to port **5000** and is the primary gateway to Keystone. All users and services rely on Keystone for authentication. The OpenStack environment's relational database management system (typically MariaDB, a fork of MySQL) contains a Keystone database that stores data for all the various Keystone resources.

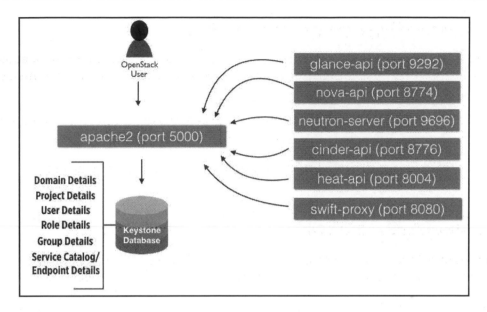

Figure 3.1: Keystone is the central OpenStack authentication service and utilizes the Apache web server for its frontend web server. All users and OpenStack services are required to authenticate to Keystone

Keystone concepts

Let's take a look at some common Keystone terminology. If you are a bit confused by the introduction of these concepts, don't worry. We will cover all of them in more detail as we work through specific exam objectives and perform tasks in our lab environment.

- **Domains:** Domains are high-level logical containers used for users, groups, and projects. Consider a new IT company wanting to create an OpenStack public cloud. If this company really wanted to make an impact in the IT world, they would need to host and support more than one customer signing up for their very own OpenStack account. The company would most likely put each new customer in their own domain. Similar to popular public clouds such as Amazon Web Services or Google Cloud Platform, each customer would create resources that are segregated from other customers residing in the same environment. The customer would not only be able to create their very own virtual resources, such as virtual machines or networks, but also create their very own users, projects, and groups within that domain.

Almost every resource or object in OpenStack gets a **universal unique identifier (UUID)**. Although we can assign human-readable names to these resources, the UUID is used to uniquely identify resources and objects in logs, databases, and other areas of the OpenStack infrastructure.

- **Projects:** A project represents an area where resources get created. Consider our previously mentioned company running an OpenStack public cloud. They set up each customer in their own domain and within that domain allow the customer to create multiple **projects**. See *Figure 3.2*. These projects would most likely be representations of various business units so that they could easily segregate resources. Users existing in other projects would not be able to see resources created in your project unless explicitly shared. Accounting, finance, or human-resources are examples of projects possible in real-world OpenStack projects. A user could certainly belong to one or more projects, but they can only be authenticated to one project at one time. The concept of authenticating oneself to a single project is called **scope**. Any resource an authenticated user creates is always owned by the project to which the user is currently scoped. There are a few exceptions, but we will discuss them later in the book.

Don't get confused if you hear people in the OpenStack world use the word **tenant**. In previous versions of OpenStack, "tenant" was used to describe what we now know as projects. You may even hear someone referring to projects as accounts! **Projects**, **tenants**, and **accounts** all mean the same thing in the OpenStack world.

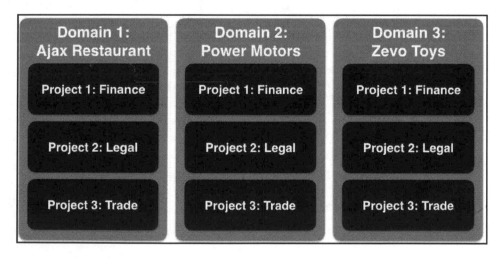

Figure 3.2: Domains are high-level logical containers used for users, groups, and projects. Projects live inside domains and represent an area where virtual resources get created

- **Users:** Users are that have been created for individual people in an organization. Users typically reside in the Keystone database, but could possibly live in an Active Directory or LDAP server. Each domain can contain any number of users; because each resource is assigned a UUID, two user accounts existing in different domains can have the exact same name. Another thing to keep in mind is that you will always see user accounts residing inside Keystone that are not human users! Remember how we saw that Keystone provides a common authentication system across the entire OpenStack cloud? Well, not only do users authenticate against Keystone, but OpenStack services such as Glance, Neutron, and Nova do as well. There will almost always be a project called **service** in any OpenStack cloud. The service project will always contain user accounts for each OpenStack service (Glance, Neutron, and so on) installed in that particular OpenStack environment. When a service wants to talk to another service, it must authenticate via its user account residing in the **service** project. Keystone is the only user account you will not see in the service project, because Keystone does not need to authenticate against itself.

- **Roles:** Roles are labels that are applied directly to a user or a group. Remember when we discussed that Keystone has nothing to do with authorization? A role is just a label associated with a user on a project. A file called `policy.json` handles authorization by determining what a user with a specific role can or cannot do. See *Figure 3.3*. When user **lisad** authenticates to Keystone and gets scoped to the **Trade** project, she has the **_member_** role. If Lisa wanted to boot a virtual machine, the `policy.json` file found in the **nova** configuration directory (`/etc/nova/policy.json`) would define whether the **_member_** role can boot instances (without modifications, a user with **_member_** should be able to boot instances). We also see that user **frankd** has the **read-only** role on the **Legal** project. If Frank authenticates and scopes to the Legal project, he may want to create a Neutron network, but unfortunately will not be able to do so because of the Neutron `policy.json` file—which explicitly declares the read-only role as only being capable of listing networks. As an OpenStack Administrator, you may have some part to play in defining these roles via the `policy.json` file, but your customers never will. A customer only has the ability to see which roles exist and apply them to users on a project.

TIP Don't get too caught up editing configuration files such as `policy.json`. There are no exam objectives regarding configuration file modification in the current official COA objective requirements.

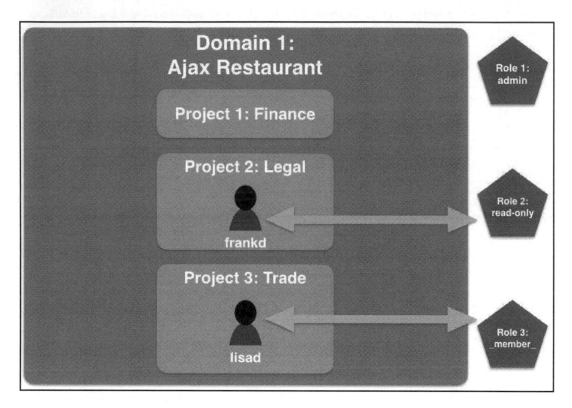

Figure 3.3: Roles are labels that get applied directly to a user or group on a specific project. When a user is scoped to a project, they receive their associated role

- **Groups:** Groups are a newer Keystone concept that provide an easy way to apply an existing role to multiple users. They are optional and were created to eliminate the hassle of applying roles to one user at a time. See *Figure 3.4*. User **frankd** is a part of the **Interns** group on the **Legal** project. Because the **read-only** role is assigned to the **Interns** group on the **Legal** project, Frank automatically gets the **read-only** role when he authenticates and scopes to the **Legal** project. User **lisad** is a member of the **Operators** group. Lisa will get the **_member_** role when she authenticates and scopes to the Trade project.

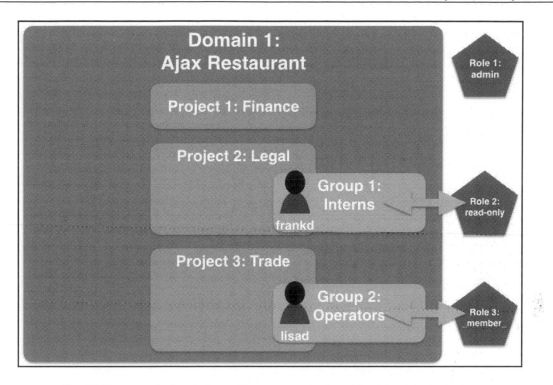

Figure 3.4: Groups are an optional container for users. They are an easy way to apply an existing role to multiple users at one time

- **Quotas**: Quotas determine the quantity or size of resources that can be created within a specific project. They act as guardrails by preventing users from exceeding capacity. Although each OpenStack service keeps track of the utilization of these resources, adjusting quotas is easily done within the Keystone panel of the Horizon dashboard (which will be shown later in this chapter).
- **Service Catalog/Endpoints**: The Service Catalog is a map stored in Keystone that contains a list of services and endpoints. I like to think of the Service Catalog as the *OpenStack telephone book*. It provides a listing of API endpoints for all services installed in the environment. There are three URLs provided for each service in the catalog: public, internal, and admin; we will talk about this in more depth when we discuss the Keystone exam objectives.

Keystone in your virtual appliance

Figure 3.5 shows you the Keystone layout of the COA virtual appliance provided with this book. As you can see, there are two domains present: **Default** and **Heat**. When one initially sets up an OpenStack environment, the default domain is just that: the default domain! In the case of our lab environment, the various projects we will work with are all within the default domain.

Notice how the users in our cloud have the **_member_** role. This role, although not explicitly defined in the `policy.json` file for each respective service, is simply a way to give users regular operator rights. With this role, users can create, read, update, and delete resources, as long as they own that resource. Notice how the admin user has the admin role assigned to it and has access to all projects in the domain. The admin role is defined in all `policy.json` files as having full admin access to all projects within all domains. I know this seems to be a bit non-secure, but keep in mind that we would never give the admin role to a customer in an environment with customers in each domain. To work around this, OpenStack administrators create **domain_admin** roles. This is outside the scope of COA prep, but for more information on this, visit `https://wiki.openstack.org/wiki/Horizon/DomainWorkFlow`.

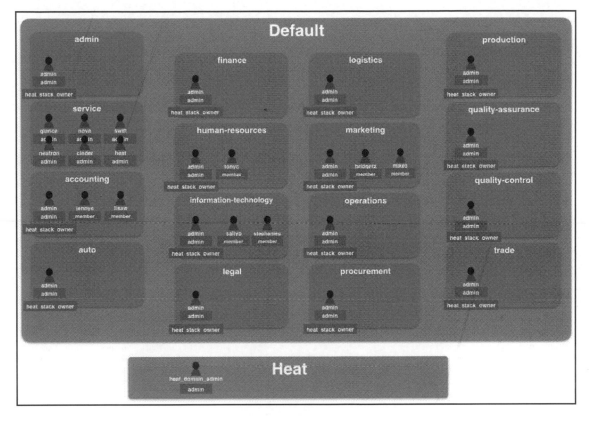

Figure 3.5: The Keystone layout for the virtual appliance included with this book

The **heat_stack_owner** role is required for any user that wants to manage Heat stacks. You will learn more about Heat in Chapter 9, *Heat Orchestration Service*.

Authentication in action

Now that you have your OpenStack environment up and running, open up your web browser and navigate to the Horizon dashboard at http://192.168.56.56/horizon. The login screen is where you would submit the username and password provided to you by your OpenStack administrator. An OpenStack administrator needs to provision this account, along with a password, email address, and a few other options.

You can log in to the provided environment with the following credentials:

User Name: admin

Password: admin

Congratulations! You have been properly authenticated by Keystone and have been granted access to the Horizon dashboard overview screen. *Figure 3.6* shows you how clicking on the *Connect* button automatically sends an API request containing your domain, username, and password to the Keystone API endpoint. Once connected you will automatically be scoped to a project to which you belong.

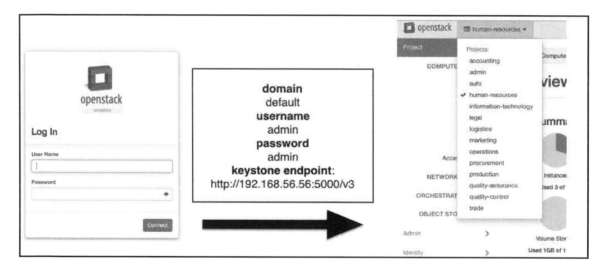

Figure 3.6: Interacting with Keystone by logging into the Horizon dashboard

You may have noticed that the login screen does not have a field for entering the domain name. This is because multi-domain is turned off in the Horizon dashboard. If you are an advanced user and would like to change this, go to `/etc/openstack-dashboard/local_settings.py` and set **OPENSTACK_KEYSTONE_MULTIDOMAIN_SUPPORT** to **True**. Make sure you restart Apache by running `sudo systemctl restart apache2`.

Project scope via the dashboard

Now that you are logged in, find the **Project** dropdown at the top of the screen. You will notice that there are a variety of projects: **accounting**, **logistics**, **marketing**, **operations**, **trade**, and more. These projects represent different business areas in our domain and are areas where resources get created. As you can see, the admin user you are logged in with belongs to a variety of projects. See *Figure 3.7*. By selecting a specific project, the user is scoping themselves to that project. Once a user is scoped to a project, any resources that the user creates (instances, volumes, networks, routers, and so on) will be owned by that project. There are a few exceptions to this rule, but we will talk about that later.

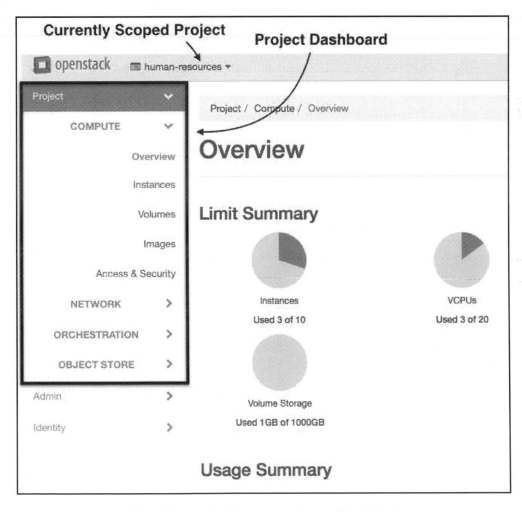

Figure 3.7: A user scoped to the human-resources project on the Horizon dashboard

The admin life

The admin user in our virtual appliance environment has the admin role on every project in the environment. Because we are logged in with a user who has the admin role, the Horizon dashboard exposes an **Admin Panel Group**, in addition to the **Project Panel Group**. Users who do not have the admin role will not see the admin panel group. See *Figure 3.8.*

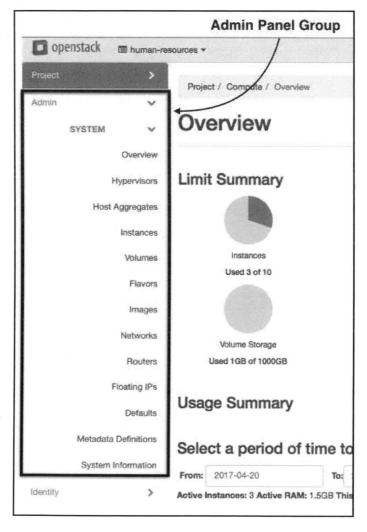

Figure 3.8: By default. the Horizon dashboard admin panel group is only seen by users with the admin role

The admin panel group will allow the logged-in user to see *all resources* created in *all projects* across *all domains*. It's very important to not forget this when performing exam objectives. Some exam objectives *may* require access to the admin panel and we will explore this in upcoming chapters.

The Identity panel

The Identity panel is presented to all users, regardless of role. Users with the admin role will have more visible options, including the ability to create additional projects within the default domain and create new users, groups, and roles.

Selecting **Projects** shows you all users across all domains in the environment.

It's important to note that with multi-domain turned off in this environment, you will lack the ability to create new domains or add new resources to any domain other than default. This is where the flexibility of the OpenStack CLI comes into play.

Keystone and the OpenStack CLI

95% of the COA objectives can be completed via the Horizon dashboard, but there still some tasks that require using the CLI.

Let's begin our work on the CLI. Open up your terminal client and SSH into your virtual appliance (see
Chapter 2, *Setting Up Your Practice Exam Environment*, for instructions on how to do this).

Recall that an OpenStack user needs to ask their OpenStack administrator (that's you!) for the initial authentication information to get started using OpenStack and the CLI. So what's the minimal amount of information a user would need to authenticate against OpenStack?

- **Keystone authentication endpoint:** A URL location of the Keystone API daemon. In production OpenStack environments, it is typically a resolvable name like https://mycloud.example.com:5000/v3, or an external IP address.
- **Domain**: The domain your user lives in.
- **Project**: The project to which you want to be scoped.
- **Username**: Your Keystone username.
- **Password**: Your Keystone password.

There are two primary ways a user can provide authentication information to OpenStack with the CLI:

1. CLI arguments
2. Bash variables

Here is an example of an admin user using `python-openstackclient` with CLI arguments to get a list of all users in the environment:

```
$ openstack --os-auth-url http://192.168.56.56:5000/v3 --os-user-domain-
name default    --os-project-name marketing --os-username admin --os-
password admin --os-identity-api-version 3 user list
```

You should get the following output:

```
+-----------------------------------------------+--------------------+
| ID                                            | Name               |
+-----------------------------------------------+--------------------+
| 0111fd06259949da89b1eaf090dfa299              | swift              |
| 10d009379e92472fa0737f05a8d17a65              | sallyp             |
| 1a4862a86ea7410a977befc927b741f2              | mikeo              |
| 214ad6d7786e4ce59474466a3f281d7c              | admin              |
| 2a0c974a13b042e9849a9366a2e5b589              | lisaw              |
| 5caa55bf0e0d4a8b9ef87f9fe3d0db58              | stephanieu         |
| 5e06fe65b4564e25bf78f3a0247de866              | jennys             |
| abf83d3121d6400a94605cf5f6f86d2e              | heat               |
| b20191a5687b4e19973f91a4e53b7350              | bridgetz           |
| b5891f82de404b78a2f01e5623f2fd27              | nova               |
| c56e3b63db334e169ea4aade4625379c              | cinder             |
| dee729ec8187474c89eaaf08ea0696a1              | glance             |
| e351bac843f841ab860ba68f4203e3e5              | tonyc              |
| e8dff9476b994c05b49ff42dd1b1551b              | heat_domain_admin  |
| eb02e27293be40a881edeaa4e6597549              | neutron            |
+-----------------------------------------------+--------------------+
```

Figure 3.9: Output from the 'openstack user list' command

In this example, the domain, user, password, and project CLI arguments are being sent to the Keystone authentication endpoint. Your credentials are validated and your role (admin) is evaluated in comparison to Keystone's `policy.json` file. Recall that the admin role gives access to everything, so you are seeing a list of all users in the environment, across all domains.

Can you imagine needing to put CLI arguments into your commands every time you want to interact with OpenStack? It would be pretty annoying. This is why many people rely on the alternate way of suppling these credentials: Bash variables.

In the Openstack user home directory (`/home/openstack`), you should see a file called `openrc`. This file contains the authentication information necessary to interact with OpenStack via the CLI. I've provided this file for you so you don't need to mess around with creating your own.

Run the following to set the credentials in your current Bash session:

```
$ source openrc
```

You can verify the variables have been set by running the following command to show all variables, and piping them to `grep` to filter based off the `OS` prefix.

```
$ export | grep OS
```

After verifying the variables have been set, you can now run a command without manually providing credentials:

```
$ openstack user list
```

You should see the same output as *Figure 3.9.*

Again, we are seeing users across the entire OpenStack environment across all domains. If we wanted to narrow the scope of users within a specific project only, we could run the following:

```
$ openstack user list --domain heat
```

You should see output similar to *Figure 3.10*:

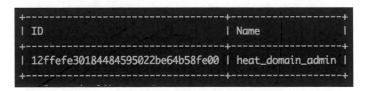

Figure 3.10: Output from the 'openstack user list --domain heat' command

It's important to note that these variables are temporary and only remain for the duration of the Bash session. If you are connecting to a real-world production OpenStack environment, be careful not to expose your variables to anyone around you. You don't want anyone stealing your password!

CLI arguments always take priority over Bash variables. If there is a CLI argument missing, `python-openstackclient` will look to the variables in the Bash session for the value.

Project scope via CLI

For objectives that require the CLI, it's critical that you understand how to scope yourself to a project. The easiest way to scope to a project on the CLI is by simply changing the project or tenant variables inside your credential file.

Let's try changing the project scope from the admin project to the legal project. Let's first copy our original `openrc` file to `openrc-legal`:

```
$ cp openrc openrc-legal
```

Now that we've made a copy, let's edit the `openrc-legal` file and update the project and tenant name variables to reflect our desired scope to the **legal** project. If you are more comfortable with `vim`, `emacs`, or any other editor, feel free to use it here.

```
$ nano openrc-legal
```

Change the following variables to `legal` and save the file. To exit and save your changes with `nano`, hit *Ctrl + X*, and then *Y* to save.

```
export OS_PROJECT_NAME=legal
export OS_TENANT_NAME=legal
```

We are changing the `OS_TENANT_NAME` variable since some of the older service-based clients may rely on it.

Now that we have created a new credential file for the **legal** project, let's source the file:

```
$ source openrc-legal
```

Verify that the variables have been properly set:

```
$ export | grep OS
```

Using the `openstack token issue` command, confirm you can properly authenticate against Keystone and get a token scoped to the legal project.

```
$ openstack token issue
```

You should see output similar to *Figure 3.11*:

```
+-----------+------------------------------------------------------------------+
| Field     | Value                                                            |
+-----------+------------------------------------------------------------------+
| expires   | 2017-07-05 07:25:01+00:00                                        |
| id        | gAAAAABZXIY99hTGxYft1ECIUn4hi3aberAf4kLGHxUK4gZwAMEKcsr           |
|           | jYT0B7TshBtV9hx-OMGSiZDXTlG6W_MIFKp7GCnnrr_bBKh_0u40soR           |
|           | dN5aAOZ3rEG7GMSaJxMpr24Go1Ow5eRlQgsl078Y8ewI5Vl1PYh8bmB           |
|           | 5s6qwxp7Gh_9kp5sp4                                                |
| project_id| 2ef4c75a3f544be38aa6df8de1a7ff13                                 |
| user_id   | 214ad6d7786e4ce59474466a3f281d7c                                 |
+-----------+------------------------------------------------------------------+
```

Figure 3.11: Output from the 'openstack token issue' command

The `project_id` should match the the ID of the legal project. Confirm by running the following command:

```
$ openstack project list
```

Service-based clients versus OpenStack client

One of the biggest questions from OpenStack newcomers is whether to use python-openstackclient or the older service-based clients such as Neutron (python-neutronclient), Nova (python-novaclient), or Cinder (python-cinderclient). Any time we interact with the Keystone v3 API, you must use the python-openstackclient. All Keystone-related COA objectives that cannot be performed on the Horizon dashboard will require you to use python-openstackclient.

Exam objectives

Now that we have a good idea of how to authenticate and scope ourselves to a specific project with Keystone via the Horizon dashboard and CLI, let's take a look at the exam objectives.

Figure 3.12 breaks down various objectives from the official objective list shown in `Chapter 1, Introducing OpenStack and the Certified OpenStack Administrator Exam,` and are available at `http://www.openstack.org/coa/requirements`. As you can see, a majority of the tasks can be completed via the Horizon dashboard, but there are still some that must be done via the CLI. You will find that many of the dashboard objectives are extremely intuitive, while some of the CLI objectives require a little more research.

Objectives	Dashboard	Command-Line
Modify Quotas	✓	✓
Create Domains	▣	✓
Edit/List Domains	▣	✓
Delete Domains	▣	✓
Create Roles	✓	✓
Edit/List/Delete Roles	✓	✓
Create Projects (Default Domain)	✓	✓
Create Projects (Other Domains)	▣	✓
Edit/List/Delete Projects (Default Domain)	✓	✓
Edit/List/Delete Projects (Other Domains)	✓	✓
Create Users (Default Domain)	✓	✓
Create Users (Other Domains)	▣	✓
Edit/List/Delete Users (Other Domains)	✓	✓
Create Groups (Default Domains)	✓	✓
Create Groups (Other Domains)	▣	✓
Edit/List/Delete Groups (Default Domain)	✓	✓
Edit/List/Delete Groups (Other Domains)	✓	✓
Create Service Catalog Services & EndPoints	▣	✓
Edit Service Catalog Services & EndPoints	▣	✓
List Service Catalog Endpoints	✓	✓

Figure 3.12: Some Keystone-related objectives must be completed via the CLI

Exam objective - adjusting quotas

Quotas determine the maximum quantity or size of resources within a specific project. As you can see from *Figure 3.13*, any resource a user creates is owned by the project to which they are scoped.

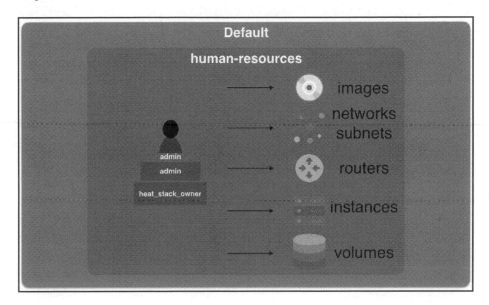

Figure 3.13: Images, networks, routers, and instances are owned by the project to which a user is scoped. In this example, the admin user is scoped to the human-resources project with the admin and heat_stack_owner roles

Quotas are an OpenStack feature that act as guardrails for the project. Quotas need to be in place to prevent users from exceeding capacities set by the OpenStack infrastructure engineers and/or OpenStack administrators. In a vanilla, out-of-the-box OpenStack environment, you must have the **admin** role in order to control quotas. See *Figure 3.14*.

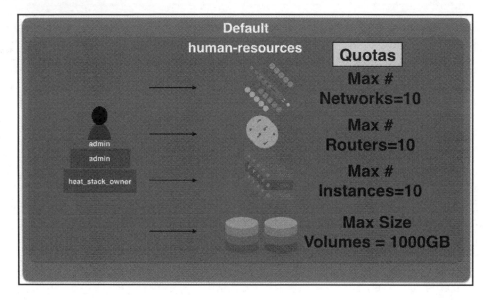

Figure 3.14: Quotas act as guardrails for the project, allowing an OpenStack Administrator to set specific quantities or capacities of virtual resources

Horizon dashboard

See *Figure 3.15*. From the OpenStack dashboard, you can modify quotas by doing the following:

1. Select the **Identity** panel.
2. Select **Projects**. This shows all projects in the environment, across all domains.

3. Select the drop-down arrow next to the **production** project and select **Modify Quotas**.

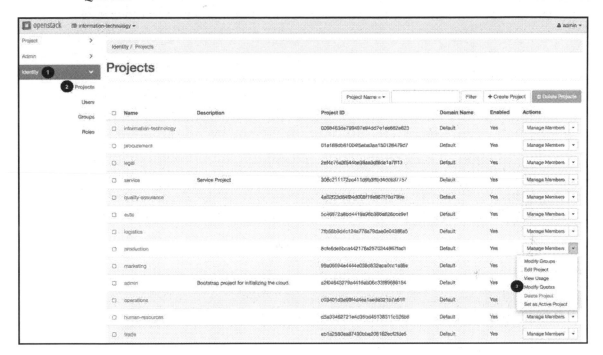

Figure 3.15: Modifying quotas from the project dropdown

4. See *Figure 3.16*. Increase the number of **instances** that can be created in the **Production** project to 20.

5. Select **Save**.

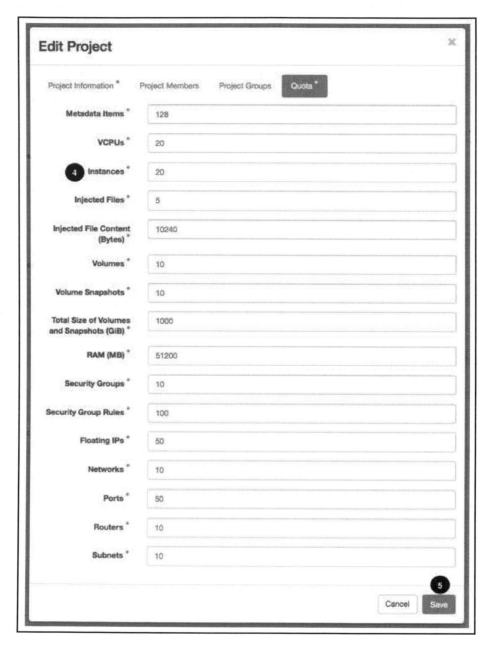

Figure 3.16: Quotas can be easily adjusted from the Horizon dashboard

Congratulations! You have just successfully allowed a total of 20 virtual machine instances to be booted within the production project. Keep in mind that this is the total number of instances within the production project and *not* per user.

CLI

To get a comprehensive list of default quotas for a specific project, use `python-openstackclient`. First ensure that you have sourced your `openrc` file:

```
$ source openrc
```

Verify that the variables have been set:

```
$ export | grep OS
```

Get a list of all projects in the environment:

```
$ openstack project list
```

Find the **Trade** project UUID. The UUID in your environment may be different than what appears here. Use the `openstack quota show` command to see all the default quotas for the trade project.

```
$ openstack quota show eb1a2580ea87490bbe206162ecf2fde5
```

You should see output similar to *Figure 3.17*:

```
+-----------------------+------------------------------------+
| Field                 | Value                              |
+-----------------------+------------------------------------+
| backup_gigabytes      | 1000                               |
| backups               | 10                                 |
| cores                 | 20                                 |
| fixed-ips             | -1                                 |
| floating-ips          | 50                                 |
| gigabytes             | 1000                               |
| gigabytes_lvm         | -1                                 |
| injected-file-size    | 10240                              |
| injected-files        | 5                                  |
| injected-path-size    | 255                                |
| instances             | 10                                 |
| key-pairs             | 100                                |
| networks              | 10                                 |
| per_volume_gigabytes  | -1                                 |
| ports                 | 50                                 |
| project               | eb1a2580ea87490bbe206162ecf2fde5   |
| properties            | 128                                |
| ram                   | 51200                              |
| rbac-policies         | 10                                 |
| routers               | 10                                 |
| secgroup-rules        | 100                                |
| secgroups             | 10                                 |
| server-group-members  | 10                                 |
| server-groups         | 10                                 |
| snapshots             | 10                                 |
| snapshots_lvm         | -1                                 |
| subnetpools           | -1                                 |
| subnets               | 10                                 |
| volumes               | 10                                 |
| volumes_lvm           | -1                                 |
+-----------------------+------------------------------------+
```

Figure 3.17: Output from the 'openstack quota show' command shows all default quotas

This is a comprehensive list of quotas and will show you anything lacking in the dashboard quota view. To modify a quota via the CLI, you have two options. Let's take a look at the first.

Check out the following to see the available parameters/arguments:

```
$ openstack help quota set
```

```
usage: openstack quota set [-h] [--class] [--properties <properties>]
                           [--server-groups <server-groups>] [--ram <ram>]
                           [--key-pairs <key-pairs>] [--instances <instances>]
                           [--fixed-ips <fixed-ips>]
                           [--injected-file-size <injected-file-size>]
                           [--server-group-members <server-group-members>]
                           [--injected-files <injected-files>]
                           [--cores <cores>]
                           [--injected-path-size <injected-path-size>]
                           [--gigabytes <gigabytes>] [--volumes <volumes>]
                           [--snapshots <snapshots>]
                           [--subnetpools <subnetpools>] [--vips <vips>]
                           [--members <members>] [--ports <ports>]
                           [--subnets <subnets>] [--networks <networks>]
                           [--floating-ips <floating-ips>]
                           [--health-monitors <health-monitors>]
                           [--secgroup-rules <secgroup-rules>]
                           [--secgroups <secgroups>] [--routers <routers>]
                           [--rbac-policies <rbac-policies>]
                           [--volume-type <volume-type>]
                           <project/class>
openstack quota set: error: too few arguments
```

Figure 3.18: Output from the 'openstack help quota set' command

If you wanted to increase quotas for the maximum number of instances within the trade project, you could do the following:

```
$ openstack quota set --instances 20 eb1a2580ea87490bbe206162ecf2fde5
```

There will not be any output.

Run the `openstack quota show` command again to verify that the instance quota has gone up to 20:

```
$ openstack quota show eb1a2580ea87490bbe206162ecf2fde5
```

You should see output similar to *Figure 3.19*:

```
| injected-file-size  | 10240
| injected-files      | 5
| injected-path-size  | 255
| instances           | 20
| key-pairs           | 100
| network             | 10
| per_volume_gigabytes | -1
| port                | 50
```

Figure 3.19: The quotas for the trade project should now reflect the ability to create up to 20 instances

One great way to see the raw API calls being made behind the scenes is by using the `--debug` option. Append it to any `python-openstackclient` command to see calls to the OpenStack APIs!

For your convenience, *Figure 3.20* shows a comprehensive list of available quotas, their definitions, default values, and the service responsible for managing the quota.

Quota Name	Definition	Quantity/Size	Service
Fixed IPs	Max # of fixed ip addresses within the	-1	Neutron
Floating IPs	Max # of floating ip addresses within the	50	Neutron
Keypairs	Max # of SSH key pairs within the	100	Nova
Injected File Content	Max file size (bytes) that can be injected	10240	Nova
Injected Files	Max # of files that can be injected into	5	Nova
Injected Path Size (KB)	Max size (kilobytes) of the injected file	255	Nova
Instances	Max # of virtual machines that can	10	Nova
Metadata Items	Max # of metadata key-value pairs that	128	Nova
Networks	Max # of networks within the project.	10	Neutron
Ports	Max # of ports within the project.	50	Neutron
RAM	Max size (MB) of all RAM assigned to all	51200	Nova
RBAC Policy	Max # of RBAC policies rules within	10	Neutron
Routers	Max # of routers within the project.	10	Neutron
Security Groups	Max # of security groups within the	10	Neutron
Security Group Rules	Max # of security group rules within	100	Neutron
Server Groups	Max # of server groups within the	10	Nova
Server Group Members	Max # of server group members	10	Nova
Subnets	Max # of subnets within the project.	10	Neutron
Subnet pools	Max # of subnets pools within the	-1	Neutron
Total Size of Volumes and	Max size (GB) of all volumes and	1000	Cinder
VCPUs	Max # of cores assigned to all	20	Nova
Volumes	Max # of volumes that can be created	10	Cinder
Volume Size	Max size (GB) of each volume within	-1	Cinder
Volume Backups	Max # of of volume backups within the	10	Cinder
Volume Backup Size	Max size (GB) of all volume backups	1000	Cinder
Volume Snapshots	Max # of volume snapshots within the	10	Cinder
Volumes	Max # of volumes within the project.	10	Cinder

Figure 3.20: A full list of all available quotas. The -1 value means 'no limit'

Where's Glance? Glance images are not controlled by quotas. To set a limit on Glance images, advanced users can look for the `image_member_quota` value in `/etc/glance/glance-api.conf`

Exam objective - managing users

Managing Keystone users is quite simple and intuitive. Remember that by default, you must have the **admin** role to manage user accounts.

Horizon dashboard

See *Figure 3.21*. From the OpenStack dashboard, you can create new users by doing the following:

1. Click on the **Identity** panel.
2. Click on **Users**. This shows all users in the environment, across all domains. You can click on the **User Name** field to put the user names in ascending order. This view can be annoying because it doesn't specify the domain or project the user account belongs to. To get that information, we need to click on the **Edit** button.
3. Click on **Create User**.

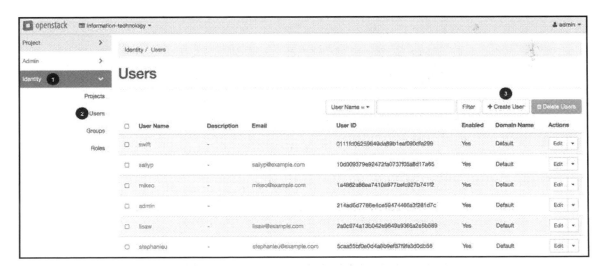

Figure 3.21: Creating a new user from the Horizon dashboard

4. **Domain ID**: the user's domain UUID. Because multi-domain is disabled, we can create a user in a domain other than default by using the CLI.
5. **Domain Name**: the user's domain name.
6. **User Name** (required): a name for the user. We will insert `johnnyc-dashboard`.
7. **Description** (optional): a description for the user. Type in `Developer`
8. **Email** (optional): an email address for the user. By default, there are no email services installed with OpenStack so this is simply data for the administrator. Type in `johnnyc@example.com`.
9. **Password** (required): a password for the user. Type in `openstack`.
10. **Confirm Password** (required): confirm the password by typing it again.
11. **Primary Project** (optional): the primary project associated with a user. Recall that a user can belong to zero or 5,000 projects. The primary project is the first project the user was setup to be associated with and has no visible effect on the user Openstack experience. Select **trade**.
12. **Role** (optional): the role the user should have on the selected primary project. Select **_member_**.
13. **Enabled** (required): whether the user's account is turned on or off. Ensure it is **enabled**.
14. Select **Create User**.

Figure 3.22: Adding details about a new OpenStack user on the Horizon dashboard

See Figure 3.23. You should now see **johnnyc-dashboard** on the list of users on the Horizon dashboard.

	stephanieu	-	stephanieu@example.com	5caa55bf0e0d4a8b9ef87f9fe3d0db58	Yes	Default	Edit ▾
	jennys	-	jsmith@example.com	5e06fe65b4564e25bf78f3a0247de866	Yes	Default	Edit ▾
	johnnyc-dashboard	Developer	johnnyc@example.com	661a4e52f3c842c685aab94841831f03	Yes	Default	Edit ▾
	heat	-		abf83d3121d6400a94605cf5f6f86d2e	Yes	Default	Edit ▾
	bridgetz	-	bridgetz@example.com	b20191a5687b4e19973f91a4e53b7350	Yes	Default	Edit ▾

Figure 3.23: The newly created user will appear in the list of users

You can easily update the **Name**, **Description**, **Email**, and **Project** of a user by selecting the **Edit** button next shown in *Figure 3.23*. To delete or disable an account, use the dropdown next to the **Edit** button.

CLI

We can add users via the CLI with `python-openstackclient`. Ensure you have sourced the admin user credentials:

```
$ source openrc
```

We will create a new user with the name `johnnyc-cli`.

Before running the command, explore the help for the user create command:

```
$ openstack help user create
```

Let's now create the user via `python-openstackclient`:

```
$ openstack user create --domain default --project trade \
--description "Developer" --email johnnyc@example.com \
--password openstack johnnyc-cli
```

It is not necessary to use the enable flag because the user is enabled by default. To disable the user upon creation, use the `--disable` flag.

Confirm the user was successfully created:

```
$ openstack user list
```

The `johnnyc-cli` user will not be able to create resources until it has a role in the project.

Run the following command. You will not receive any output.

```
$ openstack role add --user johnnyc-cli --project trade _member_
```

Verify that the `_member_` role was assigned to the user on the `trade` project by running the following command:

```
$ openstack role assignment list --names
```

Exam objective - creating domains, projects, groups, and roles

Recall that any time we log in to the Horizon dashboard with multi-domain disabled, we log in to the **Default** domain. We can easily create new projects, groups, and roles via the Horizon dashboard within the **Default** domain, but creating them under a domain other than **Default** is not possible unless we use `python-openstackclient`.

Let's dive into the process.

CLI

We will focus only on exam objectives and not complex use cases of multi-domain environments.

To create a new domain called `acme-corp` via python-openstackclient, run the following command:

```
$ openstack domain create acme-corp
```

We can now confirm that the domain has been created:

```
$ openstack domain list
```

Let's create a new user within this domain called edgarp:

```
$ openstack user create --domain acme-corp edgarp --password openstack
```

We can now proceed to create a new project within the acme-corp domain. Let's create one called development:

```
$ openstack project create --domain acme-corp development
```

Let's now create a new group in the acme-corp domain called interns:

```
$ openstack group create --domain acme-corp interns
```

Let's now add edgarp to the group:

```
$ openstack group add user --group-domain acme-corp interns edgarp
```

Verify that edgarp is in the interns group:

```
$ openstack group contains user --group-domain acme-corp interns edgarp
```

In order to get edgarp access to the development project within the acme-corp domain, we must apply a role to the interns group on the development project:

```
$ openstack role add --project-domain acme-corp --project development --group interns _member_
```

You will not receive any output from this command. We can confirm that it worked properly by first verifying that the interns group has the _member_ role on the development project within acme-corp domain:

```
$ openstack role assignment list --group interns --names
```

Figure 3.24 shows a visual of what we just created:

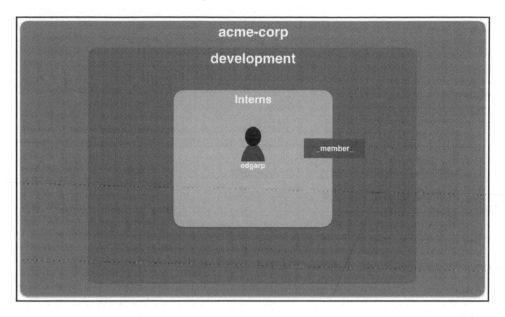

Figure 3.24: A project called development within the acme-corp domain. The edgarp user has the _member_ role on the development project

 Because Horizon dashboard multi-domain is turned off, edgarp will need to rely on the CLI for authentication to the acme-corp domain.

Exam objective - managing the service catalog - services and endpoints

For those new to OpenStack, the concept of the **service catalog** is confusing because most novice OpenStack users and administrators indirectly interact with OpenStack service APIs via the dashboard or CLI.

You can think of the catalog as a listing of URLs that are stored in Keystone. This listing shows the API URLs (otherwise known as *endpoints*) for all services currently installed in the OpenStack environment. Although not part of the exam objectives, let's take a big picture look at how a user interacting directly with the API would use the service catalog:

1. The OpenStack operator/developer decides they want to directly interact with the API, so they receive the Keystone authentication URL, username, password, domain, and project directly from their OpenStack administrator. They send this information via an API request (using a tool such as `curl` or `wget`) to Keystone.

2. Keystone responds back with two things: a token scoped to the specific project and a service catalog.

3. The user browses the service catalog much like browsing the menu at their favorite restaurant, deciding which meal to purchase. In this case, they are deciding which service they want to use. The service catalog shows the location of all the services' APIs in the OpenStack environment. If they decide they want to create a new instance, they look up how to make their API call from the Nova API documentation available at `http://developer.openstack.org`.

4. The OpenStack operator/developer then sends the token they received in **step 2** along with the API request for creating a server directly to the Nova API public URL endpoint.

5. If the user's role has been granted the authorization to create servers, the Nova service would fulfill the request to create a server, and the user would receive an `HTTP 200 OK` from the Nova API—confirming the request was successfully fulfilled.

Some services use the catalog to do lookups on how to send API calls to other services.

It's interesting to see how this is done directly via the API. The great thing about the dashboard, CLI, SDKs, and Heat is that they do not require any explicit fumbling with tokens, service catalogs, or direct API calls.

As an OpenStack administrator, you may be responsible for advertising a newly installed OpenStack service to users of the environment. Once this service gets installed by the OpenStack infrastructure engineer, you need to add it to the service catalog so that users know the service is available. Adding new services and endpoints to the catalog can easily be done via `python-openstackclient`.

There are three endpoints for each service in the service catalog:

- **Public**: The URL that users would use for externally accessing the API. This would typically be a external IP address (or name that resolves to an external IP address). One can imagine being at a coffee shop or somewhere external to the OpenStack environment. Even a smartphone app can use the public endpoint to make API calls to the service.
- **Internal**: The URL typically used by services for internal communication. This would typically be an internal IP address only accessible from within the OpenStack cluster. There is no need for a user or service to use a public endpoint if they are inside the OpenStack environment. An OpenStack administrator or infrastructure engineer who has SSH'd into an OpenStack server could also use this endpoint.
- **Admin**: The URL is used to expose special admin-only features for a service, although it is typically the same URL/port as internal. In fact, Keystone is the only service installed in the included virtual appliance that advertises a different port for the admin URL (port `35357`). Previous versions of Keystone unlocked special functionality on this port, but as of the Newton release, there is no functional difference between the `5000` and `35357` if one is using the v3 Keystone API.

Horizon dashboard

It's important to note that as of the Newton version of OpenStack, one can only **view** the service catalog via the Horizon dashboard. You can view the service catalog in the Horizon in two areas:

1. **Admin Panel Group** | **System Information** (see *Figure 3.25*)

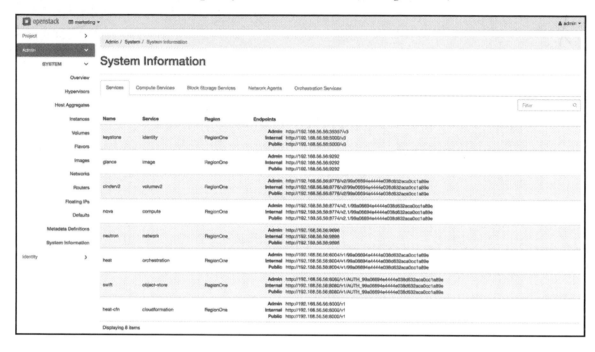

Figure 3.25: The System Information section of the Admin panel group will show all endpoints in the service catalog

2. **Access & Security** | **API Access** (see *Figure 3.26*)

Figure 3.26: The Access & Security section of the Project panel group lists all public endpoints in the catalog

CLI

We must rely on the OpenStack CLI for adding and removing entries from the service catalog. Let's consider a scenario where an OpenStack administrator would be required to edit the catalog. Imagine the OpenStack infrastructure engineers have just installed a brand new service in the OpenStack environment. The service is Trove, which allows OpenStack users to easily create both relational and NoSQL databases. How are we going to let our OpenStack users know that they now have the ability to create these databases? By advertising it in the service catalog, of course!

In order to view the entire catalog, ensure you source your `openrc` file and run the following:

```
$ openstack catalog list
```

You should see the complete service catalog as shown in *Figure 3.27.*

```
+-------------+----------------+--------------------------------------------------------------------------------+
| Name        | Type           | Endpoints                                                                      |
+-------------+----------------+--------------------------------------------------------------------------------+
| keystone    | identity       | RegionOne                                                                      |
|             |                |   internal: http://192.168.56.56:5000/v3                                       |
|             |                | RegionOne                                                                      |
|             |                |   admin: http://192.168.56.56:35357/v3                                         |
|             |                | RegionOne                                                                      |
|             |                |   public: http://192.168.56.56:5000/v3                                         |
|             |                |                                                                                |
| glance      | image          | RegionOne                                                                      |
|             |                |   public: http://192.168.56.56:9292                                            |
|             |                | RegionOne                                                                      |
|             |                |   internal: http://192.168.56.56:9292                                          |
|             |                | RegionOne                                                                      |
|             |                |   admin: http://192.168.56.56:9292                                             |
|             |                |                                                                                |
| cinderv2    | volumev2       | RegionOne                                                                      |
|             |                |   internal: http://192.168.56.56:8776/v2/a2f04643279a4416ab06c33f89686154      |
|             |                | RegionOne                                                                      |
|             |                |   admin: http://192.168.56.56:8776/v2/a2f04643279a4416ab06c33f89686154         |
|             |                | RegionOne                                                                      |
|             |                |   public: http://192.168.56.56:8776/v2/a2f04643279a4416ab06c33f89686154        |
|             |                |                                                                                |
| nova        | compute        | RegionOne                                                                      |
|             |                |   public: http://192.168.56.56:8774/v2.1/a2f04643279a4416ab06c33f89686154      |
|             |                | RegionOne                                                                      |
|             |                |   admin: http://192.168.56.56:8774/v2.1/a2f04643279a4416ab06c33f89686154       |
|             |                | RegionOne                                                                      |
|             |                |   internal: http://192.168.56.56:8774/v2.1/a2f04643279a4416ab06c33f89686154    |
|             |                |                                                                                |
| neutron     | network        | RegionOne                                                                      |
|             |                |   public: http://192.168.56.56:9696                                            |
|             |                | RegionOne                                                                      |
|             |                |   internal: http://192.168.56.56:9696                                          |
|             |                | RegionOne                                                                      |
|             |                |   admin: http://192.168.56.56:9696                                             |
|             |                |                                                                                |
| heat        | orchestration  | RegionOne                                                                      |
|             |                |   internal: http://192.168.56.56:8004/v1/a2f04643279a4416ab06c33f89686154      |
|             |                | RegionOne                                                                      |
|             |                |   admin: http://192.168.56.56:8004/v1/a2f04643279a4416ab06c33f89686154         |
|             |                | RegionOne                                                                      |
|             |                |   public: http://192.168.56.56:8004/v1/a2f04643279a4416ab06c33f89686154        |
|             |                |                                                                                |
| swift       | object-store   | RegionOne                                                                      |
|             |                |   internal: http://192.168.56.56:8080/v1/AUTH_a2f04643279a4416ab06c33f89686154 |
|             |                | RegionOne                                                                      |
|             |                |   public: http://192.168.56.56:8080/v1/AUTH_a2f04643279a4416ab06c33f89686154   |
|             |                | RegionOne                                                                      |
|             |                |   admin: http://192.168.56.56:8080/v1/AUTH_a2f04643279a4416ab06c33f89686154    |
|             |                |                                                                                |
| heat-cfn    | cloudformation | RegionOne                                                                      |
|             |                |   internal: http://192.168.56.56:8000/v1                                       |
|             |                | RegionOne                                                                      |
|             |                |   public: http://192.168.56.56:8000/v1                                         |
|             |                | RegionOne                                                                      |
|             |                |   admin: http://192.168.56.56:8000/v1                                          |
|             |                |                                                                                |
+-------------+----------------+--------------------------------------------------------------------------------+
```

Figure 3.27: The 'openstack catalog list' command shows the entire service catalog

To view all the individual services in the catalog, run the following command:

```
$ openstack service list
```

To view the URL endpoints that make up the list, use this:

```
$ openstack endpoint list
```

Let's now imagine that our engineers give us the following API URL information about the newly installed Trove service listening on port 8779 in our environment:

- **RegionOne: public endpoint**:
  `http://192.168.56.56:8779/v1.0/$(tenant_id)s`
- **RegionOne: internal endpoint**:
  `http://192.168.56.56:8779/v1.0/$(tenant_id)s`
- **RegionOne: admin endpoint**:
  `http://192.168.56.56:8779/v1.0/$(tenant_id)s`

The Region in the service catalog represents a full Openstack deployment, including its own public, internal, and admin API endpoints. Different Regions can share one set of Keystone and Horizon services, to provide access control and a Web interface. All services in our environment use one region: RegionOne.

Let's begin our advertisement of Trove by creating a listing for the service. This will include the name of the service, a description, and a type:

```
$ openstack service create --name trove --description "OpenStack Trove"
database
```

Let's now advertise the provided URLs so our OpenStack users will know how to contact the Trove API. We will advertise the public, internal, and admin API endpoints:

```
$ openstack endpoint create --region RegionOne database public
http://192.168.56.56:8779/v1.0/
$ openstack endpoint create --region RegionOne database internal
http://192.168.56.56:8779/v1.0/
$ openstack endpoint create --region RegionOne database admin
http://192.168.56.56:8779/v1.0/
```

Confirm that the Trove service and endpoints have been added to the catalog:

```
$ openstack catalog list
```

You should see Trove in the service catalog output:

```
+-----------+-----------+-----------------------------------------------+
| Name      | Type      | Endpoints                                     |
+-----------+-----------+-----------------------------------------------+
| trove     | database  | RegionOne                                     |
|           |           |   internal: http://192.168.56.56:8779/v1.0/   |
|           |           | RegionOne                                     |
|           |           |   admin: http://192.168.56.56:8779/v1.0/      |
|           |           | RegionOne                                     |
|           |           |   public: http://192.168.56.56:8779/v1.0/     |
|           |           |                                               |
+-----------+-----------+-----------------------------------------------+
```

Figure 3.28: The service catalog should now advertise the newly added Trove service and public, internal, and admin endpoints

 If you add a new service and public endpoint via the CLI, it will not show up on the Horizon dashboard until you sign out and sign back in with your username and password.

Summary

You should now have a solid understanding of Keystone and the Keystone-centric objectives required for the COA exam. Remember the importance of changing one's project scope via the Horizon dashboard and CLI. We need to use the `python-openstackclient` when creating any new domains outside of default and placing projects, users, and groups in those domains. We will also need the CLI when adding or removing entries from the service catalog.

In the next chapter, we will use discuss the Glance image service and work through all Glance exam objectives via the CLI and Horizon dashboard. Let's go!

4

Glance Image Service

In the previous chapter, we discussed the Keystone identity service, as well as the Keystone-related objectives for the Certified OpenStack administrator exam. Now we will discuss Glance. Glance is the OpenStack image service and it provides the registration, storage, and delivery of cloud images.

In this chapter, we will cover the following topics:

- Cloud Images
- Image file formats
- Glance architecture
- Glance image properties versus Glance metadata definitions
- Exam objective - creating Glance images
- Exam objective - downloading Glance images
- Exam objective - sharing Glance images with specific projects
- Exam objective - updating Glance metadata

After this chapter, you should have a solid understanding of Glance and the skills necessary to successfully fulfill all Glance-related objectives on the exam.

What is a cloud image?

If you are new to the elastic cloud world, you may be a bit confused by the concept of a cloud image. Think about the process of creating a virtual machine instance (if you haven't done this yet, you will do so in the next chapter). You typically provide a name for the instance as well as the memory size, virtual CPU count, local disk size, and an image. The virtual machine cannot boot without an operating system or something to read from the local disk.

In the past, it was customary to download your favorite operating system as an ISO, a single archive file of an optical disc. After getting your virtual machine booted, you perhaps provided answers during an install menu and went through an install wizard.

It's important to understand that in the elastic cloud world, agility is the priority and we rarely waste time with installers! When one boots an instance in an OpenStack environment, it is always required to provide a disk image (we can alternately supply an existing volume or Nova snapshot, but more on that later). Nova then proceeds to send an API request to retrieve the image from Glance. The image is placed on the compute node and the virtual machine is booted.

Unlike a typical ISO, cloud images that exist in Glance are typically snapshots of a disk's contents. These images have been previously configured by a person or script that has gone through the initial installation procedure and has installed specific programs and configuration files to ensure it is cloud aware.

Glance can store these images in a variety of backends called **data stores**. Glance supports a variety of data stores, including the local filesystem, NFS, or an OpenStack Swift container.

Building cloud images

Although outside the scope of the COA exam, it's important that we understand that the process of building these cloud images is done *outside* of OpenStack. Let's take a quick look at a few popular methods for creating a cloud image:

- **OpenStack disk image builder project**: The OpenStack disk image builder project is a tool for automatically building customized operating system images for use in clouds. It includes support for building images based on Ubuntu, Red Hat, CentOS, SUSE, and many others (`https://github.com/openstack/diskimage-builder`).
- **Hashicorp Packer**: Packer automates the building of any type of image and connects into existing configuration-management frameworks such as Chef and Puppet (`packer.io`).
- **Oracle VirtualBox**: Although extremely tedious, you can use Oracle VirtualBox to build cloud images by setting up a virtual machine to your desired state and uploading it into Glance (`virtualbox.org`).

Image file formats

Disk images store all the contents of a hard drive and come in a variety of file formats. Here are a few of the most popular options:

- **QCOW2 (QEMU Copy-On-Write)**: Used with the QEMU and QEMU-KVM hypervisors and named after their disk storage optimization strategies, which delay allocation of storage until actually needed.
- **VMDK (Virtual Machine Disk)**: Initially designed to be used with VMware's line of hypervisors but now an open format compatible with other non-VMware hypervisors such as VirtualBox.
- **VHD and VHDX (Virtual Hard Drive)**: Originally created by the Connectix Corporation for the Type-2 hypervisor *Virtual PC*, acquired by Microsoft in 2003. It's commonly used with Microsoft-related products and services, such as Hyper-V and Azure.
- **VDI (Virtual Disk Image)**: Used by Oracle's VirtualBox.
- **ISO (International Organization for Standardization, ISO9660)**: An archive file of an optical disc. It is composed of the data contents from every written sector on an optical disc, including the optical disc filesystem.
- **RAW**: An uncompressed disk image. Nova will uncompress any compressed cloud image and place it into raw format at the time of booting a virtual machine instance.

 Although we use Glance to register, store, and retrieve images, it *does not care about the type of data it stores*. In fact, Glance will store a `.txt`, `.doc`, or any other file type you throw at it. It's up to the OpenStack administrator to ensure Glance images are compatible with with the hypervisor (or hypervisors) deployed in the environment.

Glance architecture

See *Figure 4.1*. Glance is comprised of two primary daemons:

1. **glance-api**: The primary gateway to Glance. One must interact with `glance-api` to store and retrieve disk images.
2. **glance-registry**: Responsible for storing metadata associated with the image in the relational database. Examples of image metadata include the image name, image location, UUID, image size, owner (project ID), availability status, and disk format.

Glance can store images in a variety of data stores, including Swift, Amazon S3, the local filesystem on which the `glance-api` daemon resides, or even a publicly accessible web server.

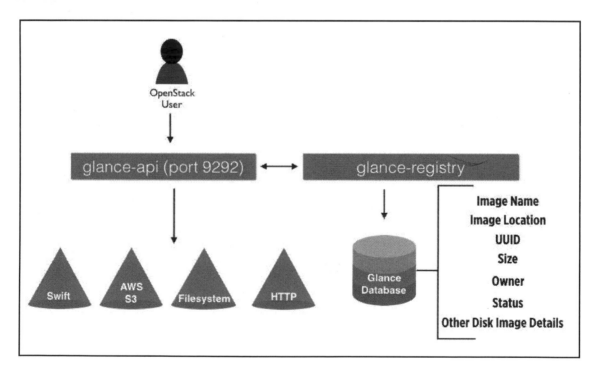

Figure 4.1: High-level diagram of the Glance architecture

The virtual appliance provided with this book configures `glance-api` to use the Swift data store. This is the most common data store used in production OpenStack environments.

Glance on the Horizon dashboard

Glance appears on the left side of the **Project Panel Group** in the Horizon dashboard. See *Figure 4.2*. In the provided virtual appliance, you can see a previously uploaded cloud image called **Cirros**. Cirros is a lightweight, minimal operating system image designed for use as a test image for clouds. You would never run production workloads on Cirros, but it's great for cloud education, development, and testing! This particular Cirros image is owned by the admin project. Also take careful note of the **visibility** column. This particular Cirros image's **visibility** is set to *public*, therefore making it accessible and thus bootable to all projects across all domains. **Visibility** is fundamental to understanding Glance and passing the Glance-related COA objectives.

Let's break down the possible visibility statuses for an image:

- **Public:** Images that are public are available to all projects, across all domains in the OpenStack environment. The default Glance `policy.json` file only allows a user with the admin role to set an image as public. Public images cannot be modified or deleted unless you are scoped to the project that owns the image.
- **Private:** Based on the default Glance `policy.json` file, any user with any role can upload images to Glance. In order to create/upload an image to Glance, a user must be scoped to a project. Once the image is successfully created/uploaded, it is owned by the project to which the user was scoped at that time and will be shown as *Private*. Any user within that project can now modify the image's properties or boot the image. Any users outside the project that owns the private image will not be able to see the image, unless it has been explicitly shared with a project.

- **Shared with Project:** If a user has the admin role, they have the ability to share an image with one specific project. If a user explicitly shares an image with your project, it will show as *Shared with Project*. You cannot modify or delete images shared with your project unless you are scoped to the project that owns the image.

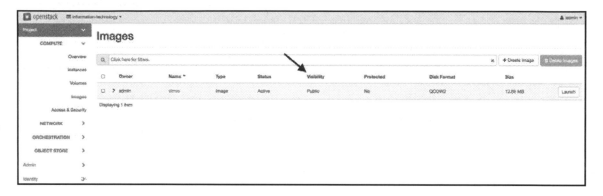

Figure 4.2: The visibility column on the Horizon dashboard determines whether a Glance image is Public, Private, or Shared with Project

Glance image properties versus Glance metadata definitions

When an image is uploaded to Glance, a user can modify metadata associated with the image as long as the user is scoped to the project that owns the image. Modifying Glance image properties can be a little confusing at first because there are two options for doing so on the Horizon dashboard.

See *Figure 4.3*. Selecting the **Edit Image** option from the Horizon dashboard allows a user to edit the **Name**, **Description**, **Format, Minimum Disk/Minimum Ram**, **Public**, and **Protected** properties. These are *not* definitions set by the Glance metadata definitions service, but simply image properties native to Glance images.

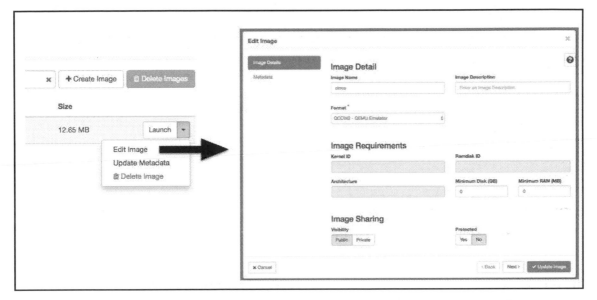

Figure 4-3: Editing Glance image properties on the Horizon dashboard

Glance metadata definitions, on the other hand, are properties that can be set on OpenStack resources. The default Glance `policy.json` file only allows users with the admin role to manage the metadata definitions, while all other users with any other role can apply those definitions to all allowed resources in OpenStack.

Figure 4.4 shows the **Metadata Definitions** panel available in the **Admin-System** panel group:

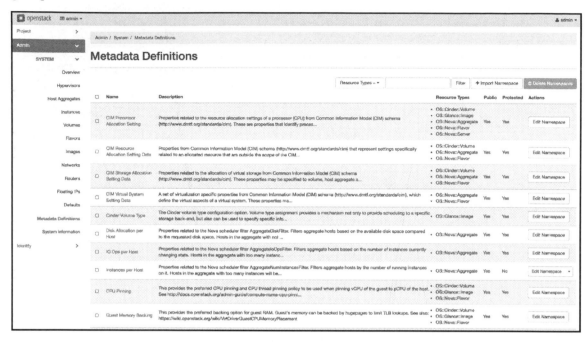

Figure 4.4: The default Glance metadata definitions template loaded by an OpenStack administrator

As you can see, the OpenStack administrator has loaded in the default templates. These metadata definition templates are available at `github.com/openstack/glance/etc/metadefs`.

A typical OpenStack user will be able to apply these loaded properties to resources they create in OpenStack. Here's an example: consider a multi-hypervisor OpenStack environment consisting of KVM, Hyper-V, and XEN hypervisors. If a user creates a Glance image, they could set metadata on that image to only allow booting it on a hypervisor compatible with the image file format.

To apply this metadata to an image, a user uploads their image and can then click on **Update Metadata** in the **Actions** dropdown. You can now select the **hypervisor_type** property from the left-hand **Available Metadata** pane and add it to the image.

You can then select the appropriate hypervisor value:

Figure 4.5: Updating metadata definitions associated with a Glance image on the Horizon dashboard

Exam objectives

After reviewing some basic details of the Glance image service, we can see that it's pretty straightforward. Similar to the Keystone exam objectives, not all of the Glance-related objectives can be performed on the dashboard.

The following chart breaks down various objectives from the official objective list shown in *Chapter 1, Introducing OpenStack and the Certified OpenStack Administrator Exam,* and is available at http://www.openstack.org/coa/requirements:

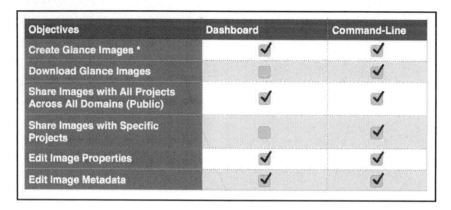

Objectives	Dashboard	Command-Line
Create Glance Images *	✓	✓
Download Glance Images		✓
Share Images with All Projects Across All Domains (Public)	✓	✓
Share Images with Specific Projects		✓
Edit Image Properties	✓	✓
Edit Image Metadata	✓	✓

Figure 4.6: Glance exam objectives

 To upload images to Glance on the Horizon dashboard, the images must be accessible via your local filesystem.

Exam objective - creating Glance images

As an OpenStack administrator, you will be responsible for creating (also known as *uploading*) Glance images so that your OpenStack users can use them to boot instances.

Let's take a look at how to do this via the OpenStack dashboard and python-openstackclient.

 We will show all Glance objectives with python-openstackclient but you are certainly free to use python-glanceclient. Remember: the exam is not concerned with how you complete objectives, as long as they successfully accomplish the task.

Horizon dashboard

Creating images via the Horizon dashboard is a fairly easy process. Let's begin by downloading a Cirros cloud image from the official website to our local laptop or desktop. It is available at `https://download.cirros-cloud.net/0.3.5/cirros-0.3.5-x86_64-disk.img`.

Now that you've downloaded Cirros, we need to ensure that we are scoped to the **procurement** project. See *Figure 4.7*.

Figure 4.7: Before we upload an image to Glance via the Horizon dashboard. ensure you are scoped to the procurement project

1. From the OpenStack overview page, scope yourself to the procurement project by selecting the top dropdown.
2. Select the **Images** panel from the **Project-Compute** panel group. If you look at the current **Public** list of images, you will notice there is currently one cloud image with visibility set to `public`. This image is currently accessible to all projects across all domains in your environment. We are going to upload a new image that will be owned only by the procurement project.
3. Select **Create Image**.
4. See Figure 4.8. **Image Nam**e (required): the display name for the image. Remember that Glance can store multiple images with the same name because it also generates an image UUID. Let's call this image `cirros-dashboard`.
5. **Image Description** (optional): Provides a description of the image you are uploading. Let's put in `Cirros Cloud Image for COA Exam Prep`.

6. **File Browse** (required): This allows us to specify the file we downloaded in the beginning of this section. Click on **Browse** and select the downloaded Cirros image from your local system.

7. **Format** (required): Specifies the disk format of the image you are uploading. We will specify QCOW2 – QEMU Emulator.

8. **Kernel** (optional): This option allows you to specify a separate kernel image for the cloud image you are uploading. Since the kernel already resides inside our Cirros Image, we will leave this empty.

9. **Ramdisk** (optional): This option allows you to specify a separate ramdisk image for the cloud image you are uploading. Since the ramdisk already resides inside our Cirros Image, we will leave this empty.

10. **Architecture** (optional): Architecture is a metadata value that is used for your OpenStack instance, but we are going to input x64 to show our OpenStack users that the image is compatible with the **x64** family of processors.

11. **Minimum Disk** (optional): Sets the minimum allowed primary disk when one boots an instance with this image. We will set this to 1. This will require anyone who boots the image to specify a flavor with primary disk size of at least 1 GB. We will discuss flavors in Chapter 5, *Nova Compute Service.*

12. **Minimum RAM** (optional): Set this to 512. This sets the minimum permitted RAM when one boots an instance with this image. Set this to 512.

13. **Visibility:** Select **Private**. Once created, this image will only be accessible to users scoped to the procurement project.

14. **Protected**: Select **No**. Let's leave this image unprotected. We could select Yes, which would prevent users from accidentally deleting the image. To delete the image, the protected flag must be removed by any user scoped to the image owner project (in this case, the procurement project).

15. Select **Create Image**.

Figure 4.8: Creating a Glance image via the Horizon dashboard

See *Figure 4.9*. The image is now available to all those within the **procurement** project. If the image takes more than a few seconds to completely load, hit **Refresh** on your web browser.

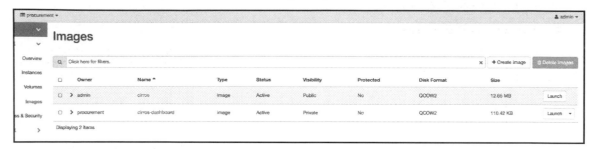

 The Newton version of OpenStack will show **all images** across **all projects** if you are logged in as a user with the admin role. Pay close attention to the **owner** column in *Figure 4.9*. This is the best way to determine which project owns a particular image.

CLI

Now that we understand how to create a Glance image on the Horizon dashboard, let's create one with `python-openstackclient`.

SSH into the provided virtual appliance. If you need instructions on how to SSH, refer to `Chapter 2`, *Setting up Your Practice Exam Environment*.

Because we are inside the appliance and not on our laptop's or desktop's filesystem, let's fetch the Cirros image and download it onto the appliance's Ubuntu 16.04 filesystem. We use the `wget` command-line utility. If you are unfamiliar with `wget`, it's a fast and convenient tool for accessing websites and downloading files from the internet.

```
$ wget https://download.cirros-cloud.net/0.3.5/cirros-0.3.5-x86_64-disk.img
```

Recall that we uploaded this image as the procurement project in the previous section. In order to scope ourselves to procurement from the CLI, we will need to provide `python-openstackclient` with the proper authentication credentials. The easiest and most convenient way for us to do this is by creating another credential file with the proper Bash variables set. Let's copy our original `openrc` file to a file called `openrc-procurement`:

```
$ cp openrc openrc-procurement
```

Now that we've made a copy, let's edit the `openrc-procurement` file and update the project and tenant name variables to reflect our desired scope to the procurement project. Feel free to use your editor of choice.

```
$ nano openrc-procurement
```

Change the following variables to `procurement` and save the file. To exit and save your changes with `nano`, hit *CTRL + X*, and then *Y* to save.

```
export OS_PROJECT_NAME=procurement
export OS_TENANT_NAME=procurement
```

 We are changing the `OS_TENANT_NAME` variable, since some of the older service-based clients rely on this rather than than `OS_PROJECT_NAME`.

Source the newly created `openrc-procurement` file:

```
$ source openrc-procurement
```

Don't forget to always verify that our variables have been properly set to scope to the `procurement` project:

```
$ export | grep OS
```

Now that we are sourced to the procurement project, run the `openstack image list` command to verify we can see if there are any available images:

```
$ openstack image list
```

See *Figure 4.10*. If you followed the previous section correctly, you should see the publicly available `cirros` image (owned by the admin project) and the `cirros-dashboard` project created via the Horizon dashboard in the previous section.

Figure 4.10: Output of the 'openstack image list' command

You can get the help for any OpenStack command by placing the word `help` after the initial command and before the action—for example: `openstack help image create`, `openstack help image list`, and `openstack help image save`.

To get more details about a specific image, you can use the `openstack image show` command. Let's see the details of the previously created `cirros-dashboard` image:

```
$ openstack image show cirros-dashboard
```

As you can see in *Figure 4.11*, in this particular image, the `owner` field shows the UUID of the procurement project along with some other details we specified in the previous section.

Before uploading our new image, we can explore some of the available arguments for this command using `help`.

```
$ openstack help image create
```

Using this information, we can now create a new Glance image via the CLI. We will use the `openstack image create` command:

```
$ openstack image create --file cirros-0.3.5-x86_64-disk.img --disk-format
qcow2 --min-disk 1 --min-ram 512 --property description='Cirros Cloud Image
for COA Exam Prep' --property architecture='x64' cirros-cli
```

`--container-format` is an optional argument that one would set if the image were in a file format that also contained metadata about the image. Container formats are not currently used by Glance or other OpenStack components, so it is safe to simply specify **bare** as the container format if you are unsure.

We should now see the output shown in *Figure 4.11*:

```
+-------------------+--------------------------------------------------------+
| Field             | Value                                                  |
+-------------------+--------------------------------------------------------+
| checksum          | f8ab98ff5e73ebab884d80c9dc9c7290                       |
| container_format  | bare                                                   |
| created_at        | 2017-08-19T23:54:00Z                                   |
| disk_format       | qcow2                                                  |
| file              | /v2/images/0505b2d1-9d42-4221-b489-04dbb4fc82cb/file   |
| id                | 0505b2d1-9d42-4221-b489-04dbb4fc82cb                   |
| min_disk          | 1                                                      |
| min_ram           | 512                                                    |
| name              | cirros-cli                                             |
| owner             | 01a169db81004f5eba3aa150126479d7                       |
| properties        | architecture='x64', description='Cirros Cloud Image for COA Exam Prep' |
| protected         | False                                                  |
| schema            | /v2/schemas/image                                      |
| size              | 13267968                                               |
| status            | active                                                 |
| tags              |                                                        |
| updated_at        | 2017-08-19T23:54:02Z                                   |
| virtual_size      | None                                                   |
| visibility        | private                                                |
+-------------------+--------------------------------------------------------+
```

Figure 4.11: Output from the 'openstack image create' command

Use this to verify that the image was successfully created by using the `openstack image list` command:

```
$ openstack image list
```

You should see output similar to *Figure 4.12* with all images set to active, verifying the image is available to be used:

```
+--------------------------------------+------------------+--------+
| ID                                   | Name             | Status |
+--------------------------------------+------------------+--------+
| 0505b2d1-9d42-4221-b489-04dbb4fc82cb | cirros-cli       | active |
| 3735dc23-52ee-4ca8-b065-fd2b1274f600 | cirros-dashboard | active |
| fdcecf4e-443a-46e0-84af-af606bb5b08a | cirros           | active |
+--------------------------------------+------------------+--------+
```

Figure 4.12: Output from the 'openstack image list' command

If we wanted to delete this image, we could easily use the simple `openstack image delete` command. See `openstack help image delete` for more information.

Exam objective - downloading images

Downloading images stored in Glance is **not possible** via the Horizon dashboard in the Newton version of OpenStack. We will rely on the `python-openstackclient` to accomplish this.

CLI

Verify you are scoped to the procurement project by sourcing the `openrc-procurement` file created in the previous section:

```
$ source openrc-procurement
```

List all available images:

```
$ openstack image list
```

Download the `cirros-cli` image to the `/tmp` directory inside your virtual appliance. You can also use the image's UUID instead of the name.

```
$ openstack image save --file /tmp/mydownloadedimage.img cirros-cli
```

Verify the image successfully downloaded to the `/tmp` location:

```
$ ls /tmp
```

Exam objective - sharing images with specific projects

An OpenStack user with the admin role has the ability to share an image with a specific project. As of the Newton version of OpenStack, Horizon does not have the capability to share images with specific projects. We will do this via `python-openstackclient`.

CLI

Ensure you are scoped to the `procurement` project:

```
$ source openrc-procurement
```

Get a list of all images we currently have access to:

```
$ openstack image list
```

Get a list of all the projects in our environment so you can lookup the UUID of the marketing project:

```
$ openstack project list
```

Share the `cirros-cli` image with the `marketing` project:

```
$ openstack image add project cirros-cli 99a06694e4444e038d632aca0cc1a89e
```

After sharing the image, you should see the output similar to *Figure 4.13*:

```
+-------------+-------------------------------------------+
| Field       | Value                                     |
+-------------+-------------------------------------------+
| created_at  | 2017-07-07T13:27:47Z                      |
| image_id    | 7d9564f3-da0c-46fb-9231-94399f01a14c      |
| member_id   | 99a06694e4444e038d632aca0cc1a89e          |
| schema      | /v2/schemas/member                        |
| status      | pending                                   |
| updated_at  | 2017-07-07T13:27:47Z                      |
+-------------+-------------------------------------------+
```

Figure 4.13: Output from the 'openstack image add' command

 Although you'll see a pending status, anyone in the marketing project should now be able to see and launch the shared image. Accepting the image is not necessary with the Glance v2 API.

Any non-admin user in the marketing project will now be able to launch an instance or create a volume from the image but will **not** be able to delete the image or modify the properties/metadata associated with it.

Exam objective - setting Glance image properties and metadata definitions

It's extremely easy to set Glance image properties and metadata definitions on images that reside in Glance. Remember that you can only set metadata on images owned by the project to which you are currently scoped.

Horizon dashboard

Recall earlier in this section, where we pointed out the two specific sections for setting Glance image properties and metadata definitions.

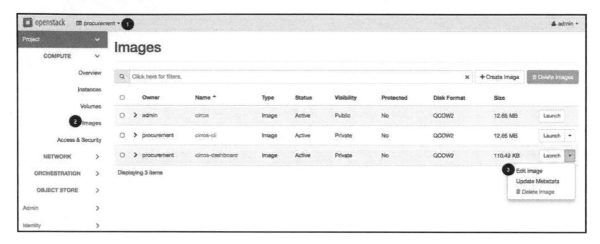

Figure 4.14: Editing Glance image properties on the Horizon dashboard

See *Figure 4.14*. Let's first update the image properties associated with the `cirros-dashboard` image:

1. Verify you are scoped to the procurement project.
2. Select the **Images** panel from the **Project-Compute** panel group.
3. Click on the `cirros-dashboard` dropdown next to the **Launch** button and select **Edit Image**.
4. See *Figure 4.15*. Lower the minimum RAM value to `256`.
5. Click on **Update Image**.

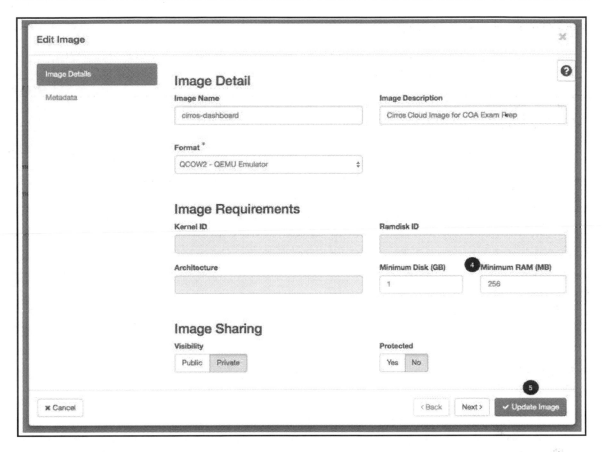

Figure 4.15: Editing Minimum Ram for a Glance image on the Horizon dashboard

Let's now apply a Glance metadata definition key/value to the image. Let's use the existing *Common Operating Systems Properties-OS Distro* metadata definition property. This will be used to help identify the specific distribution contained in the image. See *Figure 4.16*.

1. Verify you are scoped to the procurement project.
2. Select the **Images** panel from the **Project-Compute** panel group.
3. Click on the `cirros-dashboard` dropdown next to the **Launch** button and select **Update Metadata**.

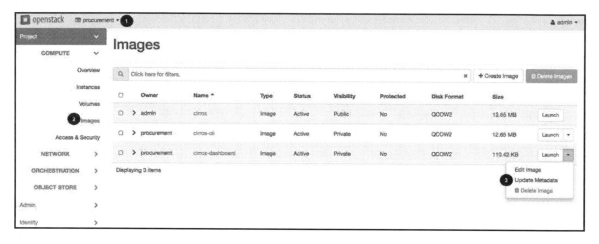

Figure 4.16: Updating Glance image metadata on the Horizon dashboard

4. See *Figure 4.17*. Select the plus sign on the left to open the **Common Operating System Properties** group. Select **OS Distro** definition. Fill in the value as `Cirros`. See *Figure 4.16*. Take note that the description we originally set on the image is a Glance metadata definition key/value pair.
5. Select **Save**.

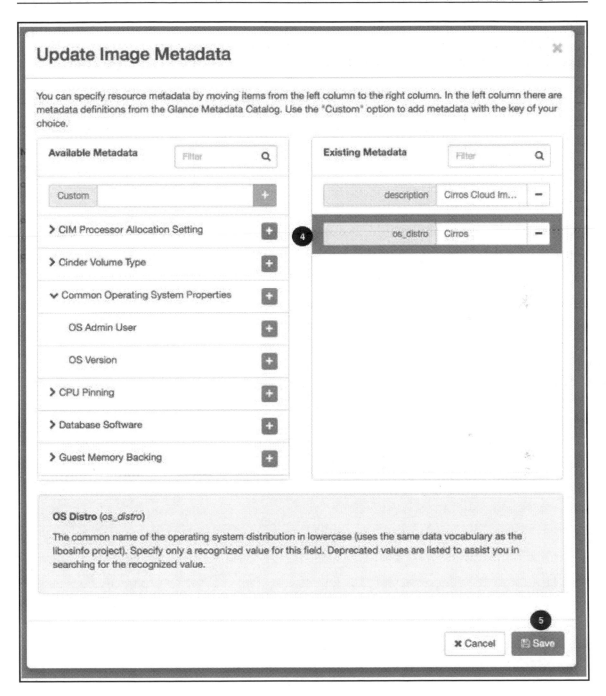

Figure 4.17: Updating metadata on an existing Glance image

To verify your work, click on the blue hyperlink for the the `cirros-dashboard` in the image list page. See *Figure 4.18*. You should see the newly updated **Min. RAM** value set to **256 MB** and the **os_distro** value set to **Cirros**.

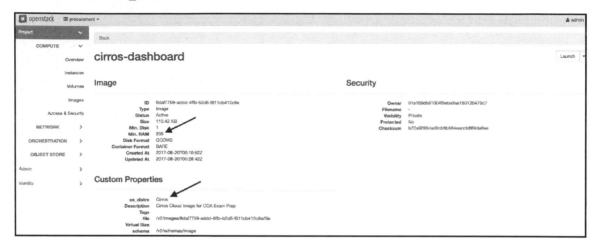

Figure 4.18: A Glance image with updated Min. RAM (image properties) and os_distro (metadata applied from metadata definitions)

CLI

Ensure you have sourced credentials for the procurement project:

```
$ source openrc-procurement
```

Verify you can get a list of all available images:

```
$ openstack image list
```

Let's set the minimum RAM requirements on the `cirros-cli` image to 256 MB. You will not receive any confirmation output from this command:

```
$ openstack image set cirros-cli --min-ram 256
```

Let's now apply the Glance metadata definition `os_distro` key/value to the image:

```
$ openstack image set cirros-cli --property os_distro='Cirros'
```

We can now verify that the Glance property and metadata definitions were properly set to the image. We should see output similar to *Figure 4.19*.

```
$ openstack image show cirros-cli
```

```
+------------------+----------------------------------------------------------------------------------------+
| Field            | Value                                                                                  |
+------------------+----------------------------------------------------------------------------------------+
| checksum         | f8ab98ff5e73ebab884d80c9dc9c7290                                                       |
| container_format | bare                                                                                   |
| created_at       | 2017-08-19T23:54:00Z                                                                   |
| disk_format      | qcow2                                                                                  |
| file             | /v2/images/0505b2d1-9d42-4221-b489-04dbb4fc82cb/file                                   |
| id               | 0505b2d1-9d42-4221-b489-04dbb4fc82cb                                                   |
| min_disk         | 1                                                                                      |
| min_ram          | 256                                                                                    |
| name             | cirros-cli                                                                             |
| owner            | 01a169db81004f5eba3aa150126479d7                                                       |
| properties       | architecture='x64', description='Cirros Cloud Image for COA Exam Prep', os_distro='Cirros' |
| protected        | False                                                                                  |
| schema           | /v2/schemas/image                                                                      |
| size             | 13267968                                                                               |
| status           | active                                                                                 |
| tags             |                                                                                        |
| updated_at       | 2017-08-20T00:26:14Z                                                                   |
| virtual_size     | None                                                                                   |
| visibility       | private                                                                                |
+------------------+----------------------------------------------------------------------------------------+
```

Figure 4.19: An image with updated Min. RAM and os_distro properties on the CLI

Summary

The Glance image service is one of the easier OpenStack services to understand and use. We've covered the basics of cloud images, image file types, Glance architecture as well as image properties and metadata definitions. It's important to remember that the only user that can make an image public (publicly accessible to all projects across all domains) must have the admin role. A user with the admin role can also share an image with a specific project. If a user does not have the admin role, they cannot modify or delete existing images *unless* that image was created by someone within the project to which they are currently scoped.

In the next chapter, we will discuss the first part of the Nova compute service and work through all objectives relating to key pairs, flavors, and the launching of virtual machines on the Horizon dashboard and `python-openstackclient`.

5
Nova Compute Service

In the previous chapter, we discussed the Glance image service and the Glance-related objectives of the Certified OpenStack Administrator exam. But what use is an image if we can't boot it? That's where Nova comes in! Nova is the OpenStack compute service and it is the core of the OpenStack cloud. It is designed to manage and automate pools of compute resources and work with a variety of existing virtualization technologies.

In this chapter, we will cover the following topics:

- Nova architecture
- Hypervisor types
- Exam objective - managing keypairs
- Exam objective - managing flavors
- Exam objective - launching instances
- Exam objective - accessing instances
- Exam objective - snapshotting instances
- Exam objective - managing instance states

After this chapter, you should have a solid understanding of Nova and the skills necessary to successfully fulfill all Nova-related objectives on the exam.

Nova - the compute orchestrator

The Nova service is the heart of the OpenStack cloud. It is a collection of daemons that work to orchestrate availability of compute resources, leveraging virtualization features that have been running on Linux machines for years! Rather than reinventing the wheel, Nova works with a variety of existing hypervisor technologies, including QEMU-KVM, QEMU, Hyper-V, VMware ESXi, Xen, and XenServer. It also supports the ability to leverage existing Linux container technologies such as LXC and Docker. When one boots an instance, Nova leverages available CPU, memory, and disk resources on compute nodes. In a production OpenStack environment, a customer may have anywhere from five to 5,000 compute nodes hosting virtual machine instances.

Nova architecture

Figure 5.1 shows a high-level diagram of Nova's architecture. Nova is made up of six daemons:

- **nova-api**: The primary gateway to Nova. One must interact with `nova-api` to create, list, delete, and manage instances.
- **nova-scheduler**: Evaluates and filters all available compute hosts to determine the best compute node for an instance you'd like to boot. The behavior of `nova-scheduler` can be modified based on specific characteristics, such as CPU architecture or a specific location in the data center.
- **nova-conductor**: A "database broker" that directly connects to the OpenStack environment's relational database. Because the compute node (or hypervisor) is the least trusted component of a multi-tenant virtualized environment, all database communication goes through `nova-conductor`.
- **nova-novncproxy**: Provides serial console access to Nova instances via a VNC client or web browser.
- **nova-consoleauth**: Receives requests from `nova-novncproxy` to authorize a user's token and maps the private host and port of an instance's VNC server.
- **nova-compute**: Manages virtual machines on the hypervisor.

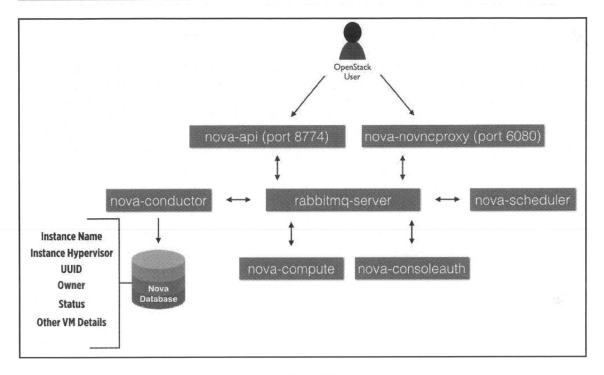

Figure 5.1: High-level diagram of Nova architecture

 In OpenStack, the term *booting* is used to refer to the creation of a virtual machine. A virtual machine booted with Nova is often called an instance. To boot an instance with Nova, one would typically provide a desired Glance image and Nova flavor. A Nova flavor is a previously provisioned profile of the CPU, memory, and local disk desired and will be discussed in more detail in the upcoming sections.

Hypervisor types

Nova is compatible with a variety of hypervisor types. Let's talk about a few of the popular ones:

- **QEMU (Quick Emulator)**: Released in 2003, QEMU is an open source hypervisor that provides full system emulation. It can emulate one or several processors without assistance from the CPU, although it does have the tendency to be a bit slow.

- **XEN**: Released in 2003 and originally a project at the University of Cambridge, Xen is open source and implements a technique called *paravirtualization* (PV). PV does not require processors with virtualization extensions, and instead relies on drivers inside the VM guests. Xen has been used by many popular public cloud offerings, including Slice Host, Rackspace, and Amazon Web Services.
- **QEMU-KVM (Quick Emulator-Kernel-based Virtual Machine)**: Released in 2006, QEMU-KVM is a fork of QEMU that continues to use QEMU to virtualize a guest's peripherals, but also takes advantage of processors with hardware-virtualization extensions. QEMU-KVM is fast because of its ability to virtualize guests at near-native speeds! This is often referred to as hardware-assisted virtualization or HVM.

Libvirt is an open source API daemon that is often used for managing any of the aforementioned hypervisors. In an OpenStack environment, `nova-compute` will utilize the Libvirt daemon, `libvirtd`, to manage virtual machines. See *Figure 5.2.*

In addition to these open source hypervisors, `nova-compute` is also compatible with Microsoft's Hyper-V hypervisor, VMware vCenter, and XenServer (a commercially supported virtualization product built on Xen).

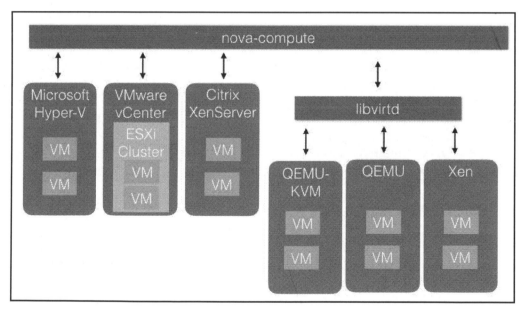

Figure 5.2: nova-compute is compatible with a variety of commercial and open source hypervisors

Your OpenStack virtual appliance provided with this book is configured to use the QEMU hypervisor. If you attempt to boot a larger cloud image (such as Ubuntu or Centos), it will run slowly. Unfortunately, VirtualBox does not allow nested virtualization, even if you have virtualization extensions turned on in the BIOS of your laptop or desktop. See `https://www.virtualbox.org/ticket/4032` for more information.

Exam objectives

Let's take a look at the Nova exam objectives.

The following table breaks down various Nova-related objectives you should know for the COA exam. As you can see, all of these tasks can be completed on both the Horizon dashboard and CLI. Remember, time is of the essence on the exam—and in many cases, it may be faster to tackle a task on the dashboard. If you feel confident using the CLI and don't need to fumble through help to discover arguments, feel free to use it!

Objectives	Dashboard	Command-Line
Create/Edit/List/Delete Flavors	✓	✓
Share Flavors with All Projects Across All Domains (Public)	✓	✓
Share Flavors with Specific Projects	✓	✓
Create/Edit/List/Delete Key Pairs	✓	✓
Launch/Suspend/Pause/Resume/Shelve/Resize/Rebuild/Lock/PowerOff Instances	✓	✓
Get Access to Instances via Remote Console	✓	✓
Create/Edit/List/Delete Boot Instance Snapshots	✓	✓

Figure 5.3: Nova exam objectives

Exam objective - managing key pairs

Key pairs are an alternative to password-based authentication when accessing an instance over SSH. A key pair consists of two keys: a **public key** and a **private key**. These keys must be used together to gain access to an instance.

When it comes to SSH keys and Nova, an OpenStack user has two options:

1. Send a request to Nova to generate a brand new SSH public and private key for you. In this case, Nova will store the public key in its database and give you the private key. Once the private key is passed to you, it can no longer be recovered. The user must keep the private key in a safe place!
2. If you have previously generated a public and private key pair using `ssh-keygen` (or another utility), you can provide your public key for Nova to store in its database.

Once your public key is registered with Nova, you select the name of the public key when you boot the instance. This implicitly grants access to anyone with the matching private key. When accessing an instance over SSH, you will specify your private key and username. If the matching public key is present on the instance, you will be granted access.

Multiple users from the same project cannot see each other's registered public keys. Unlike other resources in OpenStack, **public keys are not owned by the project**. They are owned by the user that creates or registers it. When you delete a user, you also delete the user's public key from Nova.

Horizon dashboard

Let's take a look at how to create SSH key pairs from the Horizon dashboard. See *Figure 5.4*.

1. From the OpenStack overview page, scope yourself to the **human-resources** project by selecting the top dropdown.
2. Select the **Access & Security panel** from the **Project-Compute** panel group.
3. Select the **Key Pairs** tab.
4. Select **Create Key Pair**.

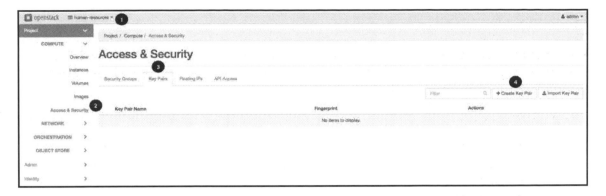

Figure 5.4: Creating a SSH key pair on the Horizon dashboard

5. Name the key pair `my-new-keypair-dashboard` and select **Create Key Pair**.

6. Horizon will automatically present the private key for you to download to your local system.

 Nova does not keep a record of the private key. Once you have navigated away from the download private key screen, you will no longer be able to retrieve it. Be sure to always keep your private keys in a safe place!

CLI

Let's create another SSH key pair in the `human-resources` project with `python-openstackclient`.

Recall that the provided openrc file contains credentials in the form of variables for proper authentication to Keystone and setting project scope.

Let's copy our original openrc file to a new file called `openrc-human-resources`.

```
$ cp openrc openrc-human-resources
```

Now that we've made a copy, let's edit the `openrc-human-resources` file, updating the project and tenant name variables to reflect our desired scope to the `human-resources` project. If you are more comfortable with another editor, feel free to use it here.

```
$ nano openrc-human-resources
```

Change the following variables to `human-resources`:

```
export OS_PROJECT_NAME=human-resources
export OS_TENANT_NAME=human-resources
```

 We are changing the `OS_TENANT_NAME` variable since some of the older service-based clients rely on it instead of `OS_PROJECT_NAME`.

Source the newly created `openrc-human-resources` file:

```
$ source openrc-human-resources
```

Verify that the proper variables are set:

```
$ export | grep OS
```

Now that we are properly scoped, let's create a a brand new key pair for the admin user. We will supply > to redirect our private-key output to a file called `my-new-keypair-cli.pem`.

```
$ openstack keypair create my-new-keypair-cli > my-new-keypair-cli.pem
```

We use > to avoid the standard-output printing of our private key and redirect it to a file called `my-new-keypair-cli.pem`.

For security, we should also change permissions on the key to only allow us, the `openstack` user logged into the virtual appliance, to read the key.

```
$ chmod 400 my-new-keypair-cli.pem
```

We can confirm that the public key has been created and stored in Nova by running the following command:

```
$ openstack keypair list
```

See *Figure 5.5*. You should see output confirming that the admin user has created two separate key pairs: one from the Horizon dashboard and one via `python-openstackclient`:

```
+------------------------------+-------------------------------------------------+
| Name                         | Fingerprint                                     |
+------------------------------+-------------------------------------------------+
| my-new-keypair-cli           | 24:92:d5:9c:88:4c:67:47:1e:2f:84:a2:cc:9b:c7:ba |
| my-new-keypair-dashboard     | 8f:f6:67:83:a3:4a:de:10:fa:a0:60:6b:c5:79:7e:78 |
+------------------------------+-------------------------------------------------+
```

Figure 5.5: Output from the 'openstack keypair list' command

Exam objective - managing flavors

In OpenStack, you always need to specify the desired RAM, local disk drive size, and virtual CPUs for your virtual machine instance. To control usage, OpenStack requires users to choose from a collection of previously defined hardware configurations called **flavors**. See *Figure 5.6*.

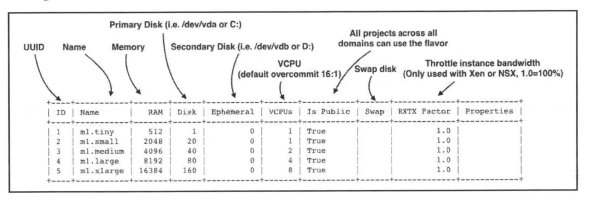

Figure 5.6: A list of Nova flavors in a typical OpenStack environment

- **ID**: UUID of the flavor.
- **Name**: Name of the flavor.
- **RAM**: Amount of RAM to use in megabytes.
- **Disk**: Amount of disk space to use for the root partition in gigabytes.
- **VCPU**: Number of virtual CPUs. By default, Nova uses a 16:1 CPU allocation ratio. This allows you to boot sixteen 1VCPU instances per physical core.
- **Ephemeral:** Amount of disk space to use for the secondary partition.
- **Swap**: Amount of disk space to use for swap in gigabytes.
- **RXTX Factor:** This is only used by Xen or NSX-based systems and allows throttling of the inbound/outbound traffic from the network attached to the instance.
- **Properties**: Any metadata set on the flavor.

By default, creating a new flavor is only granted to a user with the admin role. As an admin, it's easy to create and customize new flavors from the Horizon dashboard or `python-openstackclient`.

Horizon dashboard

Let's create a new flavor from the Horizon Dashboard. See *Figure 5.7*.

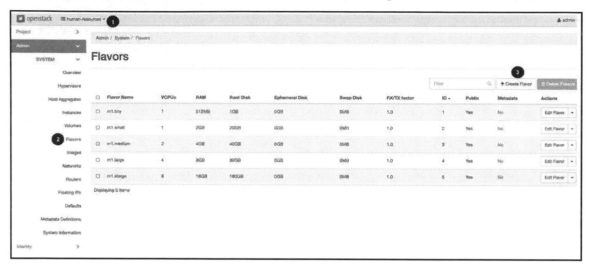

Figure 5.7: The ability to create a new flavor is only accessible to users with the admin role (by default)

1. From the OpenStack overview page, scope yourself to the **human-resources** project by selecting the top dropdown. As previously mentioned, the **Admin** panel group will be available to users with the admin role, regardless of scope. We could be scoped to any available project when creating a new flavor.

2. Select the **Flavors panel** from the **Admin-System** panel group.

3. Select **Create Flavor**.

4. **Name** (required): Name of the flavor. Type in `awesome-flavor-dashboard`

5. **ID** (optional): UUID of the flavor. Type in `100`. Leaving the ID on `auto` will automatically assign a UUID.

6. **VCPU** (required): Number of virtual CPUs to use. Type in `1`. The default overcommit ratio on a hypervisor is 16:1. This means approximately 16 vCPUs for one logical processor.

7. **RAM (MB)** (required): Amount of RAM to use in megabytes. Type in `512`.

8. **Root Disk (GB)** (required): Amount of disk space to use for the primary disk in gigabytes. Type in `1`.

9. **Ephemeral Disk (GB)** (optional): Amount of disk space to use for the secondary disk in gigabytes. Set this to `0`.

10. **Swap Disk (MB)** (optional): Amount of disk space to use for swap in megabytes. Set this to 0.

11. **RXTX Factor** (optional): This is only used by Xen or NSX-based systems and allows throttling of the inbound/outbound traffic from networks attached to the instance. If you are using one of these hypervisors, you set a base network speed in a configuration file and the factor value gets multiplied against it. To use all throughout, enter 1. If we were using one of these hypervisors and wanted to limit by half, we could enter .5.

12. **Flavor Access** (optional): Allows you to share the flavor with a specific project or group of projects. If you do not specify any projects, the flavor will be **public** and accessible to all projects across all domains. Let's keep this flavor public.

13. Select **Create Flavor.**

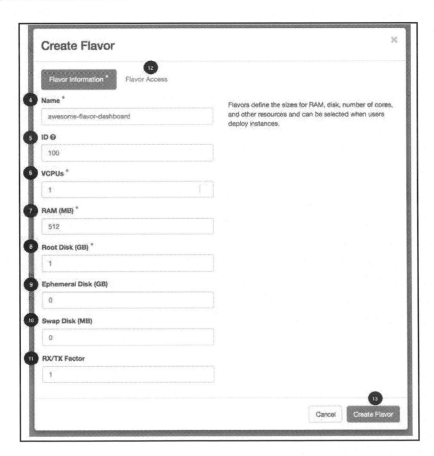

Figure 5.8: The Flavor Access tab allows you to set the flavor to be publicly accessible or shared only with specific projects

CLI

From inside your virtual appliance, verify you are the root user and source the `openrc` file:

```
$ source openrc
```

 Typing `openstack help flavor create` will provide details on all available positional and optional arguments.

Using `python-openstackclient`, create a new flavor with ID `200`, `512` MB of RAM, `1` GB primary disk, and `1` VPCU. The flavor will be public by default. Call the flavor `awesome-flavor-cli`.

```
$ openstack flavor create --id 200 --vcpus 1 --ram 512 --disk 1 "awesome-flavor-cli"
```

You should see output similar to *Figure 5.9*:

```
+-----------------------------+--------------------+
| Field                       | Value              |
+-----------------------------+--------------------+
| OS-FLV-DISABLED:disabled    | False              |
| OS-FLV-EXT-DATA:ephemeral   | 0                  |
| disk                        | 1                  |
| id                          | 200                |
| name                        | awesome-flavor-cli |
| os-flavor-access:is_public  | True               |
| properties                  |                    |
| ram                         | 512                |
| rxtx_factor                 | 1.0                |
| swap                        |                    |
| vcpus                       | 1                  |
+-----------------------------+--------------------+
```

Figure 5.9: Output from the 'openstack flavor create' command

Exam objective - launching instances

You've finally made it to the fun part: launching Nova instances. Launching instances can be done on both the Horizon dashboard and `python-openstackclient`. Let's dive into creating our first instance.

Horizon dashboard

Creating instances via the Horizon dashboard is easy. See *Figure 5.10*.

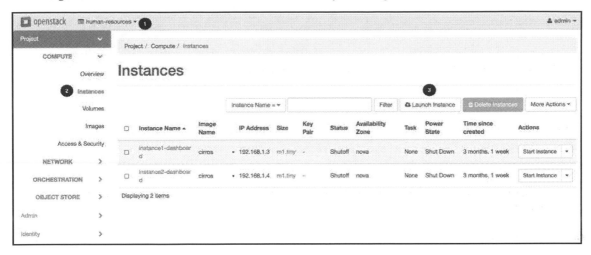

Figure 5.10: Launching an instance from the Horizon dashboard

1. From the OpenStack overview page, scope yourself to the **human-resources** project by selecting the top dropdown. When we create the instance, it will be owned by the **human-resources** project.

2. Select the **Instances** panel from the **Project-Compute** panel group. You should see two instances in the **Shutoff** state. These two instances are owned by the **human-resources** project. We will return to these in a bit.

3. Select **Launch Instance.**

4. **Details**:

   - **Instance Name** (required): The name of your instance. You can have multiple virtual machines with the same name, thanks to the UUID that automatically gets assigned to any resource you create. In this section, insert `instance3-dashboard`.

   - **Availability Zone**: Nova availability zones are used to partition your Nova deployment. This allows you to put compute hosts into logical groups to provide physical isolation or hardware differentiation. Nova is the default availability zone out of the box and contains all compute nodes in your environment.

- **Count** (required): The number of instances you'd like to boot. Specifying more than one instance will append a `-#` to the end of the virtual machine. For example, if you boot three instances named `myinstance`, they will be named `myinstance-1`, `myinstance-2`, and `myinstance-3`. Insert 1 for the instance count.

5. **Source** (required):

   - **Boot Source**: There are three primary boot sources:

     - **Boot From Image**: This is the most common type of booting and allows the user to select a specific Glance image to boot from. Select the `cirros` image.
     - **Boot From Snapshot**: Users can take snapshots of running virtual machines to capture the contents of the disk. A user has the ability to boot from an existing snapshot residing in Glance.
     - **Boot From Volume**: When a user boots an instance from a cloud image or snapshot, the primary and/or secondary drives always reside on the local storage of the compute node. Booting from a Cinder volume allows us to set an instance's primary or secondary disk off the compute node on a Cinder storage node. The advantages of this are data persistence in case of an emergency such as a hypervisor outage or planned maintenance. This will be discussed in more detail in `Chapter 7`, *Cinder Block-Storage Service*.

6. **Flavor** (required): Choose from any available flavors. Select `m1.tiny`.
7. **Networks** (required): This section allows you to choose the network on which you want to boot your instance. You can select multiple networks if you want your instance attached to multiple networks; the order of the networks determines the network interface. Select the pre-created `tenant-network1-dashboard` network.

8. **Network Ports** (optional): This section allows you to choose the port on which you want to connect your instance. You can select multiple ports if you want your instance attached to multiple ports. Unfortunately, there is no way to create new ports from this area of the panel. There should not be any available network ports.

9. **Security Groups** (optional): We will discuss security groups more in `Chapter 6`, *Neutron Networking Service*, but for now, its important that you understand that security groups control network traffic to and from a port. Even if you do not check this box, every instance that gets created will automatically get the default security group. If you create additional security groups, they will appear here. You can have more than one security group associated with an instance. Verify that the **default** security group is selected.

10. **Key Pair** (optional): This will ensure that the `cloud-init` program residing inside your requested image fetches this public key and places it into the `authorized_keys` file of the default user on the specified boot source image. Select `my-new-keypair-dashboard`.

11. **Configuration** (optional):

    - **Customization Script:** This section allows you to customize your instance by placing in a script that gets run after the instance has been launched. This is often referred to as user data and is a vast topic. The exam does not require you to fulfill user-data objectives, but you can learn more at `https://docs.openstack.org/pike/`.

    - **Disk Partition**: This option is completely ignored if you are using QEMU or QEMU-KVM as the hypervisor type. Automatic disk partitioning automatically creates a single partition from the desired flavor. In other words, if you select a flavor with a 20 GB primary disk, you will have a single 20 GB root partition (/dev/vda1) available for use. If you are running QEMU or QEMU-KVM and interested in modifying this behavior, search for the *growpart* cloud-init module. Verify that **Automatic** is selected.

- **Configuration Drive**: Checking this box automatically attaches the special OpenStack Metadata ConfigDrive when the instance boots. Selecting this should not be necessary if you already have the neutron metadata services properly set up. Verify this option is **unselected**.

12. **Server Groups** (optional): Server groups are created by the OpenStack administrator and based on whether ServerGroup Nova filters are enabled. The administrator must set up server groups to enable affinity/anti-affinity scheduling (see **Scheduler Hints** next).

13. **Scheduler Hints** (optional): Scheduling hints allow the user to influence where the virtual machine gets placed. For example, a user can use hints to ensure multiple virtual machines all get placed on the same compute node or a different one (affinity/anti-affinity). In some cases, you might want two instances on different compute nodes to keep services highly available. Server groups and scheduler hints are outside the scope of the exam.

14. **Metadata** (optional): Metadata allows the user to apply predefined Glance Metadata Definitions key/value pairs to virtual machines.

15. Select **Launch Instance**.

On the Horizon dashboard, you will not be able to boot an instance unless there is an accessible network available. Although you *can* boot an instance without a network or port via the CLIs, SDK, or directly via the API, the instance will *not have* network connectivity and will not have the ability to communicate with other instances or network resources.

The current objectives for the Newton version of the COA exam **do not** require you to set up availability zones.

Figure 5.11: There are a variety of options available when launching an instance

Be patient! Depending on the resources available on your system, this may take a bit. If all goes well, you should see your new `instance3-dashboard`. At this point, the **human-resources** project owns three instances: `instance1-dashboard` (status: Shutoff), `instance2-dashboard` (status: Shutoff), and `instance3-dashboard` (status: Active).

If you get an error when attempting to boot an instance, please verify that you do not have instances running in any other projects. The virtual appliance included with this book requires a minimum of 6GB RAM assigned, but **cannot** support many instances running at one time. If you continue to have issues booting instances, restart the virtual appliance by running `sudo reboot` from the terminal or manually shutting down the appliance within VirtualBox. If you have available memory on your laptop or desktop machine, feel free to increase the allocated RAM within VirtualBox.

CLI

Source the newly created `openrc-human-resources` file. If you have not done this yet, refer back to the `python-openstackclient` section of the previous objective.

```
$ source openrc-human-resources
```

Verify that the proper variables are set:

```
$ export | grep OS
```

Now that we are properly scoped, let's create a new virtual machine using the same parameters provided in the Horizon dashboard exercise.

```
$ openstack server create --image cirros --flavor m1.tiny --key-name my-new-keypair-cli \
\instance3-cli
```

You should see similar output as *Figure 5.12*, while the instance is building.

```
+-------------------------------------+-----------------------------------------+
| Field                               | Value                                   |
+-------------------------------------+-----------------------------------------+
| OS-DCF:diskConfig                   | MANUAL                                  |
| OS-EXT-AZ:availability_zone         |                                         |
| OS-EXT-SRV-ATTR:host                | None                                    |
| OS-EXT-SRV-ATTR:hypervisor_hostname | None                                    |
| OS-EXT-SRV-ATTR:instance_name       |                                         |
| OS-EXT-STS:power_state              | NOSTATE                                 |
| OS-EXT-STS:task_state               | scheduling                              |
| OS-EXT-STS:vm_state                 | building                                |
| OS-SRV-USG:launched_at              | None                                    |
| OS-SRV-USG:terminated_at            | None                                    |
| accessIPv4                          |                                         |
| accessIPv6                          |                                         |
| addresses                           |                                         |
| adminPass                           | 3V9KqiRu9fbb                            |
| config_drive                        |                                         |
| created                             | 2017-07-09T00:05:07Z                    |
| flavor                              | m1.tiny (1)                             |
| hostId                              |                                         |
| id                                  | b5eaa8a2-768c-4711-9ef4-3f103509df86    |
| image                               | cirros (fdcecf4e-443a-46e0-84af-af606bb5b08a) |
| key_name                            | my-new-keypair-cli                      |
| name                                | instance3-cli                           |
| os-extended-volumes:volumes_attached| []                                      |
| progress                            | 0                                       |
| project_id                          | d5a33462721e4d35bd45138311c526b8        |
| properties                          |                                         |
| security_groups                     | [{u'name': u'default'}]                 |
| status                              | BUILD                                   |
| updated                             | 2017-07-09T00:05:07Z                    |
| user_id                             | 214ad6d7786e4ce59474466a3f281d7c        |
+-------------------------------------+-----------------------------------------+
```

Figure 5.12: Output from the 'openstack server create' command

Confirm that the instance's status goes to active. The `human-resources` project should now own four instances. `instance1-dashboard` and `instance2-dashboard` were previously created on the virtual appliance. Be sure to leave them in the `SHUTOFF` state for now.

```
$ openstack server list
```

```
+--------------------------------------+-------------------+--------+----------------------------------------+------------+
| ID                                   | Name              | Status | Networks                               | Image Name |
+--------------------------------------+-------------------+--------+----------------------------------------+------------+
| b5eaa8a2-768c-4711-9ef4-3f103509df86 | instance3-cli     | ACTIVE | tenant-network1-dashboard=192.168.1.7  | cirros     |
| 2b5d2c54-570f-4eef-9735-f0ff99ff3ebb | instance3-dashboard | ACTIVE | tenant-network1-dashboard=192.168.1.5  | cirros     |
| a55e054b-9785-49a2-bd69-0d4fddb46b9e | instance2-dashboard | SHUTOFF | tenant-network1-dashboard=192.168.1.4  | cirros     |
| bf5a05f6-e45a-4619-8ea4-6442cb36c37d | instance1-dashboard | SHUTOFF | tenant-network1-dashboard=192.168.1.3  | cirros     |
+--------------------------------------+-------------------+--------+----------------------------------------+------------+
```

Figure 5.13: Output from the 'openstack server list' command

In this example, we did not need to specify the network on which we wanted to boot the instance because there was only one network available to the human-resources project. If there is more than one network available, you will not be able to boot, unless you specify the network with the `--nic` argument.

If we want to see additional details about the instance, we can run the following command:

```
$ openstack server show <instance-name-or-id>
```

Exam objective - getting access to your instance

Now that your virtual machine is up and running, let's hop inside! There are a variety of ways to do this. Let's discuss the three primary ways:

Console: Thanks to the `nova-novncproxy` and `nova-consoleauth` daemons, a user can easily gain access to the virtual machine serial console via the Horizon dashboard or an HTTP URL. The serial console provides access to an instance as if you were interacting with it directly.

You will not be able to log in to an instance via the console if password authentication is disabled or a password is not set inside the image. You must either pass user data to set a password or log in to the instance via SSH by providing your private key.

Floating IP: An alternate way of getting access to an instance is by associating a floating or external IP address with your instance and connecting via SSH from your system. Keep in mind that this not only requires configuring provider networks in your OpenStack environment but also allowing incoming traffic on port 22. We will discuss this more in Chapter 6.

Network Namespace: If you have access to the actual underlying servers where the OpenStack services are installed, you have the ability to access your instances via network namespaces. Network namespaces are a feature of the Linux kernel and allow isolation of network interfaces and routing tables. Any time an OpenStack user creates a DHCP-enabled Neutron network, a network namespace gets created. This is outside the scope of the exam, but a user with access to the OpenStack infrastructure can gain access to OpenStack instances by SSH-ing into the instance via the namespace. An example would be `ip netns exec <qdhcp-namespace_id> ssh <instance-fixed-ip-address>`.

Horizon dashboard

Let's go ahead and check out our remote serial console. See *Figure 5.14*.

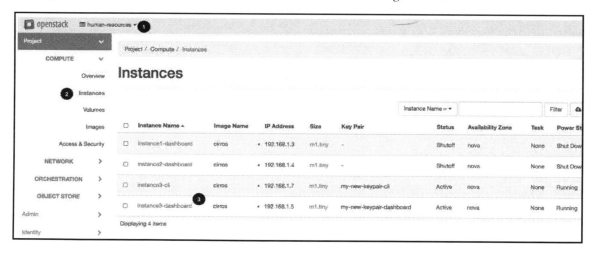

Figure 5.14. Getting access to the instance console from the Horizon Dashboard

1. From the OpenStack overview page, scope yourself to the human-resources project by selecting the top dropdown.
2. Select the **Instances** panel from the **Project-Compute** panel group.
3. Select **instance3-dashboard** from the list of instances.

4. Let's first check out the **Log** tab. The **Log** tab shows the serial console's initial bootup process. Click on **View Full Log**. Here we can see the instance's bootup process. We can see it obtain an IP address as well as obtain the public key we selected at launch. This is a great place to troubleshoot if we have issues launching instances.

5. Select the **Console** tab.

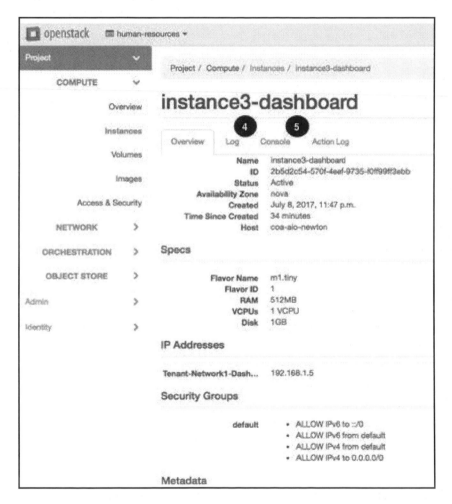

Figure 5.15: Logs and console tabs for a running instance on the Horizon dashboard

6. Select **Show Only Console**. If you still don't see anything, click on **Enter**, which should wake up the console screen.

Figure 5.16: Selecting the 'show only console' link will allow you to interact with the instance console

We can now log in to our instance:

- **Username**: `cirros`
- **Password**: `cubswin:)`

Now that we are logged in, we can run the following command to show our instance hostname.

```
$ hostname
```

You should see output similar to *Figure 5.17*.

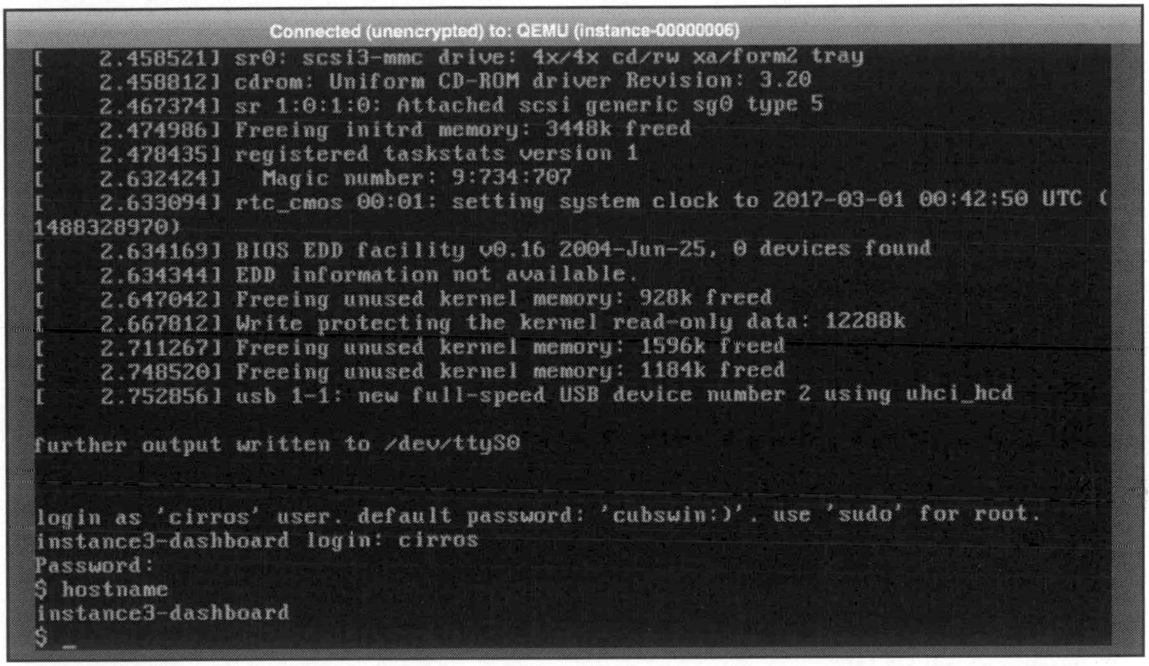

```
Connected (unencrypted) to: QEMU (instance-00000006)
[    2.458521] sr0: scsi3-mmc drive: 4x/4x cd/rw xa/form2 tray
[    2.458812] cdrom: Uniform CD-ROM driver Revision: 3.20
[    2.467374] sr 1:0:1:0: Attached scsi generic sg0 type 5
[    2.474986] Freeing initrd memory: 3448k freed
[    2.478435] registered taskstats version 1
[    2.632424]    Magic number: 9:734:707
[    2.633094] rtc_cmos 00:01: setting system clock to 2017-03-01 00:42:50 UTC (
1488328970)
[    2.634169] BIOS EDD facility v0.16 2004-Jun-25, 0 devices found
[    2.634344] EDD information not available.
[    2.647042] Freeing unused kernel memory: 928k freed
[    2.667012] Write protecting the kernel read-only data: 12288k
[    2.711267] Freeing unused kernel memory: 1596k freed
[    2.748520] Freeing unused kernel memory: 1184k freed
[    2.752856] usb 1-1: new full-speed USB device number 2 using uhci_hcd

further output written to /dev/ttyS0


login as 'cirros' user. default password: 'cubswin:)'. use 'sudo' for root.
instance3-dashboard login: cirros
Password:
$ hostname
instance3-dashboard
$ _
```

Figure 5.17: Running the hostname command from within the instance3-dashboard instance

CLI

Source the newly created `openrc-human-resources` file:

```
$ source openrc-human-resources
```

Verify that the proper variables are set:

```
$ export | grep OS
```

View all running instances:

```
$ openstack server list
```

Get the console log for `instance3-cli`. You should see the instance boot logs.

```
$ openstack console log show instance3-cli
```

Get the console URL of `instance3-cli`:

```
$ openstack console url show instance3-cli
```

You should see output similar to *Figure 5.18*.

```
+----------+---------------------------------------------------------------------------------+
| Field    | Value                                                                           |
+----------+---------------------------------------------------------------------------------+
| type     | novnc                                                                            |
| url      | http://192.168.56.56:6080/vnc_auto.html?token=7a501b75-c1b7-46ba-9d03-9ccf59671cba |
+----------+---------------------------------------------------------------------------------+
```

Figure 5.18: Output from the 'openstack console url show' command

Copy and paste the URL into your web browser.

- **Username**: `cirros`
- **Password**: `cubswin:)`

Now that we are logged in, we can run the following command to show our instance hostname.

```
$ hostname
```

Exam objective - creating instance snapshots

Nova allows users to create snapshots of instances. Snapshots, like images, are snapshots of the entire disk or disk's contents. Consider a user booting an instance from an image, then proceeding to make changes and customizations to that running instance. The user could then create a snapshot of the instance and boot an instance from this snapshot. All changes and customizations will be in place. When one creates a snapshot, it gets placed in Glance as a bootable image that is owned by the project to which the user is scoped.

Nova snapshots only contain a snapshot of the primary disk. They do not snapshot any other disks that may be associated with the instance. This includes flavors that contain a secondary or "ephemeral" storage as well as attached Cinder volumes.

Horizon dashboard

1. From the OpenStack Overview page, scope yourself to the **human-resources** project by selecting the top dropdown.
2. Select the **Instances** Panel from the Project-Compute Panel Group.
3. Select the dropdown next to **instance3-dashboard** and select **Create Snapshot**.
4. Name the snapshot **instance3-dashboard-snapshot**. See *Figure 5.19*.

Figure 5.19: Creating an instance snapshot on the Horizon dashboard

Your snapshot will be created and should now be visible in the list of Glance images owned by the **human-resources** project. See *Figure 5.20*. You may need to hit **Refresh** on your browser.

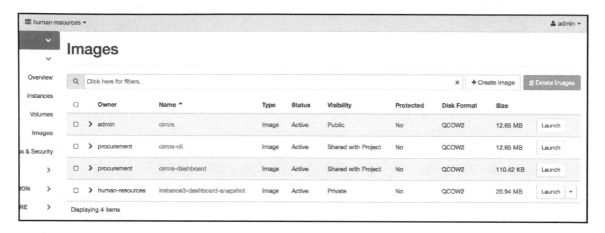

Figure 5.20: Nova instance snapshots are stored in Glance

You can now easily launch this snapshot by clicking on **Launch** instance or selecting it as a boot source when you go to create an instance.

CLI

Source the `openrc-human-resources` file:

```
$ source openrc-human-resources
```

Verify that the proper variables are set:

```
$ export | grep OS
```

First, list all your instances:

```
$ openstack server list
```

Create a snapshot from `instance3-cli` called `instance3-cli-snapshot`.

```
$ openstack server image create --name instance3-cli-snapshot instance3-cli
```

You should see output similar to *Figure 5.21*.

```
+------------------+---------------------------------------------------------------------------------------+
| Field            | Value                                                                                 |
+------------------+---------------------------------------------------------------------------------------+
| checksum         | None                                                                                  |
| container_format | None                                                                                  |
| created_at       | 2017-07-09T00:55:21Z                                                                  |
| disk_format      | None                                                                                  |
| file             | /v2/images/f2f55cdd-284e-4902-bed6-a1fe343a6646/file                                  |
| id               | f2f55cdd-284e-4902-bed6-a1fe343a6646                                                  |
| min_disk         | 1                                                                                     |
| min_ram          | 0                                                                                     |
| name             | instance3-cli-snapshot                                                                |
| owner            | d5a33462721e4d35bd45138311c526b8                                                      |
| properties       | base_image_ref='fdcecf4e-443a-46e0-84af-a160bbb5b08a', image_type='snapshot',         |
|                  | instance_uuid='b5eaa8a2-768c-4711-9ef4-3f103509df86', user_id='214ad6d7786e4ce59474466a3f281d7c' |
| protected        | False                                                                                 |
| schema           | /v2/schemas/image                                                                     |
| size             | None                                                                                  |
| status           | queued                                                                                |
| tags             |                                                                                       |
| updated_at       | 2017-07-09T00:55:21Z                                                                  |
| virtual_size     | None                                                                                  |
| visibility       | private                                                                               |
+------------------+---------------------------------------------------------------------------------------+
```

Figure 5.21: Output from the 'openstack server image create' command

Verify that the snapshot now appears in Glance:

```
$ openstack image list
```

We can verify it is owned by the human-resources project by examining the details of the image:

```
$ openstack image show instance3-cli-snapshot
```

> You can use `openstack project list` to find the UUID associated with all projects.

Exam objective - managing instance actions

There are a variety of actions we can perform on existing instances. You can see these actions by clicking on the dropdown next to the instance in the instances section of the **Project** panel. See *Figure 5.22*.

You should have two instances in the Shutoff status: `instance1` and `instance2`.

Now that these are both running, let's explore a few of the available options in the dropdown. See *Figure 5.22*.

- **Associate Floating IP**: Allows us to map a floating IP (external IP) to our instance, if available. More on this in `Chapter 6`, *Neutron Networking Service*.
- **Attach Interface**: Attach another (or the same) network to the instance. This is comparable to plugging an additional virtual NIC (or port) to the instance.
- **Detach Interface**: Remove a virtual NIC or port.
- **Edit Instance**: Rename the instance or add/remove security groups. If you completely remove all security groups from an instance's port, all ingress and egress traffic will be blocked.
- **Console**: Another way to gain console access.
- **View Log**: Another way to view the console log.
- **Pause Instance**: Store the state of the VM in memory.
- **Suspend**: Store the state of the VM on the compute node hard disk.
- **Shelve**: The instance will be stopped and snapshotted. It will then be removed from the compute node but will still appear in your list of instances with status Shelved. All the associated data and resources are kept, although the state information will be gone. It can then be unshelved and used.
- **Resize**: Specify another flavor to resize the instance.
- **Lock**: In locked state, an instance cannot be modified or terminated by non-admin users.
- **Unlock**: Unlocks an instance, allowing users within the project to modify or terminate.
- **Soft Reboot**: Triggers a graceful reboot of the instance with an ACPI event.
- **Hard Reboot**: Powers the instance off and turns it back on. Also known as a cold reboot.
- **Shut Off Instance**: Triggers a graceful shutdown of the instance with an ACPI event.
- **Rebuild Instance**: Recreates the instance from a fresh image while maintaining the same fixed and floating IP addresses, among other metadata.

- **Terminate Instance**: Completely deletes the instance.

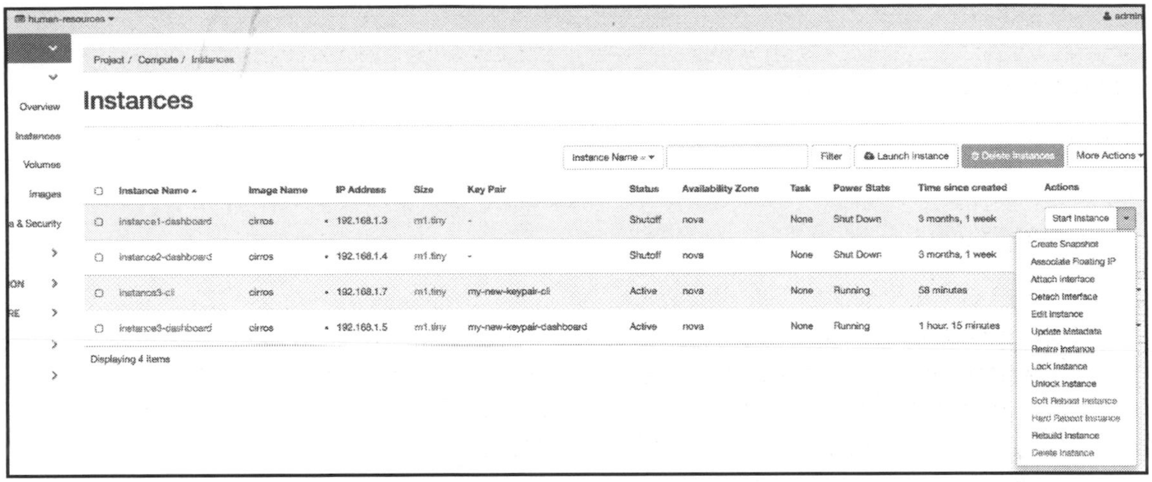

Figure 5.22: A variety of actions you can apply to a virtual machine instance on the Horizon dashboard

Horizon dashboard

1. From the OpenStack Overview page, scope yourself to the **human-resources** project by selecting the top dropdown.
2. Select the **Instances** panel from the **Project-Compute** panel group.
3. From the **Instances** section, select the drop-down next to **instance1-dashboard** and select **Start**. The instance will start up.

CLI

Source the `openrc-human-resources` file:

```
$ source openrc-human-resources
```

Verify that variables are set to scope to the human-resources project:

```
$ export | grep OS
```

List all your instances:

```
$ openstack server list
```

Let's start up instance2-dashboard.

```
$ openstack server start instance2-dashboard
```

View the status of instance2-dashboard.

```
$ openstack server show instance2-dashboard
```

The status should now be **ACTIVE**. See *Figure 5.23*.

```
+--------------------------------------+----------------------------------------------------------+
| Field                                | Value                                                    |
+--------------------------------------+----------------------------------------------------------+
| OS-DCF:diskConfig                    | MANUAL                                                   |
| OS-EXT-AZ:availability_zone          | nova                                                    |
| OS-EXT-SRV-ATTR:host                 | coa-aio-newton                                          |
| OS-EXT-SRV-ATTR:hypervisor_hostname  | coa-aio-newton                                          |
| OS-EXT-SRV-ATTR:instance_name        | instance-00000003                                      |
| OS-EXT-STS:power_state               | Running                                                |
| OS-EXT-STS:task_state                | None                                                   |
| OS-EXT-STS:vm_state                  | active                                                 |
| OS-SRV-USG:launched_at               | 2017-03-31T20:25:59.000000                             |
| OS-SRV-USG:terminated_at             | None                                                   |
| accessIPv4                           |                                                        |
| accessIPv6                           |                                                        |
| addresses                            | tenant-network1-dashboard=192.168.1.4                 |
| config_drive                         | True                                                   |
| created                              | 2017-03-31T20:25:43Z                                   |
| flavor                               | m1.tiny (1)                                            |
| hostId                               | aa59830e4c2e7e08d28d56753c964f2263466e399f3a75050b0b140a |
| id                                   | a55e054b-9785-49a2-bd69-0d4fddb46b9e                   |
| image                                | cirros (fdcecf4e-443a-46e0-84af-af606bb5b08a)          |
| key_name                             | None                                                   |
| name                                 | instance2-dashboard                                    |
| os-extended-volumes:volumes_attached | []                                                     |
| progress                             | 0                                                      |
| project_id                           | d5a33462721e4d35bd45138311c526b8                       |
| properties                           |                                                        |
| security_groups                      | [{u'name': u'default'}]                                |
| status                               | ACTIVE                                                 |
| updated                              | 2017-07-09T01:06:35Z                                   |
| user_id                              | 214ad6d7786e4ce59474466a3f281d7c                       |
+--------------------------------------+----------------------------------------------------------+
```

Figure 5.23: A running instance will show the status as ACTIVE

We should now have a total of four instances running in our virtual appliance.

Before we move on to the next chapter, let's clean up our environment and stop all running instances in the human-resources project.

```
$ openstack server delete instance1-dashboard instance2-dashboard
instance3-dashboard instance3-cli
```

Verify that the instances are no longer running in the human-resources project:

```
$ openstack server list
```

Summary

You've just learned about all the Nova-related objectives on the exam. Nova has many more features, but understanding how to manage flavors, key pairs, instances, and virtual instance actions should put you in a good position going into the exam. Remember that all Nova-related exam objectives can be completed via the Horizon dashboard. If you want to use python-openstackclient, ensure you are familiar with any positional or optional arguments. If you forget them, rely on the openstack help command. Recall that key pairs are one of the OpenStack resources that are owned by users, not the project. When you delete a user, their public key is also deleted. Nova only stores a copy of the public key. If you lose your private key, you must generate a new key pair. By default, flavors are accessible to all users in all projects across all domains. In order to make a flavor public, one must have the admin role.

In the next chapter, we will discuss Neutron, the OpenStack networking service, and work through all Neutron-related objectives on the exam.

6
Neutron Networking Service

In the previous chapter, we discussed the Nova compute service and the Nova-related objectives of the Certified OpenStack Administrator exam. Now we will discuss Neutron. Neutron is a networking service that manages the OpenStack environment's virtual networks, subnets, IP addresses, routers, firewall rules, and more. Because Neutron makes up approximately 17% of the COA objectives, fully understanding how it works from the administrator perspective is essential to passing the exam. Neutron, and **SDN** (**Software Defined Networking**) in particular, is a complex topic and spans many areas. However, it's important to remember that the exam does not require you to modify Neutron configuration files or work with configuring networks outside of the OpenStack environment.

In this chapter, we will cover the following topics:

- Neutron architecture
- Neutron concepts
- Exam objective - managing tenant networks
- Exam objective - managing tenant subnets
- Exam objective - managing security groups and rules
- Exam objective - managing routers (east/west traffic)
- Exam objective - managing provider networks
- Exam objective - managing provider subnets
- Exam objective - managing routers (north/south traffic)
- Exam objective - managing floating IPs

After this chapter, you should have a solid understanding of Neutron and the skills necessary to successfully fulfill all Neutron-related objectives on the exam.

About Neutron

In Chapter 5, we discussed the minimum requirements for booting an instance in an OpenStack environment:

- A boot source
- A flavor
- An available Neutron network

Neutron allows users to create the necessary virtual resources not only to ensure that their instances obtain internal IP addresses (also known as **fixed IPs**), but also to have the ability to map external IP addresses (also known as **floating IPs**) to instances. This allows applications residing in OpenStack instances to be externally accessible. With Neutron, users can view their own networks, subnet, firewall rules, routers, and load balancers, all through the Horizon dashboard, command-line interface, OpenStack SDKs, or directly via the API. Neutron also contains a modular framework powered by a variety of plugins, agents, and drivers, including LinuxBridge and Open vSwitch.

 This chapter provides a brief explanation of Neutron. For a deeper dive, check out *OpenStack Networking Essentials* by James Denton, Packt, 2016.

Neutron architecture

Neutron is made up of five daemons, as shown in *Figure 6.1.*

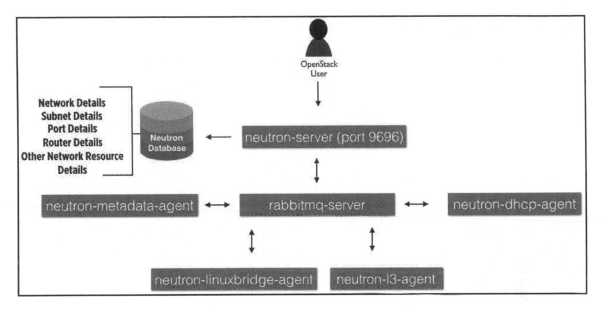

Figure 6.1: High-level view of Neutron architecture

- **neutron-server**: The API and primary gateway to Neutron. One must interact with neutron-server to create, list, delete, and manage networks and other network resources.

- **neutron-dhcp-agent**: Provides DHCP services to DHCP-enabled Neutron subnets. Behind the scenes, `neutron-dhcp-agent` actually uses `dnsmasq`, the popular lightweight DHCP server software, within a network namespace. Network namespaces are a feature of the Linux kernel and partition the use of the network, allowing segregation of network resources despite similar IP address ranges.

- **neutron-l3-agent**: Creates Neutron routers. Behind the scenes, Neutron routers are network namespaces with unique routing tables and `iptables` rules.

- **neutron-metadata-agent**: Provides metadata services to instances. The metadata service was popularized by Amazon Web Services and is a non-routable IP address (`169.254.169.254`) that a user or script can contact for personal information regarding that instance.

- **neutron-linuxbridge-agent**: Runs on each compute node in the environment. Responsible for the creation and management of all network-related functions on the compute nodes—including the creation of virtual network interfaces for newly-created instances, as well as the creation and connection of Linux bridges and `iptables` rules.

LinuxBridge plugin

In the virtual appliance provided with this book, Neutron is configured to utilize the LinuxBridge plugin. The LinuxBridge plugin utilizes existing Linux kernel features, as well as Linux programs, to provide virtual networking components. The exam does not require you to understand these relationships, but it's interesting to see the magic working behind the scenes.

Neutron feature	Existing Linux kernel feature and/or programs
neutron-dhcp-agent	network namespaces, dnsmasq
neutron-l3-agent	network namespaces, iptables (netfilter kernel module), conntrack (conntack kernel module)
neutron-plugin-agent	iptables (netfilter kernel module), iproute2 (gre, vlan, and vxlan kernel modules), bridge-utils (bridge kernel module)

Neutron concepts

Let's talk Neutron concepts. See *Figure 6.2*.

- **Network**: A network is analogous to a logical slice of the physical network. There are two primary types of networks in Neutron: **tenant networks** and **provider networks**:
    - **Tenant network**: Created by OpenStack users wishing to boot an instance on their very own virtual layer-2 broadcast domain. Tenant networks are always owned by the project to which the user is scoped during the network creation request.
    - **Provider network**: Typically managed by someone with an admin-level role. Provider networks are used to provide network access to resources outside the OpenStack environment. This resource could be something like the internet, or even a bare-metal database server that exists on a specific VLAN or VXLAN in your datacenter.
- **Subnet**: A subnet is an IPv4 or IPv6 address block associated with a specific network. A subnet allows the assignment of IP addresses to virtual machine instances or other network resources. A subnet must be associated with a network in order to boot an instance on it. Upon subnet creation, one always supplies a network CIDR. Subnets attached to tenant networks are typically DHCP enabled.

- **Port**: A port is analogous to a virtual network interface card. It represents entry and exit points for data traffic. There is always a MAC address and UUID associated with a port. A port is automatically created when one boots an instance on a network, or one can reserve a port if they prefer a specific IP address.

- **Security groups and rules**: Security groups control the traffic to and from a port. By default, all traffic is allowed out of an instance and nothing is allowed in—except another instance that contains the default security group.

- **Routers**: Routers are devices generated by the `neutron-l3-agent` daemon and allow one to connect different broadcast domains together. Neutron routers are commonly used to connect traffic from different tenant networks together (east/west traffic) as well as connecting a tenant network to a provider network in order to access something outside the environment such as the internet (north/south traffic).

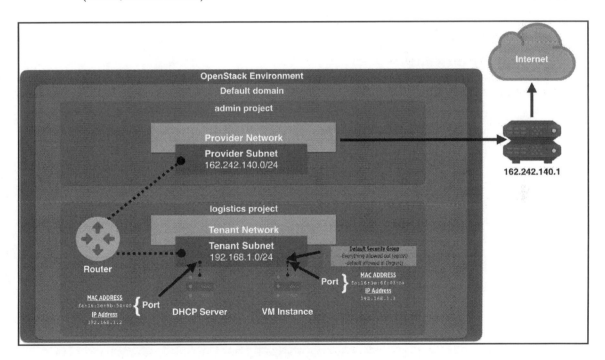

Figure 6.2: Diagram of Neutron concepts

Exam objectives

Let's take a look at the Neutron exam objectives.

The following figure breaks down various Neutron-related objectives you should know on the COA exam. As you can see in *Figure 6.3*, all of these tasks can be completed on both the Horizon dashboard and CLI. Remember: time is of the essence during the exam, and in many cases, it can be much faster to tackle a task on the dashboard.

Objectives	Dashboard	Command-Line
Create/Edit/List/Delete Tenant Networks	✓	✓
Create/Edit/List/Delete Tenant Subnets	✓	✓
Create/Edit/List/Delete Provider Networks	✓	✓
Create/Edit/List/Delete Provider Subnets	✓	✓
Create/Edit/List/Delete Ports	✓	✓
Create/Edit/List/Delete Security Groups	✓	✓
Create/Edit/List/Delete Security Group Rules	✓	✓
Create/Edit/List/Delete Routers	✓	✓
Allocate/Associate Floating IPs	✓	✓

Figure 6.3: Neutron exam objectives can be completed on the Horizon dashboard or CLI

Exam objective - managing tenant networks

Tenant networks are a necessary part of life for the OpenStack user. By default, a non-admin user can create multiple tenant networks (up to the max project quota) and attach multiple subnets to them. The same project/owner philosophy is applied to networks and subnets: any newly created network and subnet will be owned by the project to which a user was scoped at the time of its creation. Only users within the project will be able to manage the newly created networks and subnets. Although users can share networks with specific projects via RBAC rules, this is outside the scope of the COA review and not a required objective.

Horizon dashboard

Let's create a tenant network from the Horizon dashboard. See *Figure 6.4*.

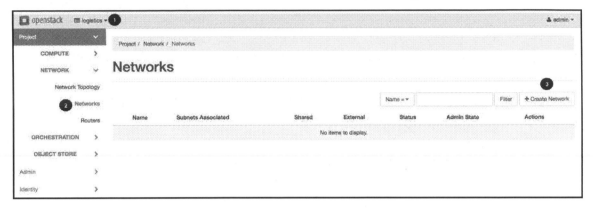

Figure 6.4: Creating a tenant network on the Horizon dashboard

1. From the OpenStack overview page, scope yourself to the **logistics** project by selecting the top dropdown.
2. Select the **Networks** panel from the **Project-Network** panel group.
3. Select **Create Network.**
4. See *Figure 6.5*. **Network Name** (optional): The name for your tenant network. Enter `tenant-network1-dashboard`.
5. **Admin State** (required):The **Admin State** controls whether the network is off or on. If you set it in the DOWN state, any subnets you associate with the network will not be functional until turned back to UP. Verify it is set to **UP**.
6. **Shared** (required): This is similar to a public option. If a tenant network is shared, all projects (even across other domains) will be able to create subnets—and thus boot instances on this network. They will not, however, be able to modify the properties of the network or delete it. We will keep this unchecked and accessible only by the users within the logistics project.

7. For the sake of this exercise, let's **uncheck Create Subnet** so we only create a network. We will create a subnet in the next section.

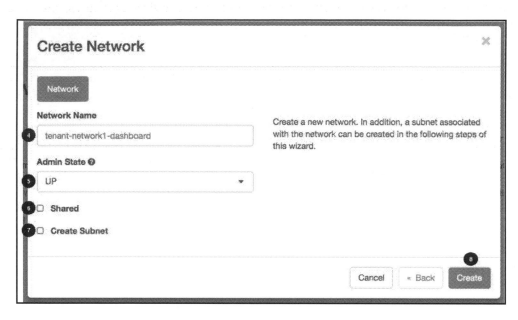

Figure 6.5: 'Create Network' properties on the Horizon dashboard

8. Select **Create**.

We should now have one tenant network owned by the logistics project. See *Figure 6.6*. It's important to note that because we have yet to associate a subnet with our new network, *we will not be able to boot an instance on it yet*.

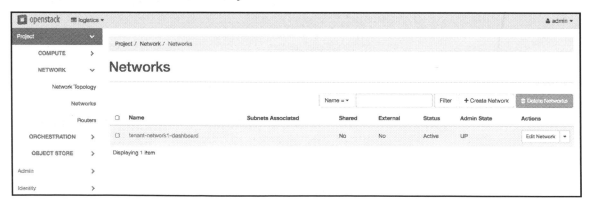

Figure 6.6: A tenant network owned by the logistics project on the Horizon dashboard

Remember, the **Admin-System** panel group provides a view of all resources in the OpenStack environment. This includes all projects across all domains. If we view the **Networks** section of the Admin-System panel group, we should be able to see the **tenant-network1-dashboard network** from the **human-resources** project in the previous chapter. See *Figure 6.7*.

Figure 6.7: The Networks section of the Admin-System Panel Group will show all networks across all projects in the environment

CLI

Recall that the provided openrc file contains credentials in the form of variables for proper authentication to Keystone and setting project scope.

In this chapter, we will do all of our Neutron-related tasks in the **logistics** project. Let's copy our original openrc file to a new file called `openrc-logistics`.

```
$ cp openrc openrc-logistics
```

Now that we've made a copy, let's edit the `openrc-logistics` file, updating the project and tenant name variables to reflect our desired scope to the logistics project. If you are more comfortable with another editor, feel free to use it here.

```
$ nano openrc-logistics
```

Change the following variables to logistics:

```
export OS_PROJECT_NAME=logistics
export OS_TENANT_NAME=logistics
```

 We are changing the OS_TENANT_NAME variable since some of the older service-based clients we use in future chapters rely on this variable.

Source the newly created openrc-logistics file:

```
$ source openrc-logistics
```

Verify that the proper variables are set and we are working within the **logistics** project:

```
$ export | grep OS
```

Now that we are properly scoped, any new network that we create from this point forward will be owned by the logistics project. One very important thing to keep in mind is that we perform all objectives in the exam as the admin user. Because we have the admin role on the logistics project, we can see all networks across all projects in the default domain. This is similar to viewing networks from the Admin-System panel group, as shown in *Figure 6.7*. For example, run the following command:

```
$ openstack network list
```

Notice how this command is displaying *all* networks in the OpenStack environment, not just within the logistics project.

One way to keep ourselves organized as admin users is to add the --long argument to the command. This will provide the project column and will let us know which project the specific network resides in.

```
$ openstack network list --long
```

You should see output similar to figure *Figure 6.8*:

Figure 6.8: A list of all networks (across all projects/domains). This view is similar to the dashboard view in *Figure 6.7*

Notice the project column? This will tell us which project owns the specific network. To get a list of the UUIDs associated with projects, run `openstack project list`.

Let's create a new tenant network within the logistics project using `python-openstackclient`. The syntax is easy!

> Use `openstack help network create` to see additional available arguments.

```
$ openstack network create tenant-network1-cli
```

Verify that the network has been successfully created and is owned by the UUID associated with the logistics project. See *Figure 6.9*.

```
$ openstack network list --long
```

Figure 6.9: Output from the 'openstack network list --long' command

We should have two tenant networks owned by the **logistics** project: `tenant-network1-dashboard` and `tenant-network1-cli`.

> Take note that we only need to supply the name for the network. The other properties associated with the network (VXLAN network types, segmentation id, and so on) are default values that have been previously configured in the Neutron configuration files at `/etc/neutron/*`.

Exam objective - managing tenant subnets

In Neutron, a subnet is an IPv4 or IPv6 address block from which IP addresses can be assigned to virtual machine instances and other network resources. Each Neutron subnet must be associated with a tenant network.

When creating subnets, users can specify a variety of parameters: the allocation pools that limit availability of which addresses in the subnet, a custom gateway address, a list of DNS servers, and individual host routes. We will discuss this in more detail in the upcoming section.

> Multiple subnets can be associated with one Neutron network, but they all must have a unique CIDR range. To create multiple subnets with the exact same IP address range, create another network. This is known as **overlapping IPs**.

Horizon dashboard

Let's create a tenant subnet from the Horizon dashboard. See *Figure 6.10*.

1. From the OpenStack overview page, scope yourself to the **logistics** project by selecting the top dropdown.
2. Select the **Networks** panel from the **Project-Network** panel group. You should see two tenant networks for us to manage:
   - **tenant-network1-dashboard**
   - **tenant-network1-cli**
3. Select the dropdown next to **tenant-network1-dashboard** and select **Add Subnet**.

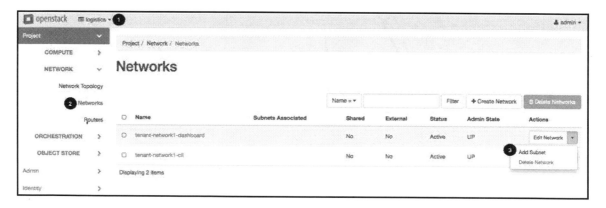

Figure 6.10: Creating a new subnet in the Horizon dashboard

4. See *Figure 6.11*. **Subnet Name** (optional): `tenant-subnet1-dashboard`

5. **Network Address** (required): `192.168.1.0/24`. This must be in **Classless Inter-Domain Routing (CIDR)** notation. CIDR notation is a compact representation of an IP address and its associated routing prefix.

Since this is one of the more confusing aspects of Neutron networking, let's take a moment to understand how this differs from real-world networking.

- In real-world networking, `192.168.1.0/24` would break down as follows:
  - `192.168.1.0`: network
  - `192.168.1.1` through `192.168.1.254`: hosts on the network
  - `192.168.1.255`: broadcast
- On a Neutron subnet, the CIDR (if all default subnet options apply) will break down as follows:
  - `192.168.1.0`: represents the network
  - `192.168.1.1`: reserved for a router (gateway) even if no router currently exists
  - `192.168.1.2`: DHCP server
  - `192.168.1.3` through `192.168.1.254`: instances or other resources
  - `192.168.1.255`: broadcast

6. **IP Version** (required): We will set this to `IPv4`.

7. **Gateway IP** (optional): Leave this blank so it will automatically default to `192.168.1.1` as the gateway address.

8. **Disable Gateway**: This should be **unchecked**. Checking this option will prevent any instances connected to the subnet from receiving default route announcements from the DHCP server.

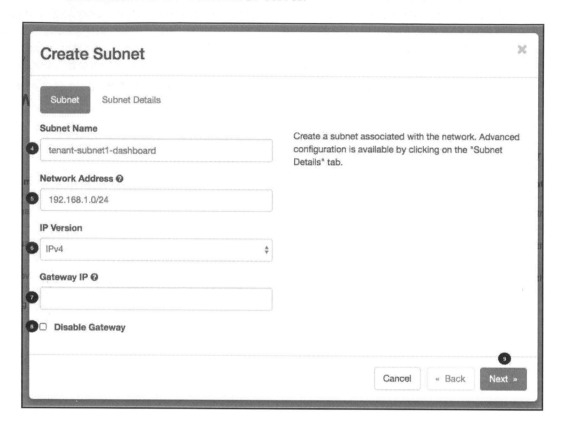

Figure 6.11: Providing subnet details on the Horizon dashboard

9. Select **Next**.
10. See *Figure 6.12*. **Enabled DHCP**: This should be checked to ensure the subnet will be DHCP enabled.
11. **Allocation Pools** (optional): This allows you to specify the IP address start and end. For example, entering an allocation pool of
    192.168.1.100,192.168.1.105 will result your DHCP server getting
    192.168.1.100 and your first instance connected to the subnet will be
    192.168.1.101. If we leave it blank, it will attempt to use most of the CIDR range, in our case: 192.168.1.2,192.168.1.254. We will keep this **blank**.

12. **DNS Name Servers** (optional): This is an IP address list of DNS name servers to be announced to the instance. Providing no value will announce the DHCP server IP as the DNS server to all instances attached to the subnet. This can automatically provide resolution of instance hostnames within OpenStack to their respective IP addresses. For resolution of names outside OpenStack, I have set the internal DNS options to use Google DNS at 8.8.8.8. There are additional DNS options within `/etc/neutron/dhcp_agent.ini`. We will keep box **blank**.

13. **Host Routes** (optional): Any additional routes announced to the hosts. We will keep this **blank**.

14. Select **Create**.

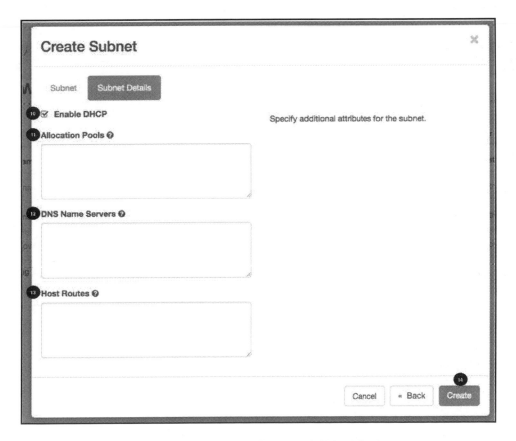

Figure 6.12: Providing DHCP options for a subnet on the Horizon dashboard

Great! We just created a brand new subnet on the Horizon dashboard! Keep in mind that you can always update this subnet from the Horizon dashboard by selecting **Edit Subnet**.

Figure 6.13: Editing/updating a subnet on the Horizon dashboard

Let's go ahead and change the default allocation pool for this subnet from the default `192.168.1.2,192.168.1.254` to `192.168.1.50-192.168.1.60`. Select **Save**. See *Figure 6.14*.

Figure 6.14: Changing the allocation pool for a subnet on the Horizon dashboard

Although the DHCP server has already been assigned to `192.168.1.2`, the first instance that gets booted on this subnet will receive the IP address `192.168.1.50`.

CLI

Let's now learn how to create a subnet with `python-openstackclient`.

Source the `openrc-logistics` file. If you have not done this yet, refer back to the beginning of this chapter.

```
$ source openrc-logistics
```

Verify that the proper variables are set:

```
$ export | grep OS
```

Let's create and attach a new subnet to the tenant network we created in the previous section, `tenant-network1-cli`:

```
$ openstack subnet create --network tenant-network1-cli --subnet-range
192.168.1.0/24 tenant-subnet1-cli
```

Let's now confirm that the new `tenant-subnet1-cli` shows up in our list. Similar to the `openstack network list` command, we will add the `--long` flag so we can verify that the logistics project owns the subnet.

```
$ openstack subnet list --long
```

You should see output similar to *Figure 6.15*.

Figure 6.15: Output from the 'openstack subnet list --long' command

Exam objective - managing security groups and rules

Now that we have our tenant networks and subnets created, let's talk about security groups. Security groups provide a profile for virtual firewall rules that control the inbound (ingress) and outbound (egress) flow of traffic to and from a port. This profile is typically associated with an instance's port.

Each project contains a default security group that allows all egress traffic but denies all ingress traffic. Security groups are frequently used to open ports that users may need to access for talking to applications outside OpenStack, as well as to prevent unnecessary east-west traffic between different applications on the same subnet—thus adding an additional layer of protection.

> Security group rules are stateful and allow established traffic. An example of this would be allowing ingress TCP port 22 for SSH. This rule automatically allows established return traffic. Another example is allowing egress ICMP for pinging out. This will automatically allow return traffic so the user can see a reply to their ping.

Horizon dashboard

1. From the OpenStack overview page, scope yourself to the **logistics** project by selecting the top dropdown.
2. Select the **Access & Security** panel on the **Project-Compute** panel group. You should automatically be set to the **Security Groups** tab. Here you should see one current security group called **default**. By default, there is one **default security group** per project.
3. Let's examine the rules in the default security group. Select **Manage Rules**.

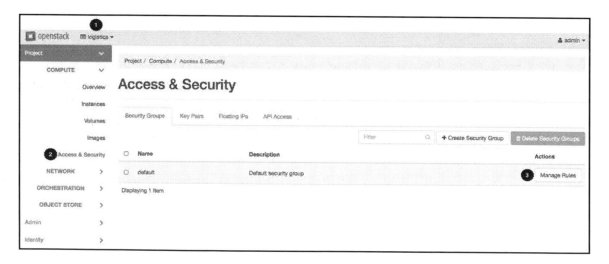

Figure 6.16: Managing security groups from the Horizon dashboard

4. See *Figure 6.17*. We should now see a list of all rules that belong to the default security group. All IPv4 and IPv6 egress traffic is allowed. All IPv4 and IPv6 ingress traffic is blocked with the exception of traffic coming from a port with the default security group. This could be another instance within the same project, for example. Let's select **Add Rule.**

5. See *Figure 6.18*. **Rule** (required): Rules define which traffic is allowed to instances assigned to the security group. We will select **ALL ICMP (ping)**.

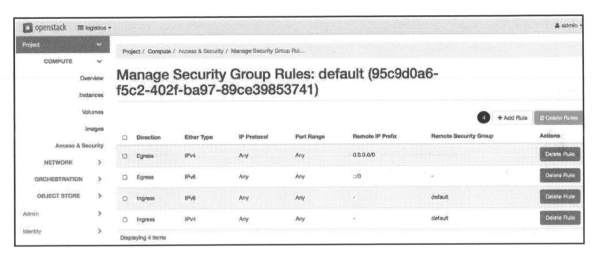

Figure 6.17: Managing security group rules from the Horizon dashboard

6. **Direction** (required): **Ingress** (inbound to the instance) or **Egress** (outbound from the instance). We will select **Ingress** to allow incoming ICMP (ping).

7. **Remote** (required): You must specify the source of traffic to be allowed. This can be an IP address block in CIDR form or a security group. Selecting a security group will allow any other instance with that security group applied.

8. **CIDR** (required): To allow incoming ping from any IP address, we can select Remote CIDR 0.0.0.0/0. Let's put that here.

9. Select **Add** to add the rule.

You can also select predefined protocols from the rule dropdown, including HTTP (22), HTTPS (443), and SSH (22). Using a **Custom TCP Rule** allows us to populate the port number ourselves.

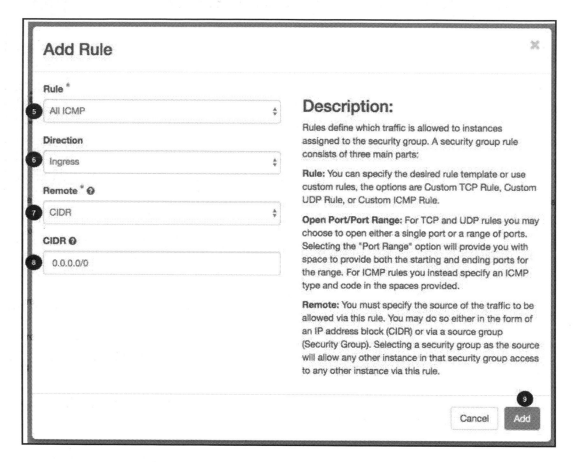

Figure 6.18: Adding a new security group rule which allows incoming ICMP from any source IP address

See *Figure 6.19*. The new ICMP should now be present in the **default** security group in the logistics project.

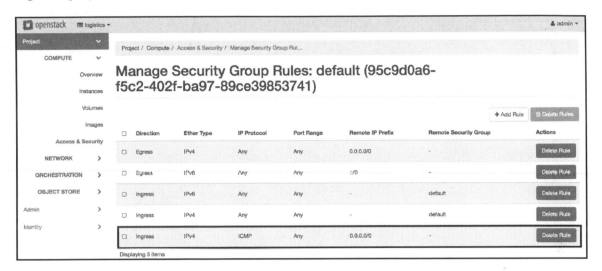

Figure 6.19: Newly created ICMP security group rule in the default security group within the logistics project

Now that we've added a new rule to the default security group, let's create an entirely new security group and add a rule to it. Many OpenStack users create brand new security groups for specific instance roles. For example, it may be appropriate to create a new security group called `database-sg`. This security group could contain a rule that would only allow TCP ingress traffic from any instance that has the `webserver-sg` security group.

Let's create a brand new security group on the dashboard called `webserver-sg-dashboard`. This security group will contain a rule that allows inbound SSH traffic (port 22) from anywhere!

1. See *Figure 6.20*. From the OpenStack overview page, scope yourself to the **logistics** project by selecting the top dropdown.
2. Select the **Access & Security** panel on the **Project-Compute** panel group. You should automatically be set to the **Security Groups** tab. Here you should see one current security group called **default**. By default, there is one **default security group** per project.

3. Select **Create Security Group**.

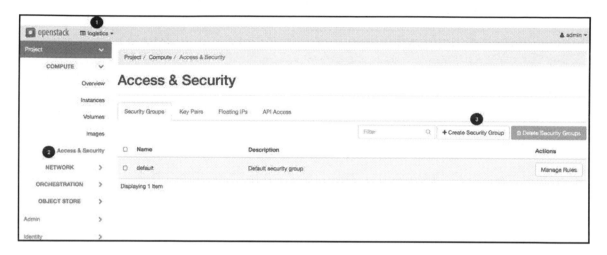

Figure 6.20: Creating a new security group from the Horizon dashboard:

4. See *Figure 6.21*. **Name** (required): The name for the security group. Keep in mind that we can have multiple security groups with the same name, thanks to UUIDs. Name the group `webserver-sg-dashboard`.

5. **Description** (optional): A description for the security group. Enter `A security group for web server instances`.

6. Select **Create Security Group**.

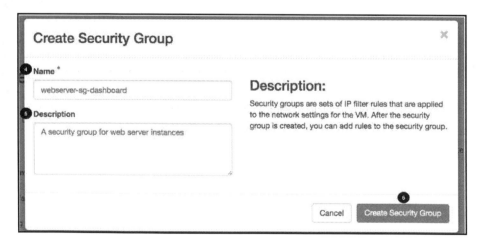

Figure 6.21: New security group options on the Horizon dashboard

You should now have a newly created security group. This group will only contain two rules, allowing all egress traffic for IPv4 and IPv6.

Let's create a new security group rule by selecting **Add Rule**. This rule will allow incoming SSH from anywhere. It should have the following:

Rule: Custom TCP Rule

Direction: Ingress

Open Port: Port

Port: 22

Remote: CIDR

CIDR: 0.0.0.0/0

See *Figure 6.22*. Once created, you should see the new rule associated with **webserver-sg-dashboard**.

Figure 6.22: A security group rule allowing incoming SSH (TCP/port 22) from any source IP address

CLI

Let's go ahead and learn how to add new groups and rules via `python-openstackclient`.

Source the `openrc-logistics` file:

```
$ source openrc-logistics
```

Verify that the proper variables are set to allow you to be scoped to the logistics project:

```
$ export | grep OS
```

Let's use `python-openstackclient` to list all security groups in our environment. You will notice we see **all security groups, across all projects in the OpenStack environment** (*one default group within every project*).

```
$ openstack security group list
```

```
+--------------------------------------+------------------------+------------------------------------------+----------------------------------+
| ID                                   | Name                   | Description                              | Project                          |
+--------------------------------------+------------------------+------------------------------------------+----------------------------------+
| 00a84fb5-f672-4ee7-93ee-2ed2324fb1bd | default                | Default security group                   | 306c211172cc411d9b3ffbd4dc637757 |
| 0d839d3d-335f-4f9c-8e51-d63ea131ce19 | webserver-sg-dashboard | A security group for web server instances| 7fb56b9d4c124a778a79dae0e04386a5 |
| 2e03372c-04af-42e3-96bb-4509cd93f788 | default                | Default security group                   | d5a33462721e4d35bd45138311c526b8 |
| 3e5ce801-bc12-4c76-ad0c-f9ca855f40b2 | default                | Default security group                   | eb1a2580ea87490bbe206162ecf2fde5 |
| 50bdb606-f2d1-4df6-80f4-00da8fba211d | default                | Default security group                   | ec527a34abee458a803c6970d6b406f1 |
| 57f8556c-612d-4faa-8440-6edf93c32409 | default                | Default security group                   | 2ef4c75a3f544be38aa6df8de1a7ff13 |
| 6b1a26f6-52fa-4859-acce-998212225b9d | default                | Default security group                   | 8cfe8de5bca442178e2570244867fad1 |
| 95c9d0a6-f5c2-402f-ba97-89ce39853741 | default                | Default security group                   | 7fb56b9d4c124a778a79dae0e04386a5 |
| 9b5ab62b-e5b5-4a7e-a05f-8341eb7a1e29 | default                | Default security group                   | a2f04643279a4416ab06c33f89686154 |
| a131a550-75d5-4954-adaa-60bff5d3b782 | default                | Default security group                   | 4a02f23d84f84d008f19e967f70d799e |
| a818e81d-87c1-43a7-973b-85f3ddb5fbc1 | default                | Default security group                   | 5c46872a8bd4419a96b386a626cce9e1 |
| ba22d83a-04d5-4fa9-9ac2-5b3abe45c600 | default                | Default security group                   | 0098463de799497e94dd7e1ee682e823 |
| c8c4d687-fc00-4046-988f-fd9d87535a84 | default                | Default security group                   | 99a06694e4444e038d632aca0cc1a89e |
| d396ea29-8ee3-4293-a8be-89f7f94042b0 | default                | Default security group                   | e127de2360954b338e17b6912583524f |
| e0512501-cb12-46c4-8f89-9a920451a8ba | default                | Default security group                   | 01a169db81004f5eba3aa150126479d7 |
| e2714bf6-84ac-4ed1-824b-34f5a207ee93 | default                | Default security group                   | c03401d3e99f4d4ea1aede321b7a61ff |
| eb67bb92-9fc6-4165-90f9-4733284e3a19 | default                | Default security group                   | fe8787fda267442bbea280391e8500d6 |
+--------------------------------------+------------------------+------------------------------------------+----------------------------------+
```

Figure 6.23: A list of all security groups in the OpenStack environment. There is one default security group per project

As we can see, the logistics project currently has two security groups: `default` and our newly created `webserver-sg-dashboard`.

Let's create a brand new security group:

```
$ openstack security group create webserver-sg-cli
```

And now we can easily add a new rule allowing inbound SSH (port 22) from anywhere.

```
$ openstack security group rule create --protocol tcp --ingress --dst-port
22 --src-ip 0.0.0.0/0 webserver-sg-cli
```

You should see output similar to *Figure 6.24*.

```
+-------------------+---------------------------------------+
| Field             | Value                                 |
+-------------------+---------------------------------------+
| created_at        | 2017-07-16T00:53:06Z                  |
| description       |                                       |
| direction         | ingress                               |
| ethertype         | IPv4                                  |
| headers           |                                       |
| id                | a13b8c1e-6e62-41c2-99cb-f583c83cfea7  |
| port_range_max    | 22                                    |
| port_range_min    | 22                                    |
| project_id        | 7fb56b9d4c124a778a79dae0e04386a5      |
| project_id        | 7fb56b9d4c124a778a79dae0e04386a5      |
| protocol          | tcp                                   |
| remote_group_id   | None                                  |
| remote_ip_prefix  | 0.0.0.0/0                             |
| revision_number   | 1                                     |
| security_group_id | 686b01c2-d300-452a-b7a6-5adbc7c5149d  |
| updated_at        | 2017-07-16T00:53:06Z                  |
+-------------------+---------------------------------------+
```

Figure 6.24: Output from the 'openstack security group rule create' command

Let's now verify that our newly created `webserver-sg-cli` security group contains our inbound SSH rule (in addition to the two rules allowing all outbound traffic for IPv4 and IPv6). See *Figure 6.25*.

```
$ openstack security group rule list webserver-sg-cli --long
```

```
+--------------------------------------+-------------+-----------+------------+-----------+-----------+-----------------------+
| ID                                   | IP Protocol | IP Range  | Port Range | Direction | Ethertype | Remote Security Group |
+--------------------------------------+-------------+-----------+------------+-----------+-----------+-----------------------+
| 1940527a-8f19-4256-82d0-c085d9edd897 | None        | None      |            | egress    | IPv4      | None                  |
| 724d62e4-1112-43ad-b270-f8d2ac09c3d5 | None        | None      |            | egress    | IPv6      | None                  |
| a13b8c1e-6e62-41c2-99cb-f583c83cfea7 | tcp         | 0.0.0.0/0 | 22:22      | ingress   | IPv4      | None                  |
+--------------------------------------+-------------+-----------+------------+-----------+-----------+-----------------------+
```

Figure 6.25: Output from the 'openstack security group rule list' command

Exam objective - managing routers - east/west traffic

In the OpenStack world, routers are virtual network devices that provide layer-3 connectivity between subnets. Routers essentially provide routing for two types of scenarios, **east/west** and **north/south** traffic.

In this section, we will focus on understanding and creating **east/west** traffic scenarios. If two virtual machine instances are on two different subnets, they will not be able to communicate with each other unless there is a router to forward traffic between them. OpenStack users can create multiple networks and subnets and connect them with routers.

Let's fulfill this objective by creating an east/west routing scenario similar to *Figure 6.26*:

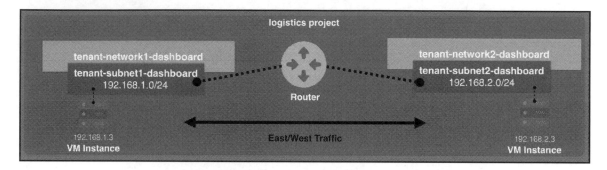

Figure 6.26: East-West traffic between two Neutron tenant networks

Horizon dashboard

At this point in our Neutron preparation, we should have one dashboard tenant network within the logistics project: `tenant-network1-dashboard`.

In order to set up our scenario in *Figure 6.26*, we will need to do the following:

- Create another dashboard tenant network called `tenant-network2-dashboard` and add a subnet called `tenant-subnet2-dashboard`
- Boot two virtual machine instances. One virtual machine instance will be attached to **tenant-network1-dashboard** and the other will be attached to **tenant-network2-dashboard**.
- Create a router
- Connect `tenant-subnet1-dashboard` and `tenant-subnet2-dashboard` to the router

Let's begin by creating our new tenant network and subnet on the dashboard. Create the network and subnet with the following details:

Create Network (*Figure 6.27*)

Verify you are scoped to the **logistics** project.

Network Name: `tenant-network2-dashboard`

Admin State: UP

Shared: unchecked

Create Subnet: checked

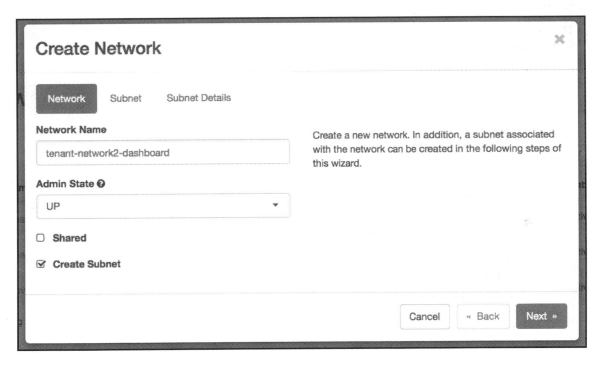

Figure 6.27: Creating tenant-network2-dashboard on the Horizon dashboard

Create Subnet (*Figure 6.28*)

Subnet Name: `tenant-subnet2-dashboard`

Network Address: `192.168.2.0/24`

IP Version: `IPv4`

Gateway IP: blank (it will automatically use `192.168.2.1`)

Disable Gateway: unchecked

Figure 6.28: Creating tenant-subnet2-dashboard on the Horizon dashboard

Subnet Details (*Figure 6.29*)

Enable DHCP: checked

Allocation Pools: blank

DNS Name Servers: blank

Host Routes: blank

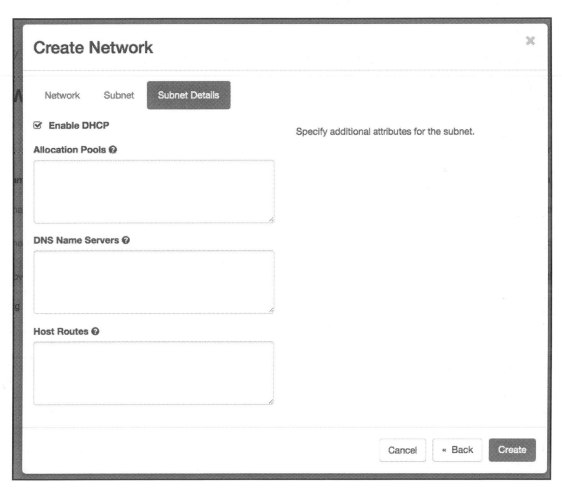

Figure 6.29: Subnet details for tenant-subnet2-dashboard on the Horizon dashboard

We should now have two tenant networks in the logistics project. See *Figure 6.30.*

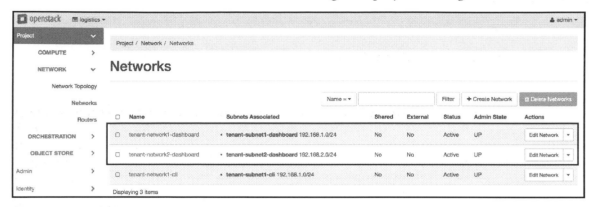

Figure 6.30: Two tenant networks (with subnets) on the Horizon dashboard

Let's now create two virtual machine instances: one in **tenant-network1-dashboard** and the other in **tenant-network2-dashboard**. Again, make sure you are scoped to the **logistics** project! Don't forget to **be patient** an give your instance time to boot!

If you get an error when attempting to boot an instance, please verify that you do not have instances running in any other projects. The virtual appliance included with this book requires a minimum of 6GB RAM assigned, but **cannot** support many instances running at one time. If you continue to have issues booting instances, restart the virtual appliance by running `sudo reboot` from the terminal or manually shutting down the appliance within VirtualBox. If you have available memory on your laptop or desktop machine, feel free to increase the allocated RAM to the virtual appliance within VirtualBox to a value greater than 6GB.

Here are the details for the instance:

Instance1 (See *Figure 6.31*)

Instance Name: `instance1-dashboard`

Availability Zone: `nova`

Count: 1

Source: `cirros`

Flavor: `m1.tiny`

Networks: `tenant-network1-dashboard`

Security Groups: `default`

Figure 6.31: Booting a new virtual machine instance on the Horizon dashboard

Instance2 (See *Figure 6.32*)

Instance Name: `instance2-dashboard`

Availability Zone: `nova`

Count: `1`

Source: `cirros`

Flavor: `m1.tiny`

Networks: `tenant-network2-dashboard`

Security Groups: `default`

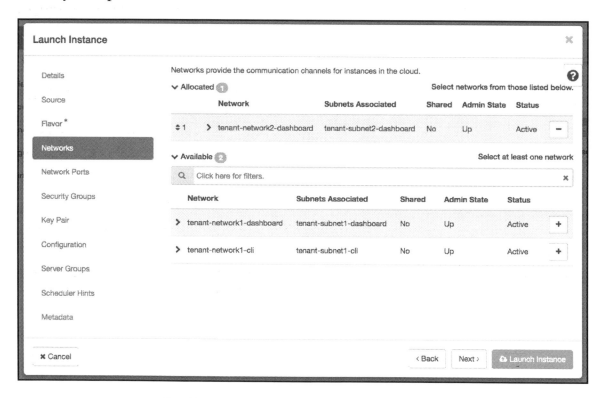

Figure 6.32: Verify that instance2-dashboard is booting on tenant-network2-dashboard

Don't be concerned if your instances do not receive a .3 IP address when booted. We are **not** guaranteed the first available IP address when simply attaching an instance to a network. If you'd like to reserve or specific a particular IP address, you can do so by creating a port via the Admin-System Networks panel or via `python-openstackclient`. For example, prior to creating your instance, you could create a port for 192.168.1.3 by running the following command: `openstack port create --network <network-uuid> --fixed-ip subnet=<subnet-uuid>,ip-address=192.168.1.3 my-new-port`. After the port has been created, specify the port (instead of a network) when booting your instance. Check `openstack help port create` for more details.

See *Figure 6.33*. We should now have two instances within the logistics project.

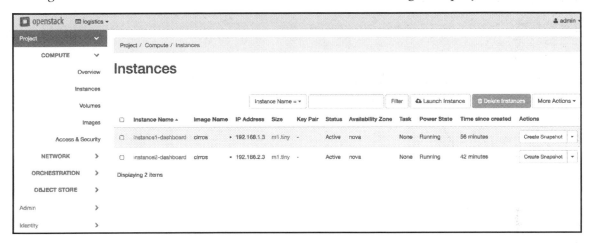

Figure 6.33: Two instances within the logistics project on the Horizon dashboard

At this point, the two subnets on these networks are completely separated from each other. In order for **instance1-dashboard** to communicate with **instance2-dashboard**, we will need to create a router.

See *Figure 6.34*. To create a router, follow these steps:

1. From the OpenStack overview page, scope yourself to the **logistics** project by selecting the top dropdown.
2. Select the **Routers** panel from the **Project-Network** panel group.
3. Select **Create Router.**

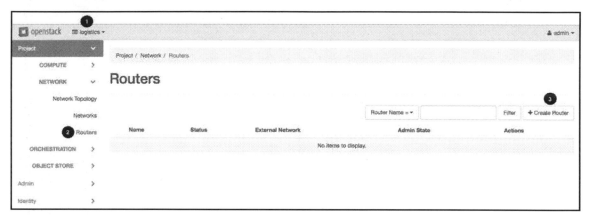

Figure 6.34: Creating a router within the logistics project

4. See *Figure 6.35*. **Router Name** (required): The name for the router. Type in `router-dashboard`.
5. **Admin State** (required): Controls whether the network is off or on. If you set it to the DOWN state, it will not route any traffic. Verify it is set to **UP**.
6. **External Network** (optional): Selects the gateway for the router. We will explore this in more detail when we get to dealing with north/south traffic. Right now, keep this one at **Select Network**.

7. Select **Create Router.**

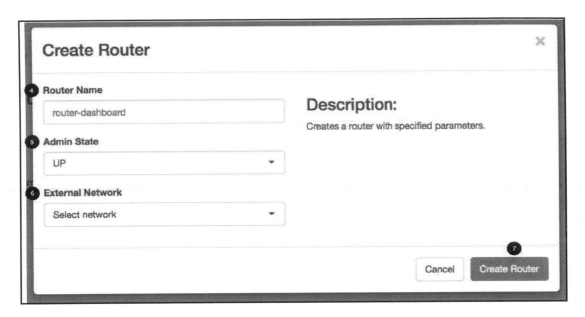

Figure 6.35: Adding router details via the dashboard

Great! We now have one router owned by the logistics project. A router can't do much by itself, so we will need to connect both of our networks to it.

1. See *Figure 6.36*. Select **router-dashboard**.

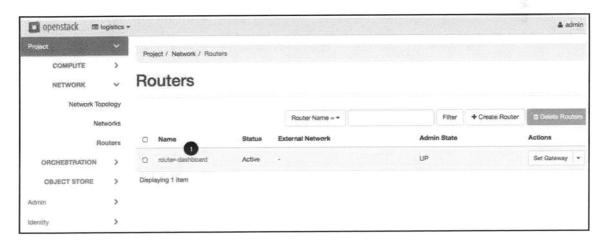

Figure 6.36: Selecting the router on the Horizon dashboard

2. See *Figure 6.37*. Select the **Interfaces** tab.

Figure 6.37: Adding an interface to a router on the Horizon dashboard

3. Select **Add Interface**.

4. See *Figure 6.38*. **Subnet** (required): Select the name of the subnet you want to connect to the router. We will select **tenant-network1-dashboard:192.168.1.0/24**.

5. **IP Address** (optional): This allows us to specify a specific IP address for the gateway. We will leave this blank since we assume it will be the default `192.168.1.1`.

6. Select **Submit**.

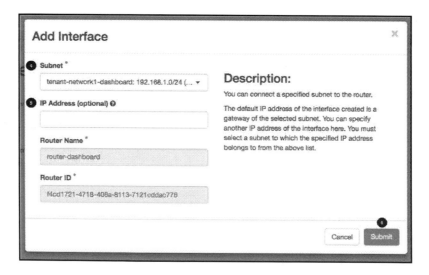

Figure 6.38: Adding interface details via the dashboard

Proceed to create **another** router interface by going through the same series of steps, but adding **tenant-network2-dashboard:192.168.2.0/24**.

The result should look something like *Figure 6.39*. **Remember**, your IP addresses may be different here because we didn't bother with manually creating a port. Just make sure you jot down the IP address for each instance.

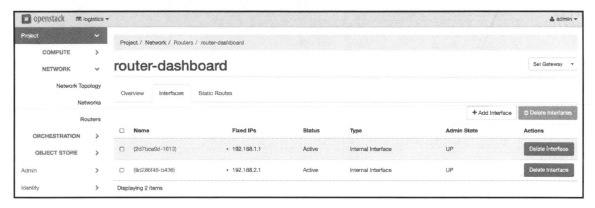

Figure 6.39: Two interfaces connected to a router on the Horizon dashboard

Let's go ahead and check connectivity between the instances. Access the `instance1-dashboard` instance via the console by following the instructions outlined in `Chapter 5`, *Nova Compute Service*.

In case you forgot, here are the Cirros login credentials:

username: `cirros`

password: `cubswin:)`

Now that we are logged in, let's attempt to ping (3 times) `instance2-dashboard` at `192.168.2.x`. If you can't remember the IP for **instance2-dashboard**, go back to the instances page on the dashboard to check!

```
$ ping -c 3 192.168.2.x
```

We should receive a reply! And see something similar to *Figure 6.40*.

```
Connected (unencrypted) to: QEMU (instance-00000006)
$ ping 192.168.2.3
PING 192.168.2.3 (192.168.2.3): 56 data bytes
64 bytes from 192.168.2.3: seq=0 ttl=63 time=1.108 ms
64 bytes from 192.168.2.3: seq=1 ttl=63 time=2.133 ms
64 bytes from 192.168.2.3: seq=2 ttl=63 time=2.275 ms

--- 192.168.2.3 ping statistics ---
3 packets transmitted, 3 packets received, 0% packet loss
round-trip min/avg/max = 1.108/1.838/2.275 ms
$
```

Figure 6.40: An instance residing on another tenant network and responding to a ping. This confirms successful east/west traffic communication

If you perform a ping without the -c count argument, you can cancel it by pressing press *Ctrl + C*.

CLI

If you plan on trying this exercise on the CLI, be sure to delete the instances you just created on the dashboard! The virtual appliance will most likely not be able to handle all these running virtual machines! If you'd like to continue with our exercises on the dashboard, feel free to skip to the next section: Managing Provider Networks on the Horizon dashboard.

Let's go ahead and set up our east/west traffic scenario using python-openstackclient.

Source the openrc-logistics file:

```
$ source openrc-logistics
```

Verify that the proper variables are set:

```
$ export | grep OS
```

Let's create our new additional network and subnet:

```
$ openstack network create tenant-network2-cli
$ openstack subnet create --network tenant-network2-cli --subnet-range
192.168.2.0/24 tenant-subnet2-cli
```

Let's boot our instances:

```
$ openstack server create --image cirros --flavor m1.tiny --nic net-
id=tenant-network1-cli instance1-cli
$ openstack server create --image cirros --flavor m1.tiny --nic net-
id=tenant-network2-cli instance2-cli
```

Confirm that the instances were successfully created:

```
$ openstack server list
```

Let's create the router:

```
$ openstack router create router-cli
```

We should see the following output:

```
+---------------------------+----------------------------------------+
| Field                     | Value                                  |
+---------------------------+----------------------------------------+
| admin_state_up            | UP                                     |
| availability_zone_hints   |                                        |
| availability_zones        |                                        |
| created_at                | 2017-07-16T23:04:12Z                   |
| description               |                                        |
| distributed               | False                                  |
| external_gateway_info     | null                                   |
| flavor_id                 | None                                   |
| ha                        | False                                  |
| headers                   |                                        |
| id                        | 89884d86-6b6d-4fa4-b164-1282dc571168   |
| name                      | router-cli                             |
| project_id                | 7fb56b9d4c124a778a79dae0e04386a5       |
| project_id                | 7fb56b9d4c124a778a79dae0e04386a5       |
| revision_number           | 2                                      |
| routes                    |                                        |
| status                    | ACTIVE                                 |
| updated_at                | 2017-07-16T23:04:12Z                   |
+---------------------------+----------------------------------------+
```

Figure 6.41: Output from the 'openstack router create' command

Let's now connect our two subnets to the router. Before we do this, let's list the available subnets:

```
$ openstack router add subnet router-cli tenant-subnet1-cli
$ openstack router add subnet router-cli tenant-subnet2-cli
```

You will not see any output from these commands. To verify our work, we can run the `openstack port list` command with the `--router` flag:

```
$ openstack port list --router router-cli
```

We should see the following output:

Figure 6.42: Output from the 'openstack port list --router' command

We can now confirm that instances should be able to successfully ping each other.

Exam objective - manage provider networks

Now that we understand how to manage tenant networks and subnets, as well as set up east/west traffic between two different tenant networks, let's create some provider networks. Provider networks are critical to any cloud environment because they enable OpenStack instances to access **external resources** beyond the OpenStack environment. Nova instances would be pretty useless if they could only talk to resources that lived inside the OpenStack environment! What good is an instance that can't talk out to the internet to download the latest operating system packages? What good is an instance if our customers can't access our web application from the outside world? Provider networks are the magic that provides network access to things that live outside OpenStack.

Horizon dashboard

Before we create a provider network on the dashboard, it's very important to remember that *by default, provider networks can only be created by users with the admin role.*

See *Figure 6.43*. Provider networks will only show up in the Admin-System panel group section of the Horizon dashboard.

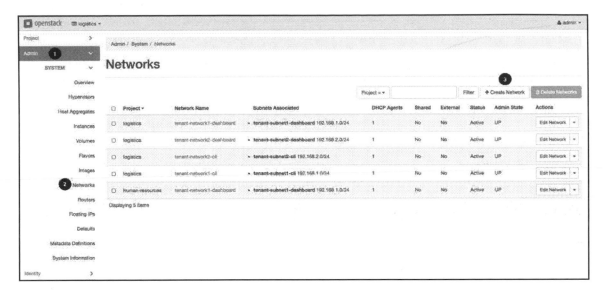

Figure 6.43: Creating a provider network from the Horizon dashboard

1. From the OpenStack overview page, select the **Admin** panel group.
2. Select the Networks Panel on the **Admin-System** panel group. Here you should see all current tenant works owned by all projects in the environment. You can identify them as tenant networks because you can see that the **External** column is set to **No**.
3. Let's create a brand new provider network. Select **Create Network**.

See *Figure 6.44*. The **Create Network** screen for provider networks is a bit different than the one for tenant networks previously reviewed in this chapter. Let's explore the options:

1. **Network Name** (optional): The name for your tenant network. Enter `provider-network-dashboard`.
2. **Project** (required): The specific project we want to own this provider network. In our environment, regular users will not be modifying the provider network, so let's place it in the **admin** project.

3. **Provider Network Type** (required): We can specify a tagging or encapsulation method for the provider network. This is useful if we want the provider network to link to a resource that resides on a specific VLAN, VXLAN, or GRE tunnel. We also have the ability to select FLAT to represent no encapsulation or tagging of the provider network traffic. Let's specify FLAT.

4. **Physical Network** (required): The name of the physical interface mapping we want associated with this provider network. This is not an interface name (such as eth0, eth1, or eth2) but rather a label defined in the file `/etc/neutron/plugins/ml2/linuxbridge_agent.ini`. I have previously created a mapping between the interface veth1 on the virtual appliance and the label *public-dashboard*. This network will provide your OpenStack environment access to the outside world, a.k.a. the internet (as long as you have internet access on your host machine). Type in *public-dashboard*.

5. **Segmentation ID** (optional): You only need to specify the segmentation ID if you specify a VLAN, VXLAN, or GRE Provider Network Type in Step 6. This could be a VLAN tag, VXLAN VNI, or GRE ID. We will leave this **blank** since we are using Provider Network Type FLAT (no encapsulation/tagging).

6. **Admin State** (required): The Admin State controls whether the provider network is off or on. If you set it in the DOWN state, any subnets you associate with the provider network will not be functional until turned back to UP. Verify it is set to **UP**.

7. **Shared** (optional): If a provider network is shared, all projects across all domains will be able to directly attach their instances to this provider network. We are only going to allow our users to set their router gateways to the provider network, so we will make sure we **uncheck** this option.

8. **External Network** (optional): This is the magic that allows our users to set their router's gateway to the network. This will allow us to get our virtual machine instances access to the resources that live outside OpenStack. Let's make sure it is **checked**.

9. Select **Submit** to create the network.

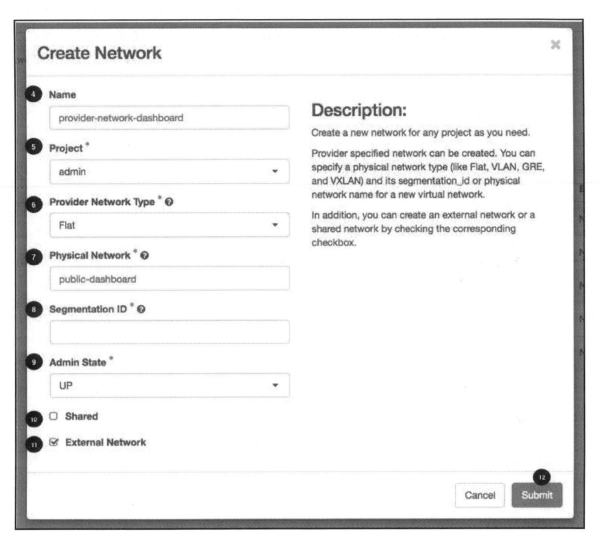

Figure 6.44: Entering provider network details on the Horizon dashboard

After you have created `provider-network-dashboard`, you should see it in the list of networks in the **Networks** panel in the **Admin-System** panel group. See *Figure 6.44*. Notice how the provider network shows **Yes** in the **External** column.

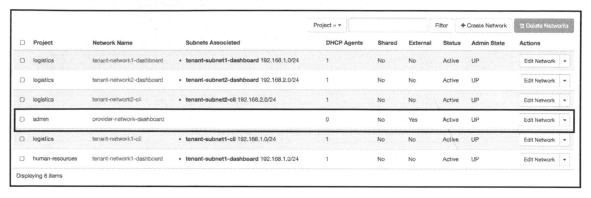

Figure 6.45: A newly created provider network on the Horizon dashboard

CLI

It's time to jump on the command line again. This time, we will be creating a provider network. Remember: we want the provider network to exist inside the **admin** project so users in other projects can't modify it. In that case, we only need to source the `openrc` file.

```
$ source openrc
```

Verify that the proper variables are set and you are scoped to the **admin** project:

```
$ export | grep OS
```

Now let's create our new provider network. This time, we will specify the `public-cli` for the provider's physical network. This is a physical network mapping that I previously provisioned for the virtual appliance. Like the `public-dashboard` physical network we used in the previous exercise, this provides your OpenStack environment with access to your system's internet connection. Also take note of the `--external` flag. Without this flag, your users will not be able to set their router's gateway to the provider network.

```
$ openstack network create --provider-physical-network public-cli --
provider-network-type flat provider-network-cli --external
```

You should see the following output:

```
+--------------------------+--------------------------------------+
| Field                    | Value                                |
+--------------------------+--------------------------------------+
| admin_state_up           | UP                                   |
| availability_zone_hints  |                                      |
| availability_zones       |                                      |
| created_at               | 2017-07-21T03:24:35Z                 |
| description              |                                      |
| headers                  |                                      |
| id                       | cafbf65d-c349-462a-a849-575df069eb2b |
| ipv4_address_scope       | None                                 |
| ipv6_address_scope       | None                                 |
| is_default               | False                                |
| mtu                      | 1500                                 |
| name                     | provider-network-cli                 |
| port_security_enabled    | True                                 |
| project_id               | a2f04643279a4416ab06c33f89686154     |
| project_id               | a2f04643279a4416ab06c33f89686154     |
| provider:network_type    | flat                                 |
| provider:physical_network| public-cli                           |
| provider:segmentation_id | None                                 |
| revision_number          | 3                                    |
| router:external          | External                             |
| shared                   | False                                |
| status                   | ACTIVE                               |
| subnets                  |                                      |
| tags                     | []                                   |
| updated_at               | 2017-07-21T03:24:36Z                 |
+--------------------------+--------------------------------------+
```

Figure 6.46: Output from the 'openstack network create' command

Confirm `provider-network-cli` was successfully created by running the following:

```
$ openstack network list --long
```

Congratulations! You've created a brand new provider network on the CLI.

Exam objective - manage provider subnets

Managing provider subnets is identical to managing tenant subnets. We will follow a very similar process to the tenant subnet creation process outlined earlier in the beginning of this chapter. One slight difference is that our provider subnet will not have DHCP enabled. **Remember: our users will not be attaching instances directly to the provider network and subnet.** When we demonstrate north/south traffic in the next section, you will only set your router gateway to the provider network/subnet.

It's also important to note that the subnet CIDR defined in the provider subnet will become the available **floating IP** address pool. We will learn about floating IP addresses in the last section of this chapter.

Horizon dashboard

1. See *Figure 6.47*. Select `provider-network-dashboard` from the Networks panel under the Admin-System panel group.

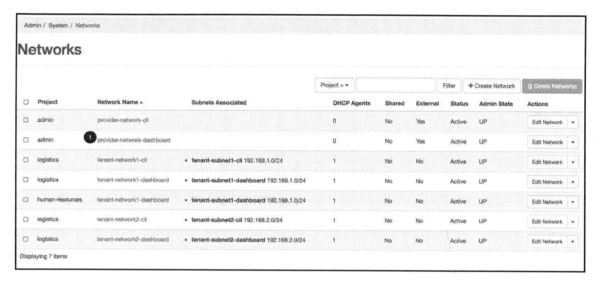

Figure 6.47: Creating a provider subnet on the Horizon dashboard

2. See *Figure 6.48*. Select the **Subnets** tab.

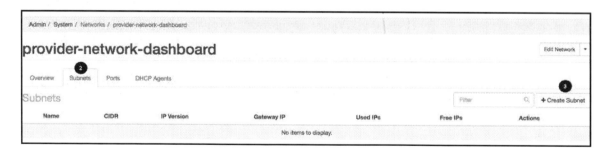

Figure 6.48: Creating a provider subnet on the Horizon dashboard

3. Select **Create Subnet**.
4. See *Figure 6.49*. **Subnet Name:** `provider-subnet-dashboard`

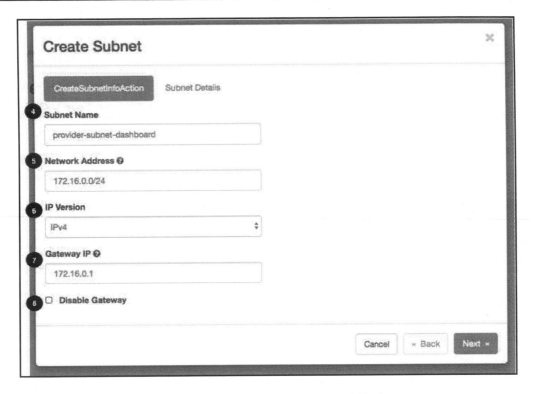

Figure 6.49: Filling in provider subnet details on the Horizon dashboard

5. Network Address: `172.16.0.0/24`. Because you most likely only have access to one public IP address in your home, we will temporarily suspend our disbelief and select an internal IP address range to act as our external provider network IP address. We are using this private network range because the virtual appliance has a previously created gateway interface, which will allow the provider network to talk out to the internet connection on the host machine. In the real world, this could be an external IP address range provided by an Internet Service Provider.

6. **IP Version**: `IPv4`

7. **Gateway IP**: This is the previously created gateway interface on your virtual appliance. This will typically be the IP of your gateway device or router that lives outside OpenStack. For the sake of this exercise, we will enter `172.16.0.1`. In your virtual appliance, this is an IP address assigned to a virtual interface that routes out to your VirtualBox NAT network and out the default gateway on your host system. You can see it by running `ip a show tap0` inside the virtual appliance.

8. **Disable Gateway**: unchecked.
9. See *Figure 6.50*. Enable **DHCP**: Users will not be booting instances on the provider network, so make sure this is **unchecked**.
10. **Allocation Pool**: This allows us to limit the range of our previously defined network address of `172.16.0.0/24`. This will become the **Floating IP** pool that will use in the last section of this chapter. Enter `172.16.0.10,172.16.0.30`.
11. **DNS Name Servers:** We will leave this blank since no instances are being attached to this provider subnet.
12. **Host Routes**: We will leave this blank since we will not be injecting any host routes.
13. Select **Create**.

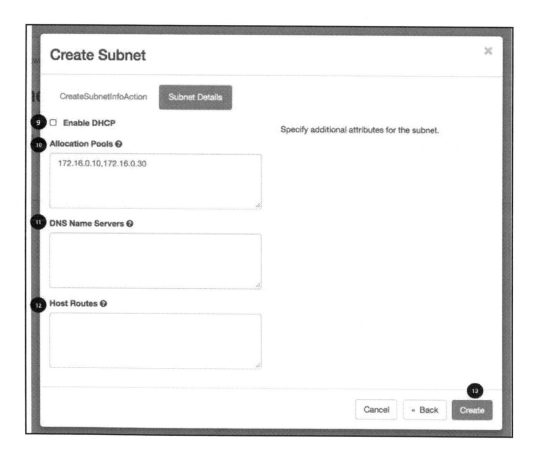

Figure 6.50: Provider subnet DHCP options on the Horizon dashboard

See Figure 6.51. We should now have a newly created subnet!

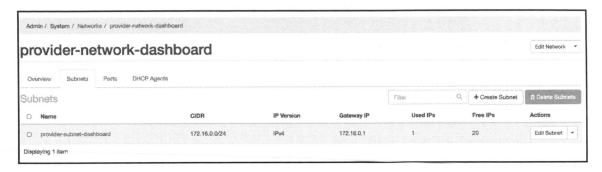

Figure 6.51: A newly provisioned provider subnet on the Horizon dashboard

CLI

Let's create our provider subnet on the CLI. We will first source the `openrc`.

```
$ source openrc
```

Verify that the proper variables are set:

```
$ export | grep OS
```

Because we are using a different provider-physical-network for our CLI examples, we will be using a different subnet, gateway, and allocation pool.

```
$ openstack subnet create --network provider-network-cli --subnet-range
172.16.1.0/24 --gateway 172.16.1.1 --no-dhcp provider-subnet-cli
```

You should see the following output:

```
+--------------------+--------------------------------------+
| Field              | Value                                |
+--------------------+--------------------------------------+
| allocation_pools   | 172.16.1.2-172.16.1.254              |
| cidr               | 172.16.1.0/24                        |
| created_at         | 2017-07-21T05:42:02Z                 |
| description        |                                      |
| dns_nameservers    |                                      |
| enable_dhcp        | False                                |
| gateway_ip         | 172.16.1.1                           |
| headers            |                                      |
| host_routes        |                                      |
| id                 | 86251a23-088d-42ba-9c3d-3f0e20e67b1c |
| ip_version         | 4                                    |
| ipv6_address_mode  | None                                 |
| ipv6_ra_mode       | None                                 |
| name               | provider-subnet-cli                  |
| network_id         | 5f14e250-abea-4c56-b27b-d4841c600f08 |
| project_id         | a2f04643279a4416ab06c33f89686154     |
| project_id         | a2f04643279a4416ab06c33f89686154     |
| revision_number    | 2                                    |
| service_types      | □                                    |
| subnetpool_id      | None                                 |
| updated_at         | 2017-07-21T05:42:02Z                 |
+--------------------+--------------------------------------+
```

Figure 6.52: Output from the 'openstack subnet create' command

Confirm `provider-network-cli` was successfully created by running the following:

```
$ openstack subnet list --long
```

Congratulations! You've created a brand new provider subnet on the CLI.

Exam objective - managing routers - north/south traffic

At this point, our east/west router traffic scenario should look similar to *Figure 6.26*. This is a great example of how Neutron routers can assist you in routing internal Neutron tenant networks. Now that we've created some provider networks, we should be able to connect our instance's tenant networks to them, thanks to our routers. Once connected, our instances will have access to the internet!

Before starting this exercise, verify that your host machine running the virtual appliance has access to wired/wireless internet. Be sure to disable any VPNs or proxies. They may interfere with external connectivity.

Horizon dashboard

It's time to connect set our router gateway to our previously created provider network so that our instances on tenant-network1-dashboard and tenant-network2-dashboard can get access to the internet:

1. See *Figure 6.53*. From the OpenStack overview page, scope yourself to the **logistics** project by selecting the top dropdown.
2. Select the panel on the **Project-Network** Panel Group. Here you should see our previously created router: **router-dashboard**.
3. Select **Set Gateway** next to **router-dashboard**.

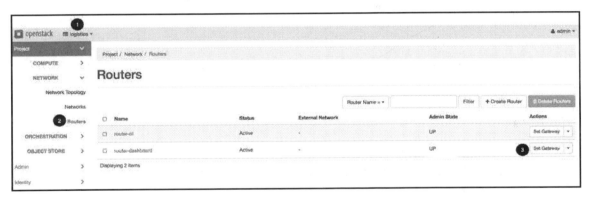

Figure 6.53: Setting the router gateway on the Horizon dashboard

4. See *Figure 6.54*. **External Network** (required): Here we will select our previously created provider network: `provider-network-dashboard`
5. Select **Submit**.

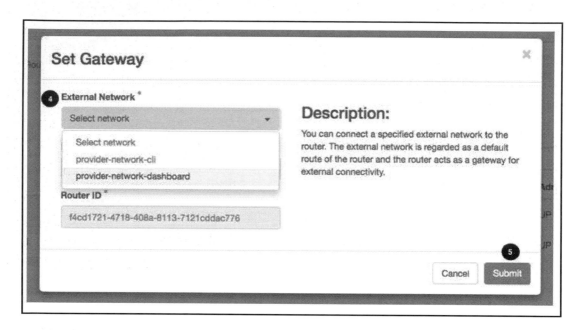

Figure 6.54: Specifying the provider network gateway for a router

Congratulations! You just have connected your instances to the internet! Before we proceed with testing connectivity, see *Figure 6.55*. This is a high-level view of our current network topology. The default gateway of the router is set to `provider-network-dashboard`. This is where all traffic *not* destined for `tenant-network-dashboard` and `tenant-network2-dashboard` will travel.

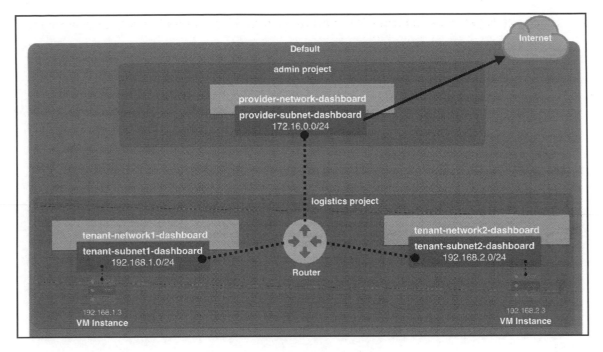

Figure 6.55: North/south traffic network toplology

> To test internet connectivity from our OpenStack instances, your personal laptop or desktop running VirtualBox must be connected to the internet.

Let's now get access to `instance1-dashboard` inside the logistics project to ensure it can access the internet:

Select the `instance1-dashboard` from the instances section.

Select the **Console** tab. Select **Show Only Console**. If you still don';t see anything, click on **Enter**, which should wake up the console screen.

We can now log in to our instance:

username: `cirros`

password: `cubswin:)`

Now that we are logged in, let's attempt to ping (3 times) openstack.org. Be patient! It may take a few moments to see the ping replies.

```
$ ping -c 3 openstack.org
```

You should see the following response:

```
Connected (unencrypted) to: QEMU (instance-00000008)
[    3.956413] rtc_cmos 00:01: setting system clock to 2017-08-20 05:35:37 UTC (
1503207337)
[    3.960748] BIOS EDD facility v0.16 2004-Jun-25, 0 devices found
[    3.960961] EDD information not available.
[    4.036329] Freeing unused kernel memory: 928k freed
[    4.136092] Write protecting the kernel read-only data: 12288k
[    4.279899] Freeing unused kernel memory: 1596k freed
[    4.370231] Freeing unused kernel memory: 1184k freed

further output written to /dev/ttyS0


login as 'cirros' user. default password: 'cubswin:)'. use 'sudo' for root.
instance1-dashboard login: cirros
Password:
$ ping -c 3 openstack.org
PING openstack.org (162.242.140.107): 56 data bytes
64 bytes from 162.242.140.107: seq=0 ttl=59 time=24.840 ms
64 bytes from 162.242.140.107: seq=1 ttl=59 time=29.029 ms
64 bytes from 162.242.140.107: seq=2 ttl=59 time=29.424 ms

--- openstack.org ping statistics ---
3 packets transmitted, 3 packets received, 0% packet loss
round-trip min/avg/max = 24.840/27.764/29.424 ms
$
```

Figure 6.56: A ping response from openstack.org confirms successful north/south traffic communication

If you perform a ping without the `-c count` argument, you can cancel it by pressing press **Ctrl + C**.

CLI

Let's set our `router-cli` to the `provider-network-cli` via python-openstackclient. This is a fairly simple command.

Before you begin, be sure to source the `openrc-logistics` credentials file, since we are working within the logistics project.

```
$ source openrc-logistics
```

Verify that the proper variables are set:

```
$ export | grep OS
```

List all available routers:

```
$ openstack router list
```

List all available networks and verify that `provider-network-cli` is listed:

```
$ openstack network list --long
```

Set the gateway of `router-cli` to `provider-network-cli`.

For this command, we will need to use the service-based client, `python-neutronclient`. This because version 2.7.12 of `python-openstackclient` does not support setting a router gateway.

To set the router-gateway with `python-neutronclient`, run the following:

```
$ neutron router-gateway-set router-cli provider-network-cli
```

 As of the writing of this book, the python-openstackclient version 3.6 supports setting the router gateway with the following command: `openstack router set router-cli --external-gateway provider-network-cli`. Beware! The exam may only contain an older version `python-openstackclient` and not support this.

Exam objective - managing floating IPs

In the previous objective, we set our router gateway to the provider network. This provided all the instances attached to networks connected to the router with access to the internet. But what if we wanted to access an application or resource on one of these instances from *outside our OpenStack environment*? Because the IP address assigned to our instances is internal and not publicly routable, Neutron allows users to associate floating IPs with their instances. Floating IPs are similar to the concept of elastic IPs in the Amazon Web Services world. Using them is a two-step process:

1. **Allocate** a floating IP to your project.
2. **Assign** the floating IP to an instance.

If you no longer need your floating IP, you can easily unassign and release it from the project, sending it back into the original floating IP address pool. Remember: the floating IP address pool was defined in the provider network subnet. In the real world, this could be an external IP address range provided by our internet service provider.

Horizon dashboard

Let's associate a floating IP address with our **instance1-dashboard** instance in the **logistics** project. We will then attempt to ping the instance from our virtual appliance via its floating IP. Because we have the admin role, we will see how to assign a specific IP address via the admin-system panel group. Let's begin!

1. See *Figure 6.57*. From the OpenStack overview page, select the **Admin-System** panel group.
2. Select the **Floating IPs** panel.

3. Select **Allocate IP to Project**.

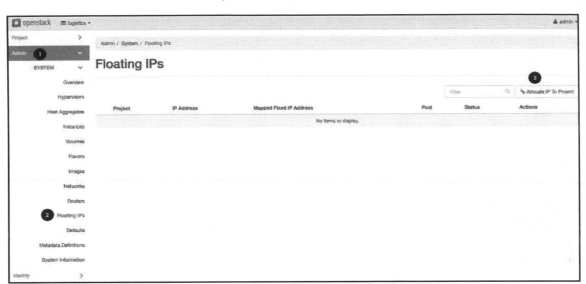

Figure 6.57: Allocating a floating IP address from the Horizon dashboard

4. See *Figure 6.58*. **Pool** (required): Select our previously created provider network, `provider-network-dashboard`.

5. **Project** (required): Select the project that will own the floating IP address. Since we have been doing all of our Neutron work in the logistics project, select `logistics`.

6. **Floating IP Address** (optional): We can specify the floating IP address we want here. In our exercise, let's request `172.16.0.100`. If we do not specify an IP address, we will be assigned a random available floating IP address from the `172.16.0.0/24` pool defined in the provider subnet we created in the **Provider Subnet** exercise.

7. Select **Allocate Floating IP** to assign the floating IP address to the logistics project.

Figure 6.58: Providing details for allocating a floating IP address on the Horizon dashboard

8. See *Figure 6.59*. Now that logistics project owns the `172.16.0.100` address, we need to assign it to **instance1-dashboard**. First, scope yourself to the logistics project.

9. Select **Associate Floating IP** from the dropdown next to the instance1-dashboard virtual machine instance.

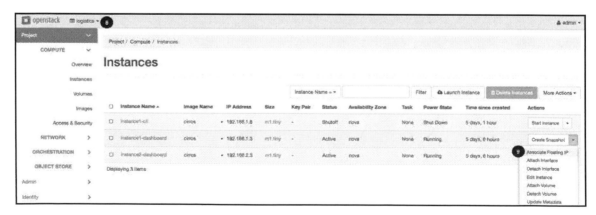

Figure 6.59: Associating an IP address with an instance from the Horizon dashboard

10. See *Figure 6.60*. **IP Address:** Any floating IP addresses that the logistics project owns will show up here. Select our previously allocated `172.16.0.100`.

11. **Port to be associated**: Here we specify the instance's port we want associated with the floating IP address. We want to ensure that **instance-1-dashboard** and its internal IP address are selected.

12. Select **Associate** to proceed with the mapping.

Figure 6.60: Providing details for associating an IP address with an instance

You did it! As you can see in *Figure 6.61*, **instance1-dashboard** now has two IP addresses:

Fixed/internal IP: `192.168.1.3`

Floating IP/external IP: `172.16.0.100`

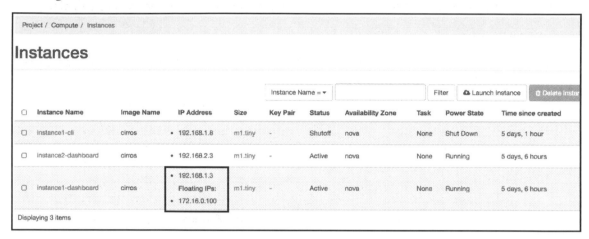

Figure 6.61: An instance with an internal IP address and floating IP address

We should now be able to ping the `172.16.0.100` IP address from **inside** the virtual appliance:

```
$ ping -c 3 172.16.0.100
```

We should get a response back. See *Figure 6.62*.

It works!

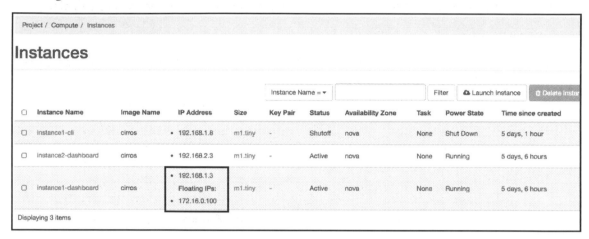

Figure 6.62: Successfully pinging instance1-dashboard via its floating IP address inside the virtual appliance

So now that we know our floating IP is working, what about SSH? Let's try to SSH into the instance.

```
$ ssh cirros@172.16.0.100
```

You'll notice that it **won't** work! We can get more information by using the SSH −v flag.

```
$ ssh cirros@172.16.0.100 −v
```

See *Figure 6.63*. Notice how our SSH client is not making a connection to the instance. What could be blocking it?

```
-bash: man: command not found
openstack@coa-aio-newton:~$ clear
openstack@coa-aio-newton:~$ ssh cirros@172.16.0.100 -v
OpenSSH_7.2p2 Ubuntu-4ubuntu2.1, OpenSSL 1.0.2g  1 Mar 2016
debug1: Reading configuration data /etc/ssh/ssh_config
debug1: /etc/ssh/ssh_config line 19: Applying options for *
debug1: Connecting to 172.16.0.100 [172.16.0.100] port 22.
```

Figure 6.63: Attempting to SSH to an instance via its floating IP from inside the virtual appliance. Something is blocking this communication!

It must be **security groups**!

By default, all incoming traffic into the instance (ingress) is blocked!

In the beginning of this chapter, we created a security group called **webserver-sg-dashboard**. We added a security group rule to this group that allows incoming SSH (TCP/port 22). Let's apply this group to **instance1-dashboard**. See *Figure 6.64*.

1. Verify you are scoped to the **logistics** project.
2. Select **Instances** from the **Project-Compute** panel.

3. Select **Edit Security Groups** from the **instance1-dashboard** dropdown.

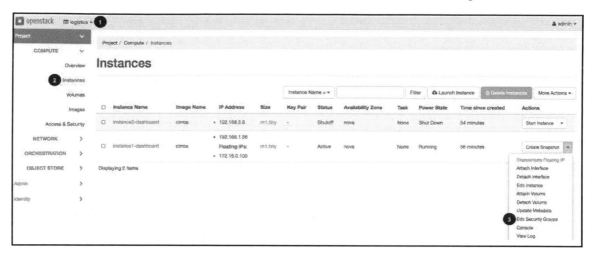

Figure 6.64: Editing the security groups associated with an instance on the Horizon dashboard

4. See *Figure 6.65*. Add the **webserver-sg-dashboard** security group to the instance.
5. Select **Save**.

Figure 6.65: Apply a security group to an instance on the Horizon dashboard

Now let's try again.

```
$ ssh cirros@172.16.0.100 -v
```

Success!

 If you have multiple security groups applied to an instance, the most permissive security group rules will take priority.

Bonus exercise

How can we go about SSH'ing to this instance without needing to put in a password? SSH keys of course!

As an extra exercise, delete **instance1-dashboard** and re-create it with the `my-new-keypair-cli` which we created in Chapter 5, *Nova Compute Service*. After associating a floating IP with our instance, we can then attempt to SSH to the instance via its floating IP address and with our **private key**! It should look something like this:

```
$ ssh -i my-new-keypair-cli.pem cirros@172.16.0.100
```

Awesome! No need to put in a password!

 If you receive a warning, you may need to remove your old known_hosts key by running `ssh-keygen -f "/home/openstack/.ssh/known_hosts" -R 172.16.0.100`

CLI

Assigning a floating IP address to an instance via `python-opentackclient` is also done following the same methodology as with the Horizon dashboard:

1. **Allocate** a floating IP address to your project.
2. **Assign** the floating IP to an instance.

Source the `openrc-logistics` file:

```
$ source openrc-logistics
```

Verify that the proper variables are set:

```
$ export | grep OS
```

Let's use `python-openstackclient` to first allocate a desired floating IP address to the logistics project:

```
$ openstack floating ip create --floating-ip-address 172.16.1.100 provider-network-cli
```

Now that the logistics project owns the `172.16.1.100` address, we can easily assign it to `instance1-cli` by running the following command:

```
$ openstack server add floating ip instance1-cli 172.16.1.100
```

Although you will not receive any output from this command, see *Figure 6.65*. You can verify the floating IP was properly associated by using the `openstack server show` command and observing the `addresses` field.

```
+-------------------------------------+------------------------------------------------------------------+
| Field                               | Value                                                            |
+-------------------------------------+------------------------------------------------------------------+
| OS-DCF:diskConfig                   | MANUAL                                                           |
| OS-EXT-AZ:availability_zone         | nova                                                            |
| OS-EXT-SRV-ATTR:host                | coa-aio-newton                                                  |
| OS-EXT-SRV-ATTR:hypervisor_hostname | coa-aio-newton                                                  |
| OS-EXT-SRV-ATTR:instance_name       | instance-0000000a                                              |
| OS-EXT-STS:power_state              | Shutdown                                                        |
| OS-EXT-STS:task_state               | None                                                            |
| OS-EXT-STS:vm_state                 | stopped                                                         |
| OS-SRV-USG:launched_at              | 2017-07-16T23:50:00.000000                                     |
| OS-SRV-USG:terminated_at            | None                                                            |
| accessIPv4                          |                                                                 |
| accessIPv6                          |                                                                 |
| addresses                           | tenant-network1-cli=192.168.1.8, 172.16.1.100                  |
| config_drive                        | True                                                            |
| created                             | 2017-07-16T23:49:38Z                                           |
| flavor                              | m1.tiny (1)                                                     |
| hostId                              | cee1fd62228d6ea2d3ffec964b4cc80b0f0641452f0f0100c8676d4d        |
| id                                  | 2e80496f-d0b6-4569-9420-1e1b68e0c27e                           |
| image                               | cirros (fdcecf4e-443a-46e0-84af-af606bb5b08a)                  |
| key_name                            | None                                                            |
| name                                | instance1-cli                                                   |
| os-extended-volumes:volumes_attached | []                                                             |
| project_id                          | 7fb56b9d4c124a778a79dae0e04386a5                               |
| properties                          |                                                                 |
| security_groups                     | [{u'name': u'default'}]                                         |
| status                              | SHUTOFF                                                         |
| updated                             | 2017-07-17T01:00:23Z                                           |
| user_id                             | 214ad6d7786e4ce59474466a3f281d7c                               |
+-------------------------------------+------------------------------------------------------------------+
```

Figure 6.66: The addresses field from the 'openstack server show' command displays an instance's fixed IP address and floating IP address

If you want to associate a security group with this instance, you could easily run the following:

```
$ openstack server add security group instance1-cli webserver-sg-cli
```

Before proceeding...

Before moving on to the next chapter, be sure to delete all running instances to free available resources. You can run the following:

```
$ openstack server list --all-projects
$ openstack server delete <server-uuid>
```

Summary

Understanding how to interact with Neutron as an OpenStack end user and administrator is critical to passing the COA exam. Neutron is a complex topic, but keep in mind that you will only be responsible for working with OpenStack networking as an OpenStack end user or administrator, not someone responsible for the underlying networking configuration. This means you do not need to worry about the details of Neutron configuration files or configuring the network infrastructure. Working through the objectives detailed in this chapter will give you the confidence you need to succeed in all Neutron-related objectives.

In the next chapter, we will discuss Cinder block storage and all the Cinder-related objectives.

7
Cinder Block-Storage Service

In the previous chapter, we discussed the Neutron networking service and the Neutron-related objectives on the Certified OpenStack Administrator exam. Now we will discuss Cinder. Cinder is the OpenStack block-storage service, and it allows users to create **persistent** volumes that can be mounted as devices by Nova virtual machine instances.

In this chapter, we will cover the following topics:

- About Cinder
- Exam objective - managing Cinder volumes
- Exam objective - attaching/detaching Cinder volumes from instances
- Exam objective - managing Cinder snapshots
- Exam objective - managing Cinder backups

After this chapter, you should have a solid understanding of Cinder and the skills necessary to successfully fulfill all Cinder-related objectives on the exam.

About Cinder

When Amazon Web Services EC2 launched in 2006, it looked a lot different than we know it today. One of the primary differences was how AWS handled virtual machine storage. At that time, AWS only offered **ephemeral** storage for virtual machine instances. Consider a user booting an EC2 instance with an instance type (or flavor) that offered a 20 GB primary disk and a 50 GB secondary disk. Any data written to those local disks (that is, /dev/xvda or /dev/xvdb inside the operating system) would reside on the compute node hosting that instance. See *Figure 7.1*.

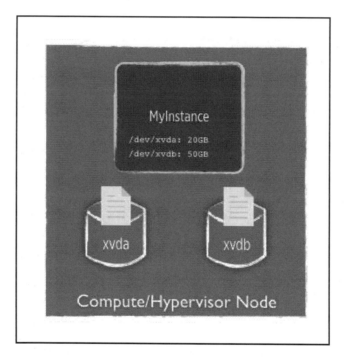

Figure 7.1: Amazon EC2 virtual machine ephemeral storage

It wasn't long before many users encountered problems:

- Data copied to the disks could not be easily transferred to other virtual machines.
- Stopping or terminating the instance meant complete data loss (once started again, the virtual machine would boot another compute node with newly provisioned disks).
- If the instance failed, your data was not accessible and could not be easily recovered.

If users were looking to **persist** their data, they were encouraged to use S3, the object storage service.

In April of 2008, AWS made a huge announcement that changed all of this forever. "Our forthcoming persistent storage feature will give you the ability to create reliable, persistent storage volumes for use with EC2" said the announcement blog post. "These volumes can be thought of as raw, unformatted drives which can be formatted and then used as desired (or even used as raw storage if you'd like)."

This was an incredible moment in IT history: the introduction of elastic cloud persistent block storage!

Similar to a portable USB drive, a user creates a block volume specified in gigabytes. Once attached to a virtual machine instance, the volume appears as a raw unformatted hard drive inside the operating system. Once the drive is formatted, it can be mounted and used like a traditional hard drive. All data written to the disk would actually reside on a dedicated server within the AWS data center, not the compute node where the instance resides. See *Figure 7.2*.

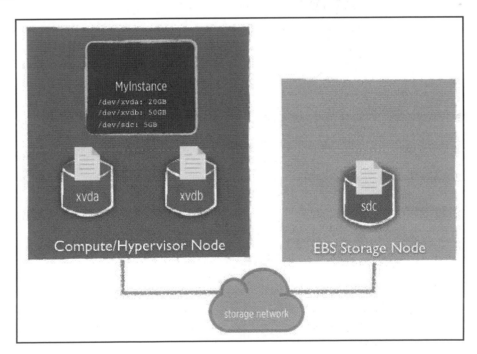

Figure 7.2: Data written to block volumes are stored on a remote storage server

Now, users also have the ability to utilize their primary drive (that is, /dev/xvda) as an EBS volume. See *Figure 7.3*. This provides full data persistence for the base operating system in the event of instance failure; it's known as an "EBS-backed" instance.

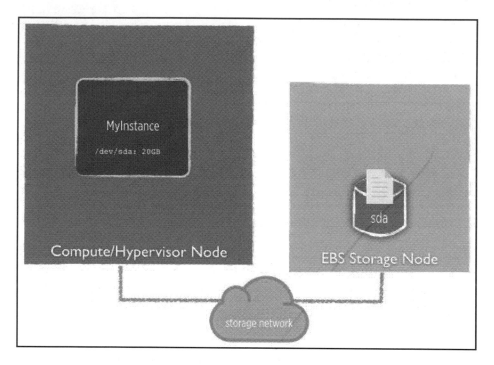

Figure 7.3: The primary hard drive can also be backed by a block volume

Inspired by AWS elastic block storage, OpenStack introduced the concept of block volumes inside the Nova project in the Bexar version in 2011. In 2012, the OpenStack Folsom release introduced block storage as its own project, called Cinder.

Cinder architecture

Cinder is made up of four daemons, as shown in *Figure 7.4*:

- **cinder-api**: The API and primary gateway to Cinder. One must interact with cinder-api to create, list, delete, and manage block volumes, snapshots, and backups.

- **cinder-scheduler**: Evaluates and filters all available storage nodes to determine the best storage node for a block volume you'd like to create. The behavior of `cinder-scheduler` can be modified based off specific characteristics such as capacity or storage capability.
- **cinder-volume**: Resides on the Cinder storage nodes and is responsible for the creation and deletion of block volumes.
- **cinder-backup**: Assists in backing up block volumes to OpenStack Swift or other third-party storage targets.

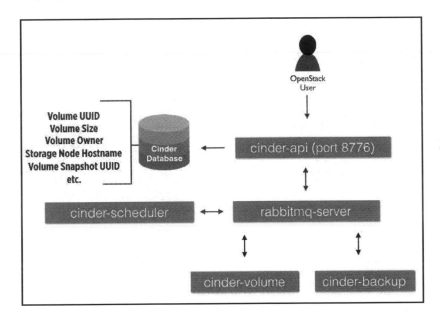

Figure 7.4: High-level view of Cinder architecture

Cinder behind the scenes

By default, Cinder is powered by two specific technologies:

1. **LVM (Logical Volume Manager)**: The LVM toolset was developed in the late 1990s to allow users to add and replace hard drives without downtime or service disruption. This is done by creating single logical volumes of entire hard disks, thus allowing dynamic resizing.
2. **iSCSI (Internet Small Computer Systems Interface)**: iSCSI is an IP-based storage standard for providing block-level access to storage devices across a network.

Consider a user creating a Cinder block volume. The user sends an API request to `cinder-api` via the Horizon dashboard or CLI. Once the `cinder-api` receives the request, it updates the Cinder database with details about the volume and places it on the message bus. `cinder-scheduler` determines the best Cinder storage node to provision the requested volume. Once selected, `cinder-volume` is responsible for generating the LVM commands to create the logical volume from a predefined volume group. The user then sends an API call to `nova-api` to attach the volume to the instance of their choice. This connection process is actually an iSCSI connection between the instance's compute node (the initiator) and the Cinder storage node (the target). See *Figure 7.5*. The user can then proceed to format the block device and write data to it within the instance's operating system. All data written to Cinder is stored in Cinder storage. The user can then detach the volume from the instance and reattach it to another instance, thus reestablishing the iSCSI connection to a different compute node.

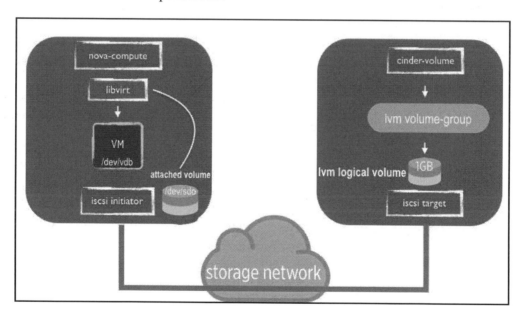

Figure 7.5: Cinder uses LVM and iSCSI to present raw block devices to Nova instances

Cinder backend software and hardware drivers

Cinder supports a variety of software and hardware drivers for the storage backend. In the case of hardware drivers, this allows users to utilize existing hardware storage devices (such as SAN or NAS) as Cinder storage nodes.

Software drivers	Hardware drivers
LVM	NetApp
NFS	Dell EqualLogic
GlusterFS	EMC V-MAX
Ceph	SolidFire

Cinder concepts

- **Volume**: A raw unformatted block device that can be attached to a Nova virtual machine instance. It can then be used as a traditional hard drive by the instance's operating system.
- **Snapshot**: A read-only, point-in-time copy of a volume's contents. A snapshot can be created from a volume that is currently in use or in an available state. The snapshot can then be used to create a new volume.
- **Backup**: A compressed, archived file of a volume's contents stored in a Swift object storage container, or another third-party provider such as Google Cloud Platform.

Exam objectives

Let's take a look at the Cinder exam objectives.

The following figure breaks down various Cinder-related objectives you should be responsible for knowing on the COA exam. As you can see, all of these tasks can be completed on both the Horizon dashboard and CLI. Remember: time is of the essence during the exam, and in many cases, it can be much faster to tackle a task on the dashboard.

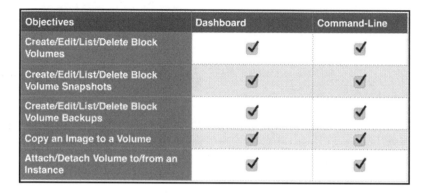

Objectives	Dashboard	Command-Line
Create/Edit/List/Delete Block Volumes	✓	✓
Create/Edit/List/Delete Block Volume Snapshots	✓	✓
Create/Edit/List/Delete Block Volume Backups	✓	✓
Copy an Image to a Volume	✓	✓
Attach/Detach Volume to/from an Instance	✓	✓

Figure 7.6: Cinder exam objectives can be completed on the Horizon dashboard or CLI

Exam objective - managing Cinder volumes

Creating Cinder volumes is incredibly simple and should be an easy way to score points on the exam. Let's take a look!

Horizon dashboard

Let's create a volume on the Horizon dashboard. See *Figure 7.7*.

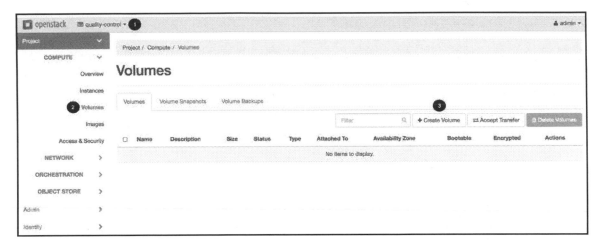

Figure 7.7: Creating a block volume from the Horizon dashboard

1. From the OpenStack overview page, scope yourself to the **quality-control** project by selecting the top dropdown.

2. Select the **Volumes** panel from the **Project-Compute** panel group.

3. Select **Create Volume**.

4. See *Figure 7.8*. **Volume Name (optional):** A name for your volume. Enter `volume-dashboard`.

5. **Description (optional):** A description for the volume. Enter `COA exam prep dashboard volume`.

6. **Volume Source (optional):** By default, any volume you create will be completely new and empty. A volume source is an existing data source that you would like copied to your volume. The following are examples of volume sources:

    1. **No Source, Empty Volume:** An empty volume. The volume must be formatted and mounted by your virtual machine instance's operating system. We will select this.

    2. **Image:** This copies the contents of an existing Glance image to your block volume. You must ensure that the size of your volume is equal to or greater than the size of the specified image. This will automatically make your image **bootable** so that you can specify it as the primary disk (boot source) when booting an instance. This is a powerful feature that will result in your `/dev/vda` folder residing on a Cinder storage node, similar to AWS EBS-backed instances.

    3. **Volume:** This copies the contents of an existing volume to your block volume. You must ensure that the size of your volume is equal to or greater than the size of the specified volume.

7. **Type (optional)**: Allows your users to specify a specific volume backend previously configured and defined by your OpenStack infrastructure engineers. An example would be a group of Cinder storage servers/nodes that only have SSD drives. Another example could be a group of Cinder storage nodes that have traditional SATA drives. This gives your OpenStack users the power of choice.

8. **Size (required):** Size of the volume in gigabytes. Enter 1.

9. **Availability Zone (optional):** Similar to Nova availability zones, Cinder availability zones are defined during installation and give you a common method for segregating cinder storage nodes. By default, all Cinder storage nodes belong to the **Nova** availability zone.

10. Select **Create Volume**.

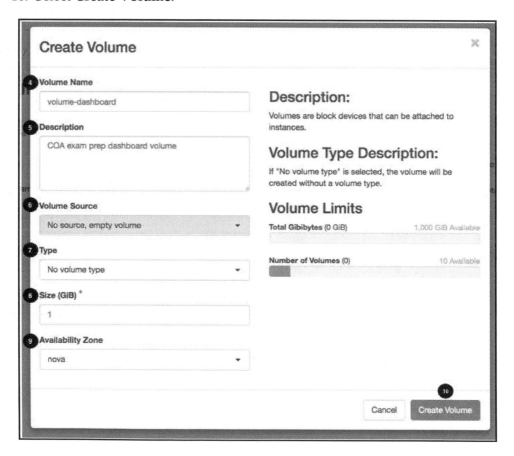

Figure 7.8: Providing block volume details on the Horizon dashboard

We should now have a newly created volume owned by the **quality-control** project. At this point, all users in the **quality-control** project should have access to modify the volume, but it cannot truly be used until it is attached to an instance.

We can only attach a block volume to one instance at a time; it's important to note that we cannot make this volume publicly accessible to all projects. What we can do, however, is transfer ownership of the volume to another project using the **Create Transfer** option in the volume panel. This will generate a special ID and authorization key that we provide to a user in an alternative project. A user in the alternate project then enter **Accept Transfer**, enter the ID and auth key, and then gain full control and ownership of the volume. After a volume has been transferred to another project, it will no longer be accessible to the original owner unless they accept the transfer back.

We also have the option of making a volume **bootable**. A bootable volume is one that can be selected as a Nova boot source. In order to be a proper boot source, the volume must contain a bootloader or instructions that the virtual machine instance BIOS can read. Select **Edit Instance** and check the **Bootable** box to make a volume bootable.

CLI

Recall that the provided `openrc` file contains credentials in the form of variables for proper authentication to Keystone and setting project scope.

In this chapter, we will do all of our Cinder-related tasks in the `quality-control` project. Let's copy our original `openrc` file to a new file called `openrc-quality-control`.

```
$ cp openrc openrc-quality-control
```

Now that we've made a copy, let's edit the `openrc-quality-control` file and update the project and tenant name variables to reflect our desired scope to the logistics project. If you are more comfortable with another editor, feel free to use it here:

```
$ nano openrc-quality-control
```

Change the following variables to quality-control:

```
export OS_PROJECT_NAME=quality-control
export OS_TENANT_NAME=quality-control
```

 We are changing the OS_TENANT_NAME variable since some of the older service-based clients may rely on the older variable, OS_TENANT_NAME.

Source the newly created openrc-quality-control file:

```
$ source openrc-quality-control
```

Verify that the proper variables are set:

```
$ export | grep OS
```

Now that we are properly scoped, any new volume that we create from this point forward will be owned by the quality-control project. Unlike some of the other python-openstackclient list commands, openstack volume list only shows volumes within the project to which we are currently scoped. This is very important to keep in mind during the exam. Run the following:

```
$ openstack volume list --long
```

We should see the volume-dashboard volume we created in the previous exercise. As an admin, we should be able to see and list all volumes across all projects in our environment. Run the following:

```
$ openstack volume list --all-projects --long
```

You should now see an additional volume that was previously created on the virtual appliance.

Let's proceed with creating a brand-new 1 GB volume with the CLI. We will name it volume-cli, with the description COA exam prep cli volume:

```
$ openstack volume create --size 1 volume-cli --description "COA exam prep
cli volume"
```

We should see output similar to *Figure 7.9*.

```
+---------------------+----------------------------------------+
| Field               | Value                                  |
+---------------------+----------------------------------------+
| attachments         | []                                     |
| availability_zone   | nova                                   |
| bootable            | false                                  |
| consistencygroup_id | None                                   |
| created_at          | 2017-07-28T23:18:04.229529             |
| description         | COA exam prep cli volume               |
| encrypted           | False                                  |
| id                  | 9ba602ef-2ca0-4a94-b89f-e21505e731bf   |
| migration_status    | None                                   |
| multiattach         | False                                  |
| name                | volume-cli                             |
| properties          |                                        |
| replication_status  | disabled                               |
| size                | 1                                      |
| snapshot_id         | None                                   |
| source_volid        | None                                   |
| status              | creating                               |
| type                | None                                   |
| updated_at          | None                                   |
| user_id             | 214ad6d7786e4ce59474466a3f281d7c       |
+---------------------+----------------------------------------+
```

Figure 7.9: Output from the openstack volume create command

Let's confirm that the volume was successfully created:

```
$ openstack volume list --long
```

We should see something similar to *Figure 7.10*.

```
+--------------------------------------+-------------------+-----------+------+------+----------+-------------+------------+
| ID                                   | Display Name      | Status    | Size | Type | Bootable | Attached to | Properties |
+--------------------------------------+-------------------+-----------+------+------+----------+-------------+------------+
| 9ba602ef-2ca0-4a94-b89f-e21505e731bf | volume-cli        | available |    1 | None | false    |             |            |
| 6faff157-8fed-463d-9526-cc1da750fb35 | volume1-dashboard | available |    1 | None | false    |             |            |
+--------------------------------------+-------------------+-----------+------+------+----------+-------------+------------+
```

Figure 7.10: Output from the 'openstack volume list --long' command

Keep in mind that this command only shows you volumes within the project to which you are scoped! To see all volumes across all projects in the OpenStack environment, use the --all-projects flag.

Horizon dashboard

In the previous Horizon dashboard exercise, we created a 1 GB Cinder block volume. In order to use the volume, we must attach it to a virtual machine instance. Before proceeding with this exercise, make sure you have no current instances running from the exercises in previous chapters.

We will need to boot one Nova instance. We will then attach our Cinder volume to this instance and write some files to it. If you forgot how to create a tenant network, subnet, and virtual machine instance, follow the instructions found in `Chapter 5` and `Chapter 6`.

Here are the details. Assume default values for anything not specified:

Network/subnet

- **Project**: `quality-control`
- **Network Name**: `tenant-network-dashboard`
- **Subnet Name**: `tenant-subnet-dashboard`
- **Network Address**: `192.168.1.0/24`

Instance

- **Project**: `quality-control`
- **Instance Name**: `instance-dashboard`
- **Source**: `cirros`
- **Flavor**: `m1.tiny`
- **Networks**: `tenant-network-dashboard`

Now that we have **instance1-dashboard** on the **tenant-network-dashboard** network within the **quality-control** project, let's attach a volume to it. See *Figure 7.11*.

Figure 7.11: Attaching a volume to an instance from the Horizon dashboard

1. From the OpenStack overview page, scope yourself to the **quality-control** project by selecting the top dropdown.
2. Select the **Instances** panel from the **Project-Compute** panel group.
3. Select **Attach Volume** from the **Actions** dropdown next to **instance-dashboard**.
4. See *Figure 7.12*. **Volume ID (required):** This is the volume you want to attach to the instance. Select `volume-dashboard`.
5. Select **Attach Volume**.
6. If we want to detach the volume, we can easily select **Detach Volume** from the **Actions** dropdown and select the volume again.

Figure 7.12: Specifying the volume to attach to the instance on the Horizon dashboard

We can verify that the volume has been successfully attached to the instance by going to the **Volumes** panel group on the dashboard and observing the **Attached To** column. See *Figure 7.13*. The volume has been mounted to the instance as `/dev/vdb`. Let's now proceed to go into the instance to see how we could use the volume.

Figure 7.13: Cinder volume successfully attached to an Nova instance

As described in `Chapter 5`, *Nova Compute Service,* access the Nova console for the **instance-dashboard** virtual machine instance.

Log in to the instance with the following default Cirros username/password:

- **Username**: `cirros`
- **Password**: `cubswin:)`

Now that we are logged in, we can use the popular `fdisk` utility to list any recognized block devices:

```
$ sudo fdisk -l
```

You should see output similar to *Figure 7.14*.

```
                Connected (unencrypted) to: QEMU (instance-0000000b)
sysfs on /sys type sysfs (rw,relatime)
devpts on /dev/pts type devpts (rw,relatime,gid=5,mode=620,ptmxmode=000)
tmpfs on /dev/shm type tmpfs (rw,relatime,mode=777)
tmpfs on /run type tmpfs (rw,nosuid,relatime,size=200k,mode=755)
$ sudo fdisk -l

Disk /dev/vda: 1073 MB, 1073741824 bytes
255 heads, 63 sectors/track, 130 cylinders, total 2097152 sectors
Units = sectors of 1 * 512 = 512 bytes
Sector size (logical/physical): 512 bytes / 512 bytes
I/O size (minimum/optimal): 512 bytes / 512 bytes
Disk identifier: 0x00000000

   Device Boot      Start         End      Blocks   Id  System
/dev/vda1   *        16065     2088449     1036192+  83  Linux

Disk /dev/vdb: 1073 MB, 1073741824 bytes
16 heads, 63 sectors/track, 2080 cylinders, total 2097152 sectors
Units = sectors of 1 * 512 = 512 bytes
Sector size (logical/physical): 512 bytes / 512 bytes
I/O size (minimum/optimal): 512 bytes / 512 bytes
Disk identifier: 0x00000000

Disk /dev/vdb doesn't contain a valid partition table
$
```

Figure 7.14: /dev/vdb is the newly attached Cinder block volume

We can then format this raw block device with the `ext3` filesystem:

```
$ sudo mkfs.ext3 /dev/vdb
```

Although our disk is formatted, it still needs to be mounted so we can use it:

```
$ sudo mount /dev/vdb /mnt
```

Now that the file is mounted, we should be able to create files on our volume. Let's use the `touch` utility to create a file called `helloworld.txt` in our volume:

```
$ sudo touch /mnt/helloworld.txt
```

 Keep in mind that our OpenStack virtual appliance is only one virtual machine, so it's acting as the hypervisor *and* Cinder storage node. In a real-world OpenStack environment, our Cinder volumes would reside on dedicated Cinder storage servers.

Let's unmount our volume from the /mnt folder:

```
$ sudo umount /dev/vdb /mnt
```

We can now easily detach this volume from **instance-dashboard** and attach it to another booted instance. Any data written to this volume will be accessible to any instance that can attach to it.

 In our exercise, we manually mounted and formatted the drive. Some operating systems may perform this process automatically upon recognizing a newly attached disk.

Be sure to detach the volume at the end of this exercise. You can do so by selecting **Detach Volume** from the **Actions** dropdown next to the virtual machine instance.

CLI

Let's create a new instance and attach a new volume via python-openstackclient.

Source the newly created openrc-quality-control file:

```
$ source openrc-quality-control
```

Verify that the proper variables are set:

```
$ export | grep OS
```

Boot a new instance within the quality-control project:

```
$ openstack server create --image cirros --flavor m1.tiny instance-cli
```

After instance-cli has been been booted and its status is ACTIVE, attach the volume-cli volume to it:

```
$ openstack server add volume instance-cli volume-cli
```

You can confirm that the volume is attached to the instance by running the following:

```
$ openstack volume list --long
```

See *Figure 7.15*. Observe the status column. This shows whether the volume is available or in use. Remember: the Newton version of OpenStack only allows you to attach a volume to one instance at a time.

```
+-----------------------+------------------+-----------+------+------+----------+-------------------------+-------------------+
| ID                    | Display Name     | Status    | Size | Type | Bootable | Attached to             | Properties        |
+-----------------------+------------------+-----------+------+------+----------+-------------------------+-------------------+
| 90e456c0-b032-48d3-902f- | volume-cli    | in-use    | 1    | None | false    | Attached to instance-cli | attached_mode='rw', |
| 2cc40a40694b          |                  |           |      |      |          | on /dev/vdb             | readonly='False'  |
| 28d0e112-bf78-4b56-8c54-9 | volume-dashboard | available | 1  | None | false    |                         | readonly='False'  |
| afa49d9daca           |                  |           |      |      |          |                         |                   |
+-----------------------+------------------+-----------+------+------+----------+-------------------------+-------------------+
```

Figure 7.15: The 'Attached to' to column shows the instance to which the volume is attached

You can get the `instance-cli` console url by running the following:

```
$ openstack console url show instance-cli
```

Feel free to format and mount the volume via the virtual machine instance console, as shown in the previous section.

To detach the volume, run the following:

```
$ openstack server remove volume instance-cli volume-cli
```

Exam objective - managing Cinder snapshots

Cinder supports volume snapshots that capture the current state of a volume. These are useful for providing backup protection and can also be used to instantiate new volumes that contain the exact data of the snapshot. Behind the scenes, Cinder snapshots are LVM snapshots that will reside in the same LVM volume group as the original logical volume. It's important to note that snapshots are not backups. Unlike Cinder snapshots, Cinder backups are stored off site. We will cover them in the next section. Let's walk through creating and restoring snapshots in the dashboard.

Horizon dashboard

See *Figure 7.16*. Let's create a volume snapshot from the Horizon dashboard.

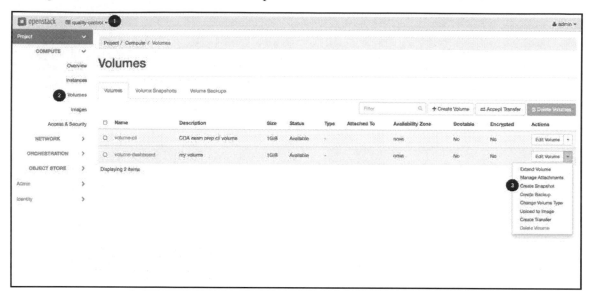

Figure 7.16: Creating a snapshot from the Horizon dashboard

1. From the OpenStack overview page, scope yourself to the **quality-control** project by selecting the top dropdown.
2. Select the **Volumes** panel from the **Project-Compute** panel group.
3. Select **Create Snapshot** next to the **volume-dashboard** dropdown.
4. See *Figure 7-17*. **Snapshot Name (required)**: A name for the snapshot. Enter `volume-snapshot-dashboard`.
5. **Description (optional)**: A description for the volume snapshot. Enter `COA exam prep dashboard volume snapshot`.

6. Select **Create Volume Snapshot**.

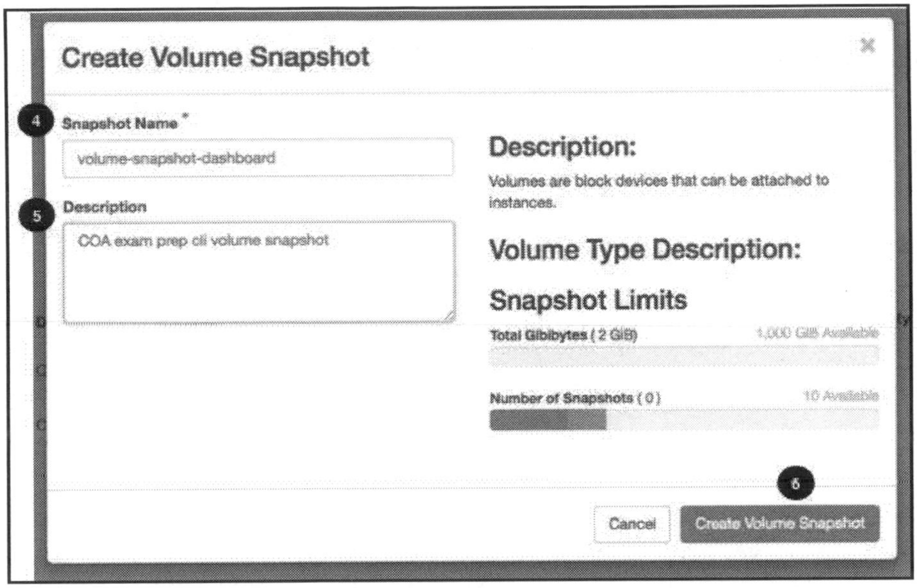

Figure 7.17: Providing the name of the source volume for the snapshot on the Horizon dashboard

You should now see your newly created volume snapshot under the **Snapshots** tab. This snapshot is owned by the `quality-control` project. You can easily create a volume from it by selecting the **Create Volume** button.

> When creating a new volume from an existing snapshot, the size of the volume must be equal to or greater than the size of the snapshot. In order to delete a volume with an associated snapshot, you must first delete the snapshot.

CLI

Let's create a new Cinder snapshot via `python-openstackclient`.

Source the newly created `openrc-quality-control` file:

```
$ source openrc-quality-control
```

Verify that the proper variables are set:

```
$ export | grep OS
```

View all current Cinder volumes:

```
$ openstack volume list
```

Take a snapshot of the `volume-cli` volume. Name the snapshot `volume-snapshot-cli`.

```
$ openstack snapshot create --name volume-snapshot-cli volume-cli
```

You should see output similar to *Figure 7.18*.

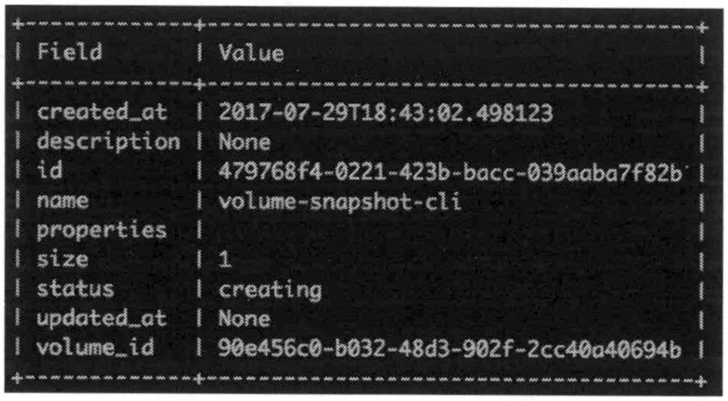

```
+-------------+--------------------------------------+
| Field       | Value                                |
+-------------+--------------------------------------+
| created_at  | 2017-07-29T18:43:02.498123           |
| description | None                                 |
| id          | 479768f4-0221-423b-bacc-039aaba7f82b |
| name        | volume-snapshot-cli                  |
| properties  |                                      |
| size        | 1                                    |
| status      | creating                             |
| updated_at  | None                                 |
| volume_id   | 90e456c0-b032-48d3-902f-2cc40a40694b |
+-------------+--------------------------------------+
```

Figure 7.18: Output from the 'openstack snapshot create' command

You can confirm the snapshot has been created by running the following command:

```
$ openstack snapshot list --long
```

If you wanted to create a volume from this snapshot, you could run the following:

```
$ openstack volume create --snapshot volume-snapshot-cli --size 1 restored-
snapshot-volume-cli
```

Exam objective - managing Cinder backups

Like Cinder snapshots, Cinder backups contain all of the data contained in a source volume. **Unlike** Cinder snapshots, Cinder backups are compressed (bz2 or zlib) archives stored off the Cinder storage node. The target backup location can exist in a variety of places depending on the driver being used. Drivers include OpenStack Swift, Google Cloud Platform, GlusterFS, or even an NFS share (just to name a few). Your virtual appliance is currently configured to utilize the OpenStack Swift deployment that is installed on the appliance. We will talk Swift in more depth in Chapter 8, *Swift Object-Storage Service*.

Horizon dashboard

Let's create a Cinder backup from the Horizon dashboard. See *Figure 7.19*.

Figure 7.19: Creating a backup on the Horizon dashboard

1. From the OpenStack overview page, scope yourself to the **quality-control** project by selecting the top dropdown.
2. Select the **Volumes** Panel from the **Project-Compute** Panel Group.
3. Select **Create Backup** next to the **volume-dashboard** dropdown.
4. See *Figure 7.20*. **Backup Name (required)**: A name for the backup. Enter volume-backup-dashboard.
5. **Description (optional)**: A description for the volume snapshot. Enter COA exam prep dashboard volume backup
6. **Container Name (optional)**: The name of the Swift object container target for the backup. Enter volume-backup-container-dashboard

7. Select **Create Volume Snapshot**.

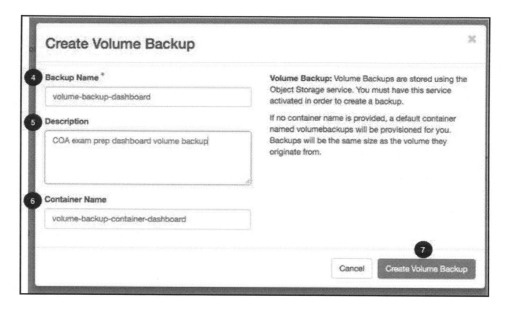

Figure 7.20: Setting the target container name for a Cinder backup on the Horizon dashboard

Once the backup has been created, we should have a new Swift object container with the contents of the volume compressed and archived.

We will discuss Swift in more detail in Chapter 8. For now, ensure you are scoped to the **quality-control** project and select the **Containers** panel in the **Project-Object Store** panel group. See *Figure 7.21*.

Figure 7.21: Output from the 'openstack volume backup list' command

To restore this backup, we can use the **Restore Backup** button in the **Volume Backups** tab.

CLI

Let's create a new Cinder backup via `python-openstackclient`.

Source the newly created `openrc-quality-control` file:

```
$ source openrc-quality-control
```

Verify that the proper variables are set:

```
$ export | grep OS
```

Create the backup:

```
$ openstack volume backup create --name volume-backup-cli --description
"COA exam prep dashboard volume backup" --container volume-backup-
container-cli volume-cli
```

After the backup completes, you should be able to confirm that the backup was successfully created:

```
$ openstack volume backup list
```

You should see output similar to *Figure 7.22*.

Figure 7.22: Output from the 'openstack volume backup list' command

If you wanted to restore the backup on the CLI, you must manually create an empty volume first, then the run the following:

```
$ openstack volume backup restore volume-backup-cli <target-volume>
```

Note

Before proceeding to the next chapter, be sure to delete all running instances to free available resources. You can run the following:

```
$ openstack server list --all-projects
$ openstack server delete <server-uuid>
```

Summary

You've just learned about all the Cinder-related objectives on the exam. As you can see, all the Cinder-related objectives can be completed on the Horizon dashboard. You can easily attach volumes to instances by using the drop down next to the instance to which you'd like to attach the volume. Recall that you can only attach a volume to one instance at a time in the Newton version of OpenStack. In the next chapter, we will discuss Swift, the OpenStack block-storage service, and work through all Swift-related objectives on the exam.

8

Swift Object-Storage Service

In the previous chapter, we discussed the Cinder block-storage service and the Cinder-related objectives on the Certified OpenStack Administrator exam. Now we will discuss Swift. Swift is the OpenStack object-storage service, and it provides users with redundant cloud storage accessible via a RESTful API.

In this chapter, we will cover the following topics:

- Swift architecture
- Swift concepts
- Exam objective - managing containers and objects
- Exam objective - setting ACLs on a container
- Exam objective - setting objects to expire

After this chapter, you should have a solid understanding of Swift and the skills necessary to successfully fulfill all Swift-related objectives on the exam.

About Swift

If you wanted to sign-up with a website hosting provider in the late 90's or early 2000's, you usually used a provider that would give you access to a server. That server would be allocated a particular amount of storage for you to use and store your files on. All for one monthly cost. You could upload your website's HTML pages, photos, and other static files via Secure SSH or an FTP client. If you needed additional storage, you would submit a request and the hosting provider would expand your capacity.

In 2006, AWS launched one of their first services: Amazon Simple Storage Service, or S3 for short. Amazon advertised S3 as "highly scalable, reliable and low-latency data storage infrastructure at very low costs." But what did this mean? Well, let's break down a few points to show why there was so much hype around S3 at that time:

- Unlike popular hosting providers at that time, a user could pay for what they actually used, as they used it (as long as they had a credit card on file). This was much like an electricity or utility bill.
- The user could store their files via a web API, allowing them to integrate programmatic uploading and downloading into their web application code (consider a photo album web application: super powerful!).
- It was incredibly cheap! Users could store thousand of objects for a few dollars a month.
- All objects were written to three different failure domains, so you were covered in the event of a server failure in an AWS data center.

Now, some of the most popular applications in the world use S3. Dropbox is a frontend that uses S3 to store your files, and Pinterest and Tumblr use S3 to host images!

In August 2009, Rackspace was inspired by Amazon S3 and began working on their very own object-storage service called Cloud Files (still available today). This project became what we know as OpenStack Swift, the open source scalable redundant storage system with a RESTful API. Like S3, Swift presents users with an object-storage service that makes storage appear limitless. It also features a lot of cool extras, such as static website hosting, object versioning, access control lists (ACLs), and object expiration.

Behind the scenes, OpenStack Swift writes the objects to multiple disk drives spread through servers in the datacenter. Swift's software (written in Python like other OpenStack services), is responsible for ensuring data replication and integrity across the cluster. Should a server or hard drive fail, Swift replicates its contents from other active nodes to new locations in the cluster. Storage clusters scale horizontally simply by adding new servers. Because OpenStack uses software logic to ensure data replication and distribution across different devices, inexpensive commodity hard drives and servers can be used.

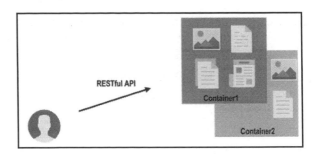

Figure 8.1: Swift allows users to upload and download files via a RESTful API

Swift architecture

Swift is made up of fourteen primary daemons, as shown in *Figure 8.2*:

- **swift-proxy-server**: The API and primary gateway to Swift and responsible for tying together the rest of the Swift architecture. One must interact with swift-proxy-server to create containers, upload objects to those containers, set ACLs, and enable special features such as object versioning or enabling static websites. For each request, it will look up the location of the account, container, or object in the ring and route the request accordingly.
- **swift-object-server**: Responsible for retriving and deleting objects stored on local drives in the Swift cluster. Objects are stored as binary files on the filesystem, with metadata stored in the file's extended attributes (xattrs). This requires that the underlying filesystem choice for object servers support xattrs on files. Each object is stored using a path derived from the object name's hash and the operation's timestamp.
- **swift-object-auditor**: Crawls the local object system checking the integrity of objects. If corruption is found, the file is quarantined, and replication will replace the bad file from another replica.
- **swift-object-expirer**: Offers scheduled deletion of objects.
- **swift-object-reconstructor**: Daemon for reconstruction of erasure code objects.
- **swift-object-replicator**: Keeps the system in a consistent state in the face of temporary error conditions such as network outages or drive failures. The replication processes compare local data with each remote copy to ensure they all contain the latest version. Object replication uses a hash list to quickly compare subsections of each partition.
- **swift-container-server**: Handles the listing of objects within a particular container. The listings are stored as SQLite database files, and are replicated across the cluster (similar to objects).

- **swift-container-auditor**: Crawls the local container system, checking the integrity of SQLite database files. If corruption is found, the file is quarantined, and replication will replace the bad file from another replica.
- **swift-container-replicator**: Similar to the swift-object-replicator, only with container SQLite database files.
- **swift-container-updater:** Updates container information in the account database. It will walk the container path in the system, looking for container SQLite files, and send updates to the account server as needed.
- **swift-container-sync**: Responsible for allowing contents of a container can be mirrored to another container through background synchronization.
- **swift-account-server**: Handles the listing of containers within a particular account. The listings are stored as sqlite database files, and are replicated across the cluster (similar to objects).
- **swift-account-auditor**: Same as the swift-container-auditor, only with account sqlite database files.
- **swift-account-replicator**: Similar to swift-container-replicator, only with account sqlite database files.
- **swift-account-reaper**: Removes accounts that have been marked for deletion by an OpenStack administrator.

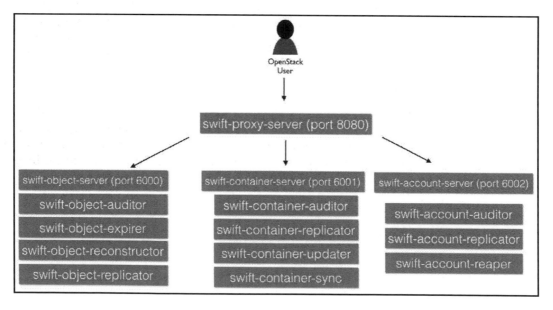

Figure 8.2: High-level view of Swift architecture

Swift concepts

- **Account**: Swift uses the term "account" to refer to an OpenStack project. Remember: in the OpenStack world, accounts, tenants, and projects all mean the same thing!
- **Container**: A "bucket" for static files (also known as **objects**). A user must create a container to upload an object into a Swift account. All containers are owned by the account (or project) to which the user was scoped when they created them. By default, all objects uploaded into a container are private.
- **Objects**: Objects are files that one uploads into a container. These are usually static files, such as pictures, movies, documents, or logs.
- **Object expiration**: One can set an object to expire at a specific time. Once an object is expired, it will no longer be accessible and is deleted from the Swift cluster. One great use case for object expiration is temporary registration codes or keys that are valid for a short time.
- **ACL (access control list)**: By default, a Swift container is private and not accessible to other users or projects. By default, a user with the admin or swiftoperator role can set ACLs at the container level and support lists for read and write access.
- **Static website hosting**: Rather than using a traditional web server such as Apache or Nginx to host a website, Swift can host static website files, such as HTML, CSS, and client-side JavaScript. By setting the web-index header on a container to the public URL of the container, it will navigate to a specified file, such as an `index.html`. One can then update their DNS to point to the URL of the publicly accessible Swift container.
- **Object versioning**: Versioning allows a user to upload multiple versions of a specific file. The user simply creates an alternate container for storing the versions. As the user uploads a file with the same name to a Swift container, the previous version gets posted to the alternate container. One can easily retrieve and restore to a previous version. If a `DELETE` request is sent to the object, the latest version gets deleted, and the previous version restored in its place.

Exam objectives

Let's take a look at the Swift exam objectives. Remember that the Certified OpenStack Administrator exam expects you to understand how to use OpenStack from the perspective of an administrator, not an infrastructure or DevOps engineer. You do not need to be overly concerned with the backend Swift configuration. This is a complex topic that you can learn more about in the book *OpenStack Object Storage (Swift) Essentials* by Packt Publishing.

The following figure breaks down various Swift-related objectives you should be responsible for knowing on the COA exam. As you can see, **only some** of these tasks can be completed on both the Horizon dashboard and CLI. When it comes to ACLs and object expiration, you will need to master the CLI commands shown in this chapter.

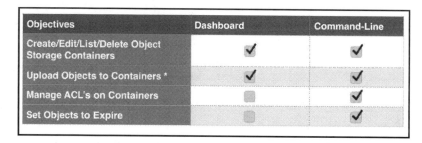

Objectives	Dashboard	Command-Line
Create/Edit/List/Delete Object Storage Containers	✔	✔
Upload Objects to Containers *	✔	✔
Manage ACL's on Containers		✔
Set Objects to Expire		✔

Figure 8.3: Swift ACLs and object expiration can only be completed via the CLI

 To upload objects to Swift on the Horizon dashboard, the files must be accessible via your local filesystem. If you want to upload files larger than 5 GB, you must use the CLI.

Exam objective - managing containers and objects

Containers are analogous to buckets in the Amazon S3 world. Containers are owned by the project (also known as an **account** in the Swift world). When it comes to permissions, Swift containers act a bit differently from traditional OpenStack resources. By default, a user must have the **admin** or **swiftoperator** role in order to create, delete, and modify containers. We will learn about how to set ACLs in the upcoming section.

Horizon dashboard

See *Figure 8.4*. Let's create a new container on the Horizon dashboard.

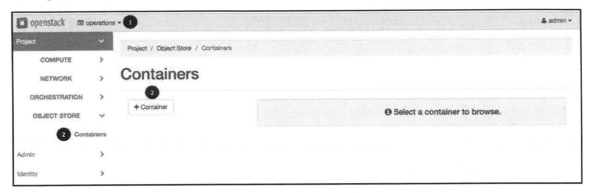

Figure 8.4: Creating a Swift container on the Horizon dashboard

1. From the OpenStack overview page, scope yourself to the **operations** project by selecting the top dropdown.
2. Select the **Containers** panel from the **Project-Object Store** panel group.
3. Select **Container**.
4. See *Figure 8.5*. **Container Name (required)**: A name for your container. Enter `container-dashboard`.
5. **Container Access Public (required)**: Makes the contents of this container accessible to the public. This means anyone in the world can browse to any of the objects within the container (as long as the swift API endpoint is publicly accessible). Lets keep this **unchecked**, thus making the container private. By default, a private container's objects are only accessible to users with the **admin** or **swiftoperator** roles. We will learn more about ACLs in the upcoming section.

6. Select **Create**.

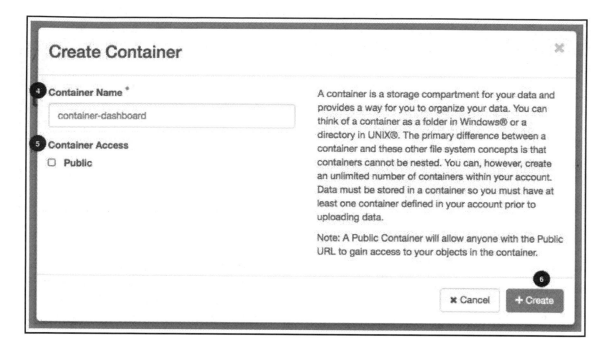

Figure 8.5: Setting a container name and access on the Horizon dashboard

After creating the container, we will now upload an object to it.

Create a text file on your local system called `object-dashboard.txt`. Inside the text file, simply write `object-dashboard` and save the file.

Choose the `object-dashboard.txt` file and select the **Upload File** icon. If your file is successfully uploaded, you should see something similar to *Figure 8.6*. *Figure 8.7* shows a visual of our object in the context of our container, project, and domain.

> If you want to upload a file larger than 5 GB, you must use `python-swiftclient`.

If we wanted to download this file, we can easily do so by selecting **Download**:

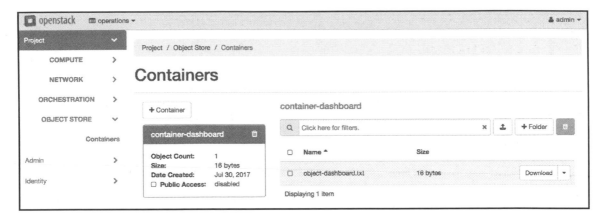

Figure 8.6: A private Swift container with one object on the Horizon dashboard

 Be careful! Swift will automatically overwrite any file you upload that contains the exact same name and file extension. We can change this behavior by enabling object versioning. This is outside the scope of the COA exam preparation, but you can learn more at `https://docs.openstack.org/swift`.

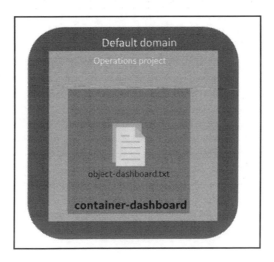

Figure 8.7: A Swift object residing in a container within the context of project and domain

CLI

Surprisingly enough, `python-openstackclient` does not currently have the functionality necessary to set ACLs on containers, although this will be featured in future versions. To be consistent and keep things simple, I am going to show you how to utilize `python-swiftclient`, which is included with `python-openstackclient`. Recall that the provided `openrc` file contains credentials in the form of variables for proper authentication to Keystone and setting project scope. In this chapter, we will perform all of our Swift-related tasks in the **operations** project. Let's copy our original openrc file to a new file called `openrc-operations`:

```
$ cp openrc openrc-operations
```

Now that we've made a copy, let's edit the `openrc-operations` file and update the project and tenant name variables to reflect our desired scope to the logistics project. If you are more comfortable with another editor, feel free to use it here.

```
$ nano openrc-operations
```

Change the following variables to operations:

```
export OS_PROJECT_NAME=operations
export OS_TENANT_NAME=operations
```

> We are changing the `OS_TENANT_NAME` variable since some of the older service-based client may rely on it.

Source the newly created `openrc-operations` file:

```
$ source openrc-operations
```

Verify that the proper variables are set:

```
$ export | grep OS
```

Now we can proceed to list our containers owned by the operations project:

```
$ swift list
```

We should see the container-dashboard container. If we wanted to list all the objects inside this container, we could run the following:

```
$ swift list container-dashboard
```

We should see the object-dashboard.txt file from the previous exercise. To download the file to our present working directory, we can run the following:

```
$ swift download container-dashboard object-dashboard.txt
```

Let's now create a new container:

```
$ swift post container-cli
```

Create a new object called object-cli.txt:

```
$ touch object-cli.txt
```

Let's add the name of the file inside the file:

```
$ echo "object-cli" > object-cli.txt
```

Now we can upload the object to the container:

```
$ swift upload container-cli object-cli.txt
```

We can confirm that the container and file have been successfully uploaded by running the following:

```
$ swift list container-cli
```

Let's create and upload another object:

```
$ touch object-deleteme.txt
```

Let's upload this file to our container:

```
$ swift upload container-cli object-deleteme.txt
```

Confirm that the file has been successfully uploaded:

```
$ swift list container-cli
```

Let's now delete this file:

```
$ swift delete container-cli object-deleteme.txt
```

That's all there to creating containers, uploading objects to those containers, and deleting objects! Pretty easy!

Exam objective: managing container ACLs

Recall that by default, the contents of a container can only be accessed by those with the **admin** or **swiftoperator** role. If one has either of these roles, they have the permission to set ACLs. ACLs work on the container level and apply to all objects within the container.

- **Read ACLs** control who can read/download the files within the container. You can also limit read/download access to all users within a specific project or one specific user.
- **Write ACLs** allow you to set upload permissions for a container. For example, you may want to allow a specific user or all users within a project to upload files to a container. You can even set a container to anonymous write, which will allow anyone, regardless of project, to upload objects into the container.

 ACLs can only be set using the raw API or via `python-swiftclient`. The only ACL one can set via the Horizon dashboard is allowing anonymous access to a container via the Public checkbox in *Figure 8.6.*

CLI

 Beware! The python-swiftclient help (`swift post --help`) does not have correct information regarding ACL syntax! A bug fix has already submitted, but don't rely on it during the exam! Be sure to the follow the ACL syntax here or official community documentation at `https://docs.openstack.org/ocata/`!

Let's source our `openrc-operations` file:

```
$ source openrc-operations
```

Verify that the proper variables are set and you are scoped to the **operations** project:

```
$ export | grep OS
```

Let's begin by listing our current containers. We should be able to see our `container-cli` container we created in the previous section:

```
$ swift list
```

To view the ACLs for this container, run the following command:

```
$ swift stat container-cli
```

We should see output similar to *Figure 8.8*.

```
         Account: AUTH_c03401d3e99f4d4ea1aede321b7a61ff
       Container: container-cli
         Objects: 1
           Bytes: 0
        Read ACL:
       Write ACL:
         Sync To:
        Sync Key:
   Accept-Ranges: bytes
 X-Storage-Policy: Policy-0
   Last-Modified: Sun, 30 Jul 2017 06:52:56 GMT
     X-Timestamp: 1501397575.81917
      X-Trans-Id: txe0c5448fccb64a909aedd-00597d8d7c
    Content-Type: text/plain; charset=utf-8
```

Figure 8.8: Output from the 'swift stat' command shows no read or write ACLs set on the container

As you can see, the **Read ACL** and **Write ACL** are empty. This means that the container is currently private and only accessible to those with the **admin** or **swiftoperator** role.

Let's begin by making a container publicly accessible so anyone on the internet can download a file from it. Let's break down the syntax for the Read ACL.

Take a look at the following syntax:

```
$ swift post container-cli --read-acl ".r:*,.rlistings"
```

The .r refers to the referrer header. The referrer header is the address of the webpage that is linked to the resource being requested. In other words, if someone linked to the object in this container on `https://www.openstack.org/`, the request to Swift for the object would contain `openstack.org` in the referrer header. The wildcard asterisk (*) suggests that the referrer header can contain any value and thus come from any website where the Swift link may be published. The .rlistings in the syntax enables the container to list all objects in the container. Let's run this command now!

You won't get any confirmation output when you set ACLs so we can verify that the read ACL has been applied by running the following:

```
$ swift stat container-cli
```

We should see output similar to *Figure 8.9*.

```
        Account: AUTH_c03401d3e99f4d4ea1aede321b7a61ff
      Container: container-cli
        Objects: 1
          Bytes: 11
       Read ACL: .r:*,.rlistings
      Write ACL:
        Sync To:
       Sync Key:
  Accept-Ranges: bytes
     X-Trans-Id: txc38d061d572f4b41b2692-00597e3f0a
 X-Storage-Policy: Policy-0
  Last-Modified: Sun, 30 Jul 2017 20:18:11 GMT
    X-Timestamp: 1501397575.81917
   Content-Type: text/plain; charset=utf-8
```

Figure 8.9: Output from the 'swift stat' command after setting public read ACLs

To verify that the container is public, we need to grab the public URL from the service catalog.

Run the following command:

```
$ openstack catalog list
```

Find the Swift public endpoint and copy and paste it into your browser. Be sure to append the container name to the end so it looks similar to this:

```
http://192.168.56.56:8080/v1/AUTH_c03401d3e99f4d4ea1aede321b7a61ff/container-cli
```

By navigating to this public Swift URL and appending the container name, you should see a listing of the object in the container. See *Figure 8.10*.

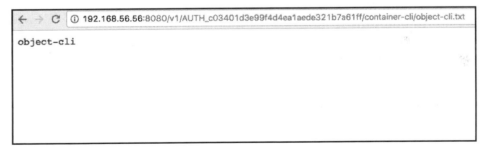

```
←  →  C   ⓘ 192.168.56.56:8080/v1/AUTH_c03401d3e99f4d4ea1aede321b7a61ff/container-cli

This XML file does not appear to have any style information associated with it. The document tree is shown below.

▼<container name="container-cli">
  ▼<object>
     <name>object-cli.txt</name>
     <hash>6e0eabcf5d7c88adf50dd30bf505f961</hash>
     <bytes>11</bytes>
     <content_type>text/plain</content_type>
     <last_modified>2017-07-30T08:21:06.852630</last_modified>
  </object>
</container>
```

Figure 8.10: Listing of objects inside a Swift container via a web browser

If we then navigate directly to the file by typing in the full path name, `http://192.168.56.56:8080/v1/AUTH_c03401d3e99f4d4ea1aede321b7a61ff/container-cli/object-cli.txt`, we should see its contents. See *Figure 8.11*.

```
←  →  C   ⓘ 192.168.56.56:8080/v1/AUTH_c03401d3e99f4d4ea1aede321b7a61ff/container-cli/object-cli.txt

object-cli
```

Figure 8.11: Navigating directly to an object via a web browser

Figure 8.12 is a visual of public users accessing the contents of our container with our read ACLs enabled:

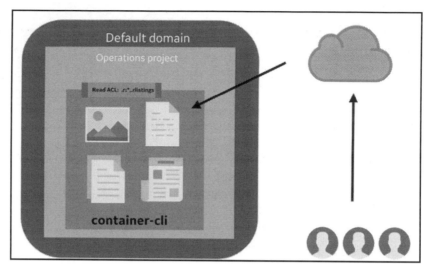

Figure 8.12: If the Swift proxy-server (API) URL is externally accessible, any user should be able
to list and grab the contents of a container with public read ACLs

What if we wanted to limit container access to users within our OpenStack environment that reside within a specific project?

We can use the following syntax: `--read-acl <project-uuid:user-uuid>`

It's important that we use the UUID. In a multi-domain environment, this is the only way our system knows the specific project and user to which we are referencing.

Let's only allow **lisaw** from the **accounting** project to be able to read/download files from the container-cli container.

 Recall from Chapter 3 that we can get a list of all users by running `openstack user list` and all projects by running `openstack project list`.

Run the following command. Your UUIDs may be different than what appear here:

```
$ swift post container-cli --read-acl \
"fe8787fda267442bbea280391e8500d6:2a0c974a13b042e9849a9366a2e5b589"
```

We can then verify the ACL was properly set by running the following:

```
$ swift stat container-cli
```

If we wanted to allow more than one specific user from the accounting project, we could use commas to separate them, like `--read-acl <project-uuid:user1-uuid,user2-uuid>`

To allow all users within the accounting project, we could use wildcard: `--read-acl <project-uuid:*>`.

To set write ACLs, we use the `--write-acl` flag.

Let's add a write ACL that allows any user from within the **accounting** project to write objects to the container:

```
$ swift post container-cli --write-acl "fe8787fda267442bbea280391e8500d6:*"
```

Verify that the write ACLs have been properly set:

```
$ swift stat container-cli
```

You should see output similar to *Figure 8.13*:

```
          Account: AUTH_c03401d3e99f4d4ea1aede321b7a61ff
        Container: container-cli
          Objects: 1
            Bytes: 11
         Read ACL: fe8787fda267442bbea280391e8500d6:2a0c974a13b042e9849a9366a2e5b589
        Write ACL: fe8787fda267442bbea280391e8500d6:*
          Sync To:
         Sync Key:
    Accept-Ranges: bytes
       X-Trans-Id: tx33c53082a5c741d78874b-00597e4516
  X-Storage-Policy: Policy-0
    Last-Modified: Sun, 30 Jul 2017 20:35:15 GMT
      X-Timestamp: 1501397575.81917
     Content-Type: text/plain; charset=utf-8
```

Figure 8.13: Read and Write ACLs set on a Swift container

Exam objective: settings objects to expire

One can set an object to expire at a specific time by setting the X-Delete-At or X-Delete-After object headers. Once an object is expired, it will be inaccessible and eventually deleted from the Swift cluster.

To expire an object at a certain time, the time and date must be in Unix Epoch format.

 To get the current time in Unix Epoch format on your system, you can run date +%s.

CLI

Let's set our object-cli.txt object to delete at Saturday, September 1, 2018 9:09:14 AM, GMT . This will convert to 1535792954 in UNIX Epoch format.

```
$ swift post container-cli object-cli.txt -H "X-Delete-At:1535792954"
```

We can verify that the expiration was set by running the following:

```
$ swift stat container-cli object-cli.txt
```

You should see output similar to *Figure 8.14*.

```
      Account: AUTH_c03401d3e99f4d4ea1aede321b7a61ff
    Container: container-cli
       Object: object-cli.txt
 Content Type: text/plain
Content Length: 11
Last Modified: Sun, 30 Jul 2017 20:58:39 GMT
         ETag: 6e0eabcf5d7c88adf50dd30bf505f961
  X-Delete-At: 1505943383
Accept-Ranges: bytes
  X-Timestamp: 1501448318.78078
   X-Trans-Id: tx17117d97648945c186795-00597e488c
```

Figure 8.14: An object set to expire at a specific date and time in Unix Epoch format

Once we hit the specified date, the file will be deleted.

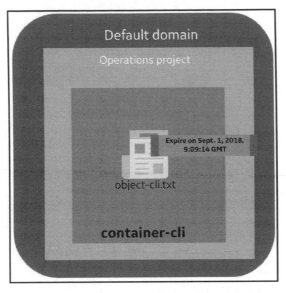

Figure 8.15: A visual of a Swift object in a container to expire at a specific time in the future

We can also set an object to delete after a certain amount of time has passed.

Let's set the object to delete in 60 seconds using the X-Delete-After header. This will overwrite the previous command and set an expiration time for 60 seconds from the current time/date of the system.

```
$ swift post container-cli object-cli.txt -H "X-Delete-After:60"
```

Verify that the expiration was set:

```
$ swift stat container-cli object-cli.txt
```

In 60 seconds, you should no longer be able to check the status of the object because it will have been deleted. You will see an error, indicating the object is no longer available. See *Figure 8.16*.

```
Object HEAD failed: http://192.168.56.56:8080/v1/AUTH_c03401d3e99f4d4ea1aede321b7a61ff/container-cli/object-cli.txt 404 Not Found
Failed Transaction ID: txb1dc424a4bf24fef9fb37-00597da398
```

Figure 8.16: You will receive a 404 'Not Found' once the object has been expired and deleted from the cluster

> You may still be able to see the deleted object when running `swift list container-cli`. Although the object has definitely been deleted from the cluster, the SQLite database listing has not been updated yet. Be patient, and it will eventually be removed from the listing!

If you want to remove an expiration header, you can easily do so by using the `X-Remove-Delete-At` header with an empty value. For example:

```
$ swift post container-cli object-cli.txt -H "X-Remove-Delete-At: "
```

Summary

In this chapter, we reviewed Swift architecture and concepts like accounts, containers, objects. It's important to remember that a majority of Swift features are not enabled on the Horizon dashboard and must be set directly via the API or via `python-swiftclient`. Don't forget: containers are private by default and can only be managed by users with the admin or swiftoperator roles. To grant public or individual OpenStack users access to containers, you must set read and/or write ACLs.

It is absolutely critical that you remember the ACL syntax! **Some older versions of** `python-swifclient` **report incorrect information in the help output!** The ACL syntax described in this chapter and does work properly. For more information on Swift, check out the official documentation at `https://docs.openstack.org/swift`.

Heat Orchestration Service

9

In the previous chapter, we discussed the Swift object storage service and all the Swift-related objectives in the COA exam. Now we will discuss Heat. Heat is the OpenStack orchestration service, and its goal is to help OpenStack users model, set up, and automate the creation and management of OpenStack resources. Due to to the minimal amount of Heat content in the exam, this chapter will be short and sweet. We will cover the following topics:

- About Heat
- Heat architecture
- Heat templates
- Exam objective - managing stacks
- Exam objective - updating stacks

After this chapter, you should have a solid understanding of Heat and the skills required to successfully fulfill all Heat-related objectives in the exam.

About Heat

In *Chapter 1*, we discussed the various ways OpenStack users can create resources with OpenStack. Up until this point in our COA exam prep journey, we've utilized the Horizon dashboard and CLI. Although these have been fun to use, working with them to deploy OpenStack resources can be pretty tedious. In fact, between 2007 and 2010, Amazon users primarily relied on the AWS console, CLI, or SDK to provision virtual resources for their applications. Many users began creating bash scripts with the CLI to automate the creation of entire environments for their applications.

This worked great for a while, but users began to run into problems if they accidentally ran the script again, wanted to delete the resources, or add just one additional change. Users then had to build the logic into their bash scripts in order to make them idempotent and add additional scripts to assist in removing the environments. It was a lot of work.

Then in February of 2011, AWS CloudFormation was released! With CloudFormation, a user could describe their desired AWS architecture in a JSON template file. They could then launch this template and deploy their "stack" while AWS took care of doing everything in the proper order, while logging all events of the creation process. After a user was done with the stack environment, they could easily add additional resources to it or destroy the whole thing by deleting it.

Heat was introduced in April 2013 with the Grizzly version of OpenStack. Like CloudFormation, Heat begins with a blueprint or Heat orchestration template that describes all the OpenStack resources to be provisioned. Heat takes care of provisioning and configuring with no need to worry about dependencies or the order of execution.

You can delete the stack just as easily, which deletes all the resources associated with the stack. If you want to make a change to the stack, you can even easily update it by providing a modified template with new parameters.

Heat architecture

Heat is made up of three daemons:

- **heat-api**: The API and primary gateway to Heat. One must interact with `heat-api` to create, list, delete, and manage stacks.
- **heat-api-cfn**: This provides an AWS-style Query API that allows services or human users to utilize CloudFormation-like functionalities, such as wait conditions and triggering autoscaling.
- **heat-engine**: This is responsible for launching stacks and managing all resources specified in the template.

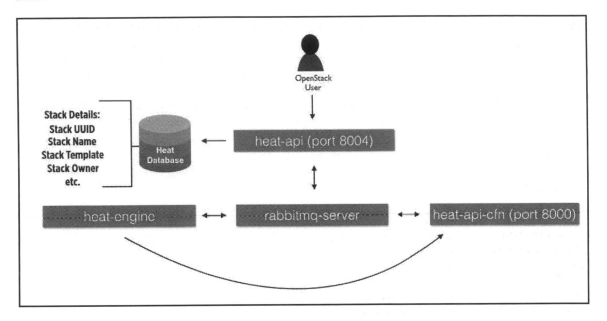

Figure 9.1: High-level view of Heat architecture

Heat templates

Heat templates (heat orchestration templates or HOT, for short) are templates that `heat-api` can consume to create virtual resources in the OpenStack environment. They describe all the desired resources and their associated parameters. After the stack has been created, the OpenStack resources are up and running. Templates are extremely convenient because they allow you to check them into a version control system such as GitHub to easily track changes and collaborate with the team. If problems occur after deploying a Heat template, simply restore to a previous version of the template.

Figure 7.2 breaks down the anatomy of a Heat template.

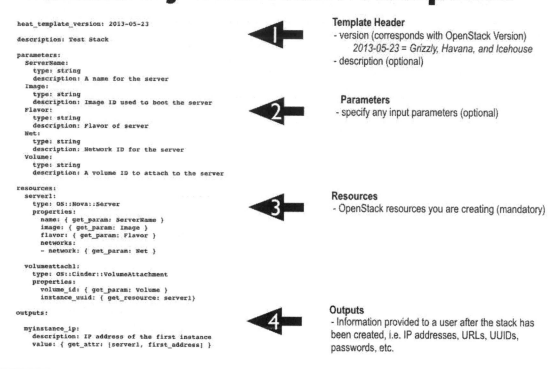

Figure 9.2: Anatomy of a Heat template

1. **Template header**: The template version is mandatory and the description is optional. Additional features and capabilities are released in every new version of OpenStack. This means that newer templates that users create may reference features not found in older versions, therefore making the templates incompatible with older environments. Here is a list of Heat template versions and the OpenStack versions they are compatible with:

Heat template version	OpenStack version
2013-05-23	Grizzly, Havana, Icehouse, and higher
2014-10-16	Juno and higher
2015-04-30	Kilo and higher
2015-10-15	Liberty and higher
2016-04-08	Mitaka and higher
2016-10-14	Newton and higher

2. **Parameters:** These are optional and can be any particular value you'd like the user to be able to insert. These values get passed in by the user at the time of deploying or "creating" the stack.

3. **Resources**: These are mandatory and represent any OpenStack resource you want to create.

4. **Outputs:** Information provided to the user after stack creation. This could be anything from an IP address to a special registration code or password.

Heat resources

Resources are mandatory and are a reference to any OpenStack resources you want to create. OpenStack resources can be anything from Nova virtual machine instances to Neutron security groups. Refer to *Figure 9.3*. You can get a complete list of compatible resources on the Horizon dashboard by navigating to the **Resource Types** panel from the **Project-Orchestration** panel group.

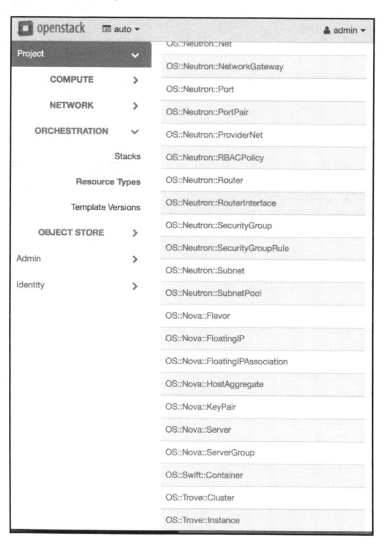

Figure 9.3: A list of available Heat resources on the Horizon dashboard

Backward compatibility with AWS

You may have noticed that some of the Heat resources have a prefix AWS::. These resources are used to make CloudFormation templates compatible with OpenStack Heat. As you know, AWS and OpenStack have many different features so I do not recommend attempting to create stacks with templates that have been designed to work with AWS environments. You would be much better off refactoring your CloudFormation templates with Heat resources. But for the curious, here are a few AWS Heat resources and what they do:

AWS Heat Resource	Action
AWS::EC2::Instance	**OS::Nova::Server** (Creates a Nova instance)
AWS::EC2::SecurityGroup	**OS::Neutron::SecurityGroup** (Creates a Neutron security group)
AWS::EC2::VPC	**OS::Neutron::Network** (Creates a Neutron tenant network)
AWS::EC2::Volume	**OS::Cinder::Volume** (Creates a Cinder volume)
AWS::IAM::AccessKey	**OS::Nova::KeyPair** (Generates a public/private key for a specified user)
AWS::S3::Bucket	Similar to **OS::Swift::Container** (Creates a Swift container)

Exam objectives

Let's a take a look at the Heat exam objectives.

Figure 9.4 breaks down various Heat-related objectives you should be responsible for knowing in the COA exam. As you can see, all of these tasks can be completed on both the Horizon dashboard and CLI. Remember that time is of the essence during the exam, and in many cases, it can be much faster to tackle a task on the dashboard.

Objectives	Dashboard	Command-Line
Create/Edit/List/Delete Heat Stacks	✓	✓
Update Heat Stacks	✓	✓

Figure 9.4: Heat exam objectives can be performed on the Horizon Dashboard or CLI

Exam objective - managing stacks

When you create a heat template, you are creating a stack. The stack is owned by the project to which the user was scoped at the time of creation. Creating a stack is fairly simple on the Horizon dashboard and CLI. Let's try the dashboard first.

This chapter assumes you have performed the exam objective exercises in Chapter 6. If you have not completed Chapter 6, *Neutron Networking Service*, go back and ensure that you have created a **tenant-network1-dashboard** and **tenant-network1-cli**.

A user must have the `heat_stack_owner` role to manage stacks. The admin user that ships with the included virtual appliance should already have this role.

Horizon dashboard

1. From the OpenStack overview page, scope yourself to **logistics** by selecting the top dropdown.
2. Select the **Stacks** panel from the **Project-Orchestration** panel group.
3. Select **Launch Stack**.

Figure 9.5: Launching a stack from the Horizon dashboard

4. See *Figure 9.6*. **Template Resource** (required): You can specify how you wish to provide the template you are going to use.

- **File**: Allows you to select a template on your local filesystem.
- **Direct Input**: Copy and paste a template into a text field.
- **URL**: Provide a URL to a publicly accessible template hosted on a site or GitHub.

5. Paste the following template. This template creates a brand new instance with our specified flavor and image, connects it to an existing tenant network, and then attaches a brand new 1 GB block volume. Be careful with the spacing when pasting into the Horizon dashboard. A copy of the template is available inside the virtual appliance and official book GitHub repo.

 YAML (YAML Ain't Markup Language) is a superset of JSON and makes setting values easier for humans. Tabs are not allowed in YAML so always be sure to use spaces. All properties and lists must be indented with 1 or more space. If you a struggle with the template, find an example Heat template online or play around with an online YAML parser at http://yaml-online-parser.appspot.com/.

```
heat_template_version: 2013-05-23
description: Test Stack

parameters:
  ServerName:
    type: string
    description: A name for the server
  Image:
    type: string
    description: Image ID used to boot the server
  Flavor:
    type: string
    description: Flavor of server
  Net:
    type: string
    description: Network ID for the server
  VolumeName:
    type: string
    description: A name for the volume

resources:
  server1:
    type: OS::Nova::Server
    properties:
      name: { get_param: ServerName }
```

```
        image: { get_param: Image }
        flavor: { get_param: Flavor }
        networks:
        - network: { get_param: Net }
  volume1:
    type: OS::Cinder::Volume
    properties:
      name: { get_param: VolumeName }
      size: 1

volumeattach1:
    type: OS::Cinder::VolumeAttachment
    properties:
      volume_id: { get_resource: volume1 }
      instance_uuid: { get_resource: server1}
```

6. Environment Resource (optional): This allows you to specify an environment file that fills in input parameters for the selected template. We will ignore this for now.

7. Select **Next**.

Figure 9.6: Providing a heat template for a stack on the Horizon dashboard

8. **Stack Name** (required): Name of the stack to be created. Let's name this stack-dashboard.

9. **Creation Timeout** (required): Minutes to wait before canceling the stack. This will automatically cancel the stack creation process if the stack does not complete. Leave this as the default.

10. **Rollback On Failure** (optional): If checked, this will undo the stack creation process, cleaning up any created resources. We will leave this unchecked.

11. **Password for user "admin"** (required): This is the password for the current user logged into the dashboard, in our case, admin. We provide this for security purposes (although it can be disabled in the Horizon dashboard with the enable_user_pass value in the dashboard config file at /etc/openstack-dashboard/local_settings.py). Enter admin.

12. **Flavor** (required): The i input parameter specified in our Heat template. The flavor we want to use for our instance. Let's use m1.tiny.

13. **Image** (required): The input parameter specified in our Heat template. The image we want to use for our instance. Let's use cirros.

When providing parameters of existing OpenStack resources to Heat, it's sometimes safer to provide their specific UUIDs rather than the names. This helps in avoiding conflicts when you may have multiple resources with the same name.

14. **Net** (required): The input parameter specified in our Heat template that refers to the network we want our instance to attach to. Let's use tenant1-dashboard.

15. **ServerName** (required): The input parameter specified in our Heat template. The name we want for our server.

16. **VolumeName** (required): The input parameter specified in our Heat template. The name of the volume we want our stack to create and attach to the instance.

17. Select **Launch**.

Figure 9.7: Providing parameters for a stack on the Horizon dashboard

Your stack status should be in **Create in Progress**. Be patient, it may take a few minutes to complete. Once complete, you will see the status change to **Create Complete.** Take a look at *Figure 9.8* for the finished product.

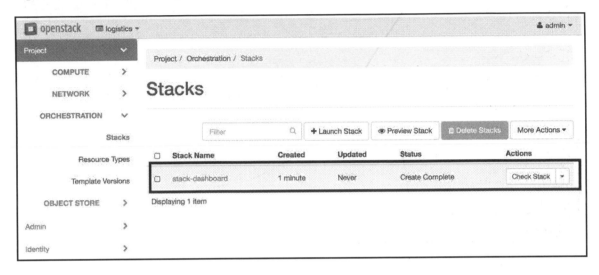

Figure 9.8: Once completed, the stack status should show 'create complete'

We should now be able to see our newly created virtual machine and attached volume.

CLI

Remember that in `Chapter 6`, we created the `openrc-logistics` file. We are going to use that file here. If you skipped Chapter 6, feel free to flip back to see how we created a new credential file that allowed us to scope to the logistics project.

Source the `openrc-logistics` file:

```
$ source openrc-logistics
```

Verify that the proper variables are set and we are scoped to logistics:

```
$ export | grep OS
```

Now that we are properly scoped, let's begin by listing any current stacks in the logistics project. We should have one stack from the previous Horizon dashboard exercise:

```
$ openstack stack list
```

You should see output similar to *Figure 9.9*:

```
+----------------------------------------+-----------------+-----------------+-----------------------+--------------+
| ID                                     | Stack Name      | Stack Status    | Creation Time         | Updated Time |
+----------------------------------------+-----------------+-----------------+-----------------------+--------------+
| e3efcd0d-47d1-4271-b8b9-13a8504c15fa   | stack-dashboard | CREATE_COMPLETE | 2017-08-09T03:59:31Z  | None         |
+----------------------------------------+-----------------+-----------------+-----------------------+--------------+
```

Figure 9.9: Output from the 'openstack stack list' command

Let's create a file called `test-stack.yaml` using the Heat template from the previous section. If you are using the virtual appliance, you may already see the `test-stack.yaml` residing in the `/home/openstack` directory.

 To find the UUIDs of the resources, use the `openstack image list` and `openstack network list --long` commands.

```
$ openstack stack create -t test-stack.yaml --parameter Flavor=m1.tiny --parameter Image=<image-uuid> --parameter Net=<network-uuid> --parameter ServerName=stackserver-cli --parameter VolumeName=stackvolume-cli stack-cli
```

You should see output similar to *Figure 9.10*.

```
+---------------------+--------------------------------------+
| Field               | Value                                |
+---------------------+--------------------------------------+
| id                  | 7b17ce40-56c3-4e48-a175-860b41fa0ad1 |
| stack_name          | stack-cli                            |
| description         | Test Stack                           |
| creation_time       | 2017-08-09T04:17:18Z                 |
| updated_time        | None                                 |
| stack_status        | CREATE_IN_PROGRESS                   |
| stack_status_reason | Stack CREATE started                 |
+---------------------+--------------------------------------+
```

Figure 9.10: Output from the 'openstack stack create' command

Run the `openstack stack list` command to check the status of the stack:

```
$ openstack stack list
```

If your stack status changes to CREATE_FAILED, use the `openstack stack show` command on the stack to see the specific error. If it's due to `No Valid Host`, ensure that there are no other instances running outside the **logistics** project. If all else fails, reboot the virtual appliance, delete the stack using the `openstack stack delete` command, and retry creating the stack.

Exam objective - updating stacks

After creating a stack, you may want to modify an aspect of it, including adding, removing, or modifying a resource. This can be easily done via the dashboard or CLI. Note that doing this on the dashboard is a bit of a hassle as we need to provide **all** original parameters.

Horizon dashboard

1. From the OpenStack overview page, scope yourself to the **logistics** by selecting the top dropdown.
2. Select the **Stacks** panel from the **Project-Orchestration** panel group.
3. See *Figure 9.11*. Select the dropdown next to **stack-dashboard** and select **Change Stack Template**.

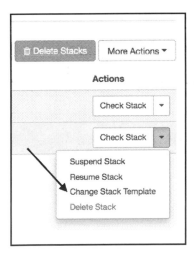

Figure 9.11: Updating a stack on the Horizon dashboard

See *Figure 9.12*. Follow the exact same instructions shown in the previous Horizon dashboard "Create Stack" section only this time, we will modify the name of our Server. Let's change it to `stackserverupdate-dashboard`.

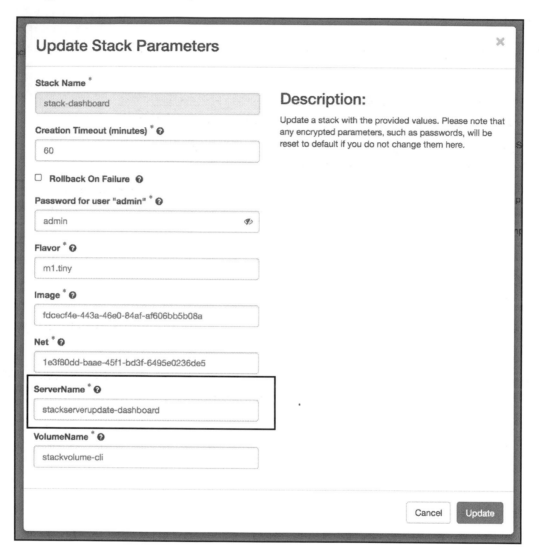

Figure 9.12: Provide the same parameters as the previous exercise, but change the ServerName

Once complete, the status of the stack should read **Update Complete**. Our stack has remained the same with the exception of the one parameter we've modified.

CLI

Source the `openrc-logistics` file:

```
$ source openrc-logistics
```

Verify that the proper variables are set and we are scoped to the logistics project:

```
$ export | grep OS
```

Let's update our stack by modifying the `ServerName` parameter. Thanks to the `--existing` flag, we do not need to re-enter all the original parameters:

```
$ openstack stack update --existing --parameter
ServerName=stackserverupdate-cli stack-cli
```

 Be sure to enter all parameter keys as they exactly appear in the Heat template! In the example above, we must type `ServerName`. It is case sensitive!

Run the following to check the stack status:

```
$ openstack stack list
```

You should see output similar to *Figure 9.13*, showing that the stack has been properly updated.

```
b8f18545-12f8-41fe-8278-de9209d6a8b7 | stack-cli    | UPDATE_COMPLETE | 2017-08-09T04:28:34Z | 2017-08-09T04:53:18Z
```

Figure 9.13: A successfully updated stack on the CLI

After you are done playing with Heat, be sure to delete your stacks by running the following:

```
$ openstack stack delete <stack-name-or-uuid>
```

Summary

Great! We just completed the Heat exam objective section of our COA prep. Remember that you can complete Horizon objectives on both the dashboard and CLI, but updating an existing stack is much easier on the CLI thanks to the `--existing` flag. Don't forget to always try to use UUIDs of virtual resources for Heat parameters. There may be multiple resources with the same name and UUIDS allow us to be specific. Do not be overly concerned with building Heat templates from scratch or overly complex Heat template scenarios. If you can kick a stack and provide the appropriate parameters, you'll be good to go! Now that we have completed all service-related objectives in the exam, let's move on to the final section: troubleshooting!

10
Troubleshooting

Congratulations! We've covered all the OpenStack service-related exam objectives in the COA exam. Knowing these objectives will put you in good shape for the exam, but keep in mind that there are also some basic OpenStack troubleshooting skills that you will need to bring to the table. In this chapter, we will cover the following:

- Debugging the CLI
- Managing OpenStack daemons
- Using the API to check component/agent status
- Exam objective - important OpenStack service directories
- Exam objective - analyzing log files
- Exam objective - managing MySQL

After this chapter, you should have a solid understanding of successfully meeting all troubleshooting-related objectives in the COA exam.

Debugging the CLI

When you use `python-openstackclient` or the traditional service-based clients (that is, `python-novaclient`, `python-neturonclient`, or `python-swiftclient`), there is a lot going on behind the scenes! To see the API calls being made, we can use the `--debug` flag to see the requests and responses in real time. Let's try using it with the following command. Ensure that you source the `openrc` file before running it.

Although understanding the `--debug` flag is not required to pass the exam, it is an invaluable tool that can really help you narrow down issues in real-world OpenStack environments.

```
$ openstack server list --debug
```

We should see output similar to Figure 10-1. Wow, that's a lot of text!

Figure 10.1: Output from using the --debug flag on the CLI

How can we decipher this? As you already know from the first chapter of this book, we communicate with RESTful APIs via the HTTP protocol. To understand the debug, we can look for the requests and responses being made to the Keystone and Nova APIs.

Figure 10.2: Initial request/response to the Keystone API

1. python-openstackclient first makes a GET call to the Keystone authentication endpoint specified in the `openrc` file. This is just to ensure that the authentication endpoint is alive and responding.

2. We can see that the Keystone API responds back with an `HTTP 200 OK`. This means that the response has succeeded and we are ready to proceed.

Figure 10.3: Request/response to get a scoped token from Keystone API

3. Although the debug output obscures the body of the request, here, `python-openstackclient` sends the username, password, domain, and project name to the authentication endpoint in order to request a scoped token.

4. The response of this request contains the scoped token (not visible on the debug output) and the entire OpenStack environment service catalog. `python-openstackclient` can use the catalog to look up the nova/compute API endpoint URL.

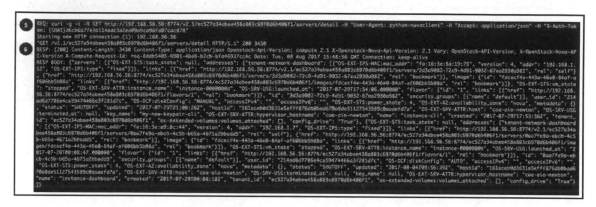

Figure 10.4: Request/Response to get a list of all running servers from Nova API

5. `python-openstackclient` then sends a request to the discovered nova/compute API endpoint URL from step 4. As you can see, there is an `X-Auth-Token` header in the request, which contains the token. The debug output shows an SHA1 hash of the token to obscure the actual token contents.

6. And finally, we see a response from `nova-api`: a list of any running instances (in the JSON format) within our project. Thanks to `python-openstackclient`, this JSON will be converted into a nicely formatted table.

Although understanding the `--debug` flag is not required to pass the exam, it's an invaluable tool that can really help you narrow down your issue in real-world OpenStack environments.

Managing OpenStack daemons

If we are using an operating system with the `systemd` init system, we can easily use the `systemctl` command to start, stop, or check the status of any OpenStack daemons running on a particular server.

For example, to check the status of the `nova-api` service, we can run the following command:

```
$ sudo systemctl status nova-api
```

We should see output similar to *Figure 10.5*.

```
• nova-api.service - OpenStack Compute API
   Loaded: loaded (/lib/systemd/system/nova-api.service; enabled; vendor preset: enabled)
   Active: active (running) since Tue 2017-08-08 09:36:05 EDT; 2h 57min ago
  Process: 3472 ExecStartPre=/bin/chown nova:adm /var/log/nova (code=exited, status=0/SUCCESS)
  Process: 3424 ExecStartPre=/bin/chown nova:nova /var/lock/nova /var/lib/nova (code=exited, status=0/SUCCESS)
  Process: 3382 ExecStartPre=/bin/mkdir -p /var/lock/nova /var/log/nova /var/lib/nova (code=exited, status=0/SUCCESS)
 Main PID: 3544 (nova-api)
   CGroup: /system.slice/nova-api.service
           ├─3544 /usr/bin/python /usr/bin/nova-api --config-file=/etc/nova/nova.conf --log-file=/var/log/nova/nova-api.log
           ├─4079 /usr/bin/python /usr/bin/nova-api --config-file=/etc/nova/nova.conf --log-file=/var/log/nova/nova-api.log
           └─4145 /usr/bin/python /usr/bin/nova-api --config-file=/etc/nova/nova.conf --log-file=/var/log/nova/nova-api.log
```

Figure 10.5: Output from the systemctl status command

This shows us that the `nova-api` service is currently running and will be started on reboot (`enabled`). If the service was stopped, we could easily start it back up by running the following:

```
$ sudo systemctl start nova-api
```

If we want to restart a service, we can run the following:

```
$ sudo systemctl restart nova-api
```

 The exam does not require you to edit any specific OpenStack configuration files—but a good rule of thumb for live OpenStack environments is to remember to restart the service any time you want new changes to configuration files to be applied.

Using the APIs to check the component status

Some OpenStack service APIs feature the ability to allow users to check the status of the service components without interacting with the daemons directly on the physical machine. These are typically admin-role-only functions and are a convenient way to verify the OpenStack component health. Let's try checking the status of nova components with the `openstack compute service list` command:

```
$ openstack compute service list
```

We should get output similar to *Figure 10.6*.

```
+----+----------------+----------------+----------+---------+-------+-----------------------------+
| ID | Binary         | Host           | Zone     | Status  | State | Updated At                  |
+----+----------------+----------------+----------+---------+-------+-----------------------------+
|  1 | nova-conductor | coa-aio-newton | internal | enabled | up    | 2017-08-08T16:42:14.000000  |
|  2 | nova-consoleauth | coa-aio-newton | internal | enabled | up  | 2017-08-08T16:42:07.000000  |
|  3 | nova-scheduler | coa-aio-newton | internal | enabled | up    | 2017-08-08T16:42:07.000000  |
|  6 | nova-compute   | coa-aio-newton | nova     | enabled | up    | 2017-08-08T16:42:14.000000  |
+----+----------------+----------------+----------+---------+-------+-----------------------------+
```

Figure 10.6: Output from the 'openstack compute service list' command

The output of this command shows us that the `nova-conductor`, `nova-consoleauth`, `nova-scheduler`, and `nova-compute` services are all up and running. In a real-world OpenStack infrastructure, we would see multiple `nova-compute` services for every hypervisor in the environment.

Here are some other services that feature component status commands:

- **Neutron**

```
$ openstack network agent list
```

- **Cinder**

```
$ openstack volume service list
```

- **Heat**

```
$ openstack orchestration service list
```

Important OpenStack service directories

When an OpenStack infrastructure engineer installs a brand new service in an OpenStack environment, that OpenStack service's package will most likely use the following directories by default:

- **Configuration files**

```
/etc/<service-name>/*
```

In this location, we find configuration files for the respective service, typically using the `.conf` file extension. These files control the behavior of the API and any associated components that may be installed on the machine. This is also the directory where the `policy.json` authorization file resides.

- **Data files**

  `/var/lib/<service-name>/*`

  Data files are where the OpenStack service will store any relevant data. For example, in `/var/lib/glance`, Glance will store images in this directory. In `/var/lib/nova`, Nova will store the actual data written to an instance's ephemeral disk as well as all associated virtual machine configuration information.

- **Log files**

  `/var/log/<service-name>/*`

  Most OpenStack services will write their log files to this directory. We will discuss logs in greater detail in the next section.

Exam objective - analyzing log files

As discussed in the previous section, OpenStack services write log files to `/var/log/<service-name>/*`. The OpenStack service operating system packages automatically set up the `logrotate` program to tar and compress old OpenStack log files, thus avoiding excessive storage consumption. The exception to this default log directory is Keystone and Swift. Keystone utilizes Apache and therefore writes log files to `/var/log/apache2/*`. Swift writes log files to `/var/log/syslog`.

Anytime a user makes a request to an OpenStack service's API, a request UUID is generated. You will sometimes see these request IDs when attempting to interact with a service on the Horizon dashboard or CLI. To get more information on service errors, you can easily browse log files for clues regarding the specific request ID.

For example, when attempting to create a new Neutron security group called `default` on the Horizon dashboard, you get an error that looks like *Figure 10.7*.

> **Error:** Unable to create security group: Default security group already exists. Neutron server returns request_ids: ['req-7c0fe7f3-12f6-4c19-81fc-994aebf31ca5']

Figure 10.7: Error with request-ID generated by attempting to create an additional default Neutron security group

We can then `grep` for that specific request ID in the `neutron-server` log file to see the specific time the request was made:

```
$ sudo grep -nar "req-017786ad-5b66-4b06-9dc5-ed35a9dff22c"
/var/log/neutron/neutron-server.log
```

We should see output similar *Figure 10.8*:

```
6545:2017-08-08 18:54:19.160 4032 INFO neutron.api.v2.resource [req-7c0fe7f3-12f6-4c19-81fc-994aebf31ca5 214ad6d7786e4ce5947446
6a3f281d7c d5a33462721e4d35bd45138311c526b8 - - -] create failed (client error): There was a conflict when trying to complete y
our request.
6546:2017-08-08 18:54:19.167 4032 INFO neutron.wsgi [req-7c0fe7f3-12f6-4c19-81fc-994aebf31ca5 214ad6d7786e4ce59474466a3f281d7c
d5a33462721e4d35bd45138311c526b8 - - -] 192.168.56.56 - - [08/Aug/2017 18:54:19] "POST /v2.0/security-groups.json HTTP/1.1" 409
335 0.014891
```

Figure 10.8: An error in the neutron-server logs when attempting to create an additional 'default' Neutron security group

> You will need to either use `sudo` or become the root (`sudo su -`) to analyze log files in your virtual appliance environment. The `openstack` user does not have permissions to these directories.

Managing MySQL

As an OpenStack administrator, you will most likely rely on an experienced database administrator for all OpenStack-related database maintenance. The official OpenStack exam requirements contain a broad objective to "analyze database servers and back up a database". Here are some basics for working with a MySQL/MariaDB, which should put you in good shape for the exam.

We can use the `mysql` command-line tool to explore MySQL on our virtual appliance.

Run the following:

```
$ sudo mysql -h localhost
```

After connecting, we can run the following command to see all the OpenStack service databases:

```
MariaDB [(none)]> show databases;
```

You should see output similar to *Figure 10.9*

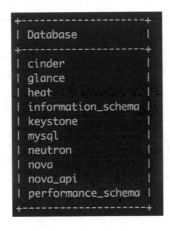

Figure 10.9: Output from the 'show databases' SQL statement

To use a specific database, we can run the following:

```
MariaDB [(none)]> use nova;
```

To see all the tables in the Nova database, we can run this:

```
MariaDB [(none)]> show tables;
```

If we wanted to see all the data regarding our virtual machine instances, we can run the following:

```
MariaDB [(none)]> select * from instances;
```

To exit the MySQL/MariaDB prompt, run the following:

```
MariaDB [(none)]> exit;
```

If we wanted to perform a SQL dump of a specific database, you can run this:

```
$ sudo mysqldump -h localhost --databases nova > nova.sql
```

To restore a SQL dump, run the following:

```
$ sudo mysql -h localhost < nova.sql
```

Summary

So there we have it! In this section, we covered some general OpenStack troubleshooting skills that will prepare you for the COA exam. Remember that the troubleshooting domain covers only about 13% of the exam, so don't expect many questions on this content. Although it's not an exam objective, you should understand how to use the `--debug` flag to provide clues when troubleshooting OpenStack issues on the CLI. I also showed you how some OpenStack service APIs allow you to check the status of their components/agents. The most important exam objective in this section is to remember the OpenStack service log file locations, and how to `grep` through them when identifying specific messages. And lastly, we ended the chapter with some very basic MySQL/MariaDB skills, including showing tables of specific databases, backing up, and restoring databases.

11
Final Tips and Tricks

Congratulations! At this point, I'm hoping you're feeling great about taking the COA. Here are some handy tips and tricks to keep in mind prior to going into the exam.

In this chapter, we will cover the following topics:

- Project scope
- Time management
- CLI help
- External monitors
- Issues during the exam
- Diving deeper into OpenStack

After reviewing these tips, you should be ready to take on the exam. Be sure to check out the practice exam in Chapter 12 before taking the real thing!

Project scope

Project scope is the most fundamental aspect of any OpenStack environment. If you are attempting an objective on the Horizon dashboard, don't forget to always scope yourself to the proper project from the top dropdown. Refer to *Figure 11.1*.

If for any reason you do not see a project from the top dropdown, you should jump to the CLI.

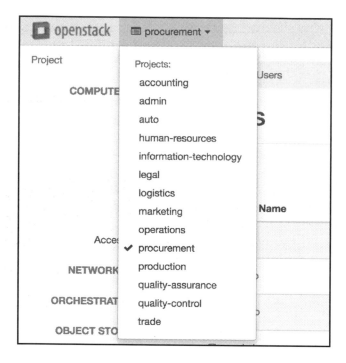

Figure 11.1: Scoping to a project on the Horizon dashboard

If you are on the CLI, the easiest way to scope yourself to a new project is using the method presented in the previous chapters of this book:

```
$ cp openrc openrc-<project-name>
```

After making a copy of the original openrc file, use the editor of your choice to fill in the proper variables for project and tenant:

```
$ nano openrc-<project-name>
```

Ensure that you set both the OS_PROJECT_NAME and OS_TENANT_NAME variables:

```
export OS_PROJECT_NAME=<project-name>
export OS_TENANT_NAME=<project-name>
```

 Although python-openstackclient needs only the OS_PROJECT_NAME variable, some older clients may rely on the legacy OS_TENANT_NAME variable. We set it here for consistency.

After saving your file with the newly set variables, source the file to set the variables in the current Bash session:

```
$ source openrc-<project-name>
```

Before running any commands, verify that the variables have been set properly!

```
$ export | grep OS
```

You should see output similar to *Figure 11.2*.

```
declare -x OS_AUTH_URL="http://192.168.56.56:5000/v3"
declare -x OS_AUTH_VERSION="3"
declare -x OS_IDENTITY_API_VERSION="3"
declare -x OS_PASSWORD="admin"
declare -x OS_PROJECT_DOMAIN_NAME="default"
declare -x OS_PROJECT_NAME="accounting"
declare -x OS_TENANT_NAME="accounting"
declare -x OS_USERNAME="admin"
declare -x OS_USER_DOMAIN_NAME="default"
```

Figure 11.2: Confirming Bash session variables are set to the proper project scope

Time management

To pass the COA, you must manage your time appropriately! Always pay attention to your remaining time in the exam console. As mentioned in Chapter 1, *Introducing OpenStack and the Certified OpenStack Administrator Exam*, you are free to use the official upstream OpenStack documentation at https://docs.openstack.org/ocata/. However, I would not rely on this during the exam. Scouring through the site for answers will eat up your precious time! If a question appears to be taking longer than 4–5 minutes to complete, you should click on the forward button and move on! Come back to it later if you still have time left!

If a task can be completed on the Horizon dashboard, it's usually much quicker than the CLI. If you are a CLI pro and don't want to dig through the `--help` commands, the CLI may be a faster choice for you.

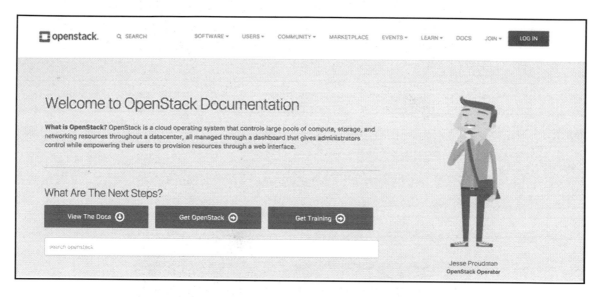

Figure 11.3: Although you are free to browse docs.openstack.org during the exam. it's a time waster!

CLI help

If you forget how a specific CLI command works, you can always rely on the help! Here are some examples of using `python-openstackclient` help.

```
dns quota list  List quotas
dns quota reset  Delete blacklist
dns quota set  Set blacklist properties
dns service list  List service statuses
dns service show  Show service status details
domain create  Create new domain
domain delete  Delete domain(s)
domain list    List domains
domain set     Set domain properties
domain show    Display domain details
ec2 credentials create  Create EC2 credentials
ec2 credentials delete  Delete EC2 credentials
ec2 credentials list  List EC2 credentials
ec2 credentials show  Display EC2 credentials details
endpoint create  Create new endpoint
endpoint delete  Delete endpoint(s)
endpoint list  List endpoints
endpoint set   Set endpoint properties
endpoint show  Display endpoint details
extension list  List API extensions
federation domain list  List accessible domains
federation project list  List accessible projects
federation protocol create  Create new federation protocol
federation protocol delete  Delete federation protocol(s)
federation protocol list  List federation protocols
federation protocol set  Set federation protocol properties
federation protocol show  Display federation protocol details
flavor create  Create new flavor
flavor delete  Delete flavor(s)
flavor list    List flavors
flavor set     Set flavor properties
flavor show    Display flavor details
flavor unset   Unset flavor properties
floating ip create  Create floating IP
floating ip delete  Delete floating IP(s)
floating ip list  List floating IP(s)
floating ip pool list  List pools of floating IP addresses
floating ip show  Display floating IP details
group add user  Add user to group
group contains user  Check user membership in group
group create   Create new group
group delete   Delete group(s)
group list     List groups
group remove user  Remove user from group
group set      Set group properties
group show     Display group details
help           print detailed help for another command
host list      List hosts
host set       Set host properties
host show      Display host details
hypervisor list  List hypervisors
hypervisor show  Display hypervisor details
hypervisor stats show  Display hypervisor stats details
```

Figure 11.4: Output from the 'openstack help' command

Using the help is a **two-step process**.

Step 1: Determine how to perform a particular action using `openstack help`.

You can filter specific actions using `grep`. Here are some examples:

```
$ openstack help | grep domain
$ openstack help | grep project
$ openstack help | grep image
$ openstack help | grep server
$ openstack help | grep network
$ openstack help | grep volume
```

Step 2: After you find out the action you want to perform, you can provide `--help` to explore all available positional arguments and flags. Here are some examples:

```
$ openstack domain create --help
$ openstack project create --help
$ openstack image add project --help
$ openstack server create --help
$ openstack network list --help
$ openstack router create --help
```

As previously mentioned in Chapter 8, *Swift Object-Storage Service*, Swift requires you to use `python-swiftclient`.

Beware! Some previous versions of `python-swiftclient` display incorrect information about how to set ACLs on containers.

Refer to Chapter 8, *Swift Object-Storage Service*, on how to properly set ACLs on a container or refer to the official upstream Swift documentation available at `https://docs.openstack.org/swift/`.

External monitors

If you are planning on taking the exam on a personal laptop, that's completely fine! Keep in mind that you are free to hook up one or many external monitors to the laptop while taking the exam. In some cases, using an external monitor will fit more details found on the Horizon dashboard and more output from the terminal. If you have an external monitor available (28" or larger), you may want to use it instead of relying on a small laptop screen.

Figure 11.5: Using an external monitor may help you fit more dashboard and terminal details on one screen

Issues during the exam

If you experience any network connectivity issues during the exam, remain calm and wait for the exam to reconnect. The proctor chat window should be available if you have any questions or if you experience any technical difficulties. If you have any concerns toward the end of the exam, ensure that you contact the proctor via the chat window before ending the exam.

Diving deeper into OpenStack

The content in this book certainly prepares you to succeed on the COA exam, but it covers only the tip of the iceberg of OpenStack knowledge! There is still a whole world to uncover on OpenStack, including topics such as high availability, building cloud-aware apps on OpenStack, and OpenStack networking. I recommend that you check out these titles if you want to dive deeper: *OpenStack Cloud Computing Cookbook - Third Edition* by Kevin Jackson, Cody Bunch, and Egle Sigler, *Troubleshooting OpenStack* by Tony Campbell, and *OpenStack Networking Essentials* by James Denton.

Summary

These tips and tricks will put you in a great position going into the exam. We reviewed the importance of project scope on the Horizon dashboard and CLI. Remember: if an objective can be completed on the Horizon dashboard, do it! It's typically faster than using the CLI unless you are a command-line pro! Time is extremely important and you only have about 4 to 5 minutes to complete each objective. With that said, don't waste your time with `http://docs.openstack.org` during the exam. Navigating the help in `python-openstackclient` is very useful in the event of forgetting some CLI arguments. Don't forget that older versions of `python-swiftclient` provide incorrect information on Swift ACLs, so use the syntax provided in this book or the `http://docs.openstack.org/swift`. And finally, be sure to check out other OpenStack books currently on the market! If this is your first OpenStack book, the cloud learning as just begun!

12
Practice Exam

Use this practice test to prepare for the Certified OpenStack Administrator exam.

Before you begin...

Be sure to delete any previously running instances prior to starting. If you need help detecting running instances and deleting them, refer to the end of Chapter 5, *Nova Compute Service*.

Instructions

Complete all objectives on the Horizon dashboard or CLI. Some questions may depend on resources created in other questions. Being able to complete all these objectives within one hour should put you in good standing for the exam. If a specific detail is not provided, assume the default value.

Question 1

Within the **accounting** project, create a new tenant network called **tenant-network1**. It should have a subnet called **tenant-subnet1** with the following details:

- **CIDR**: 192.168.5.0/24
- **DHCP**: Enabled
- **Allocation range**: 192.168.5.50 to 192.168.5.60

Question 2

From inside your terminal environment, build an `openrc` credential file for the **admin** user that will scope to the **auto** project.

Question 3

Create a new keypair in the **accounting** project called **keypair1**.

Question 4

Your infrastructure engineers just installed the Manilla service in your OpenStack environment. Create a new entry in the service catalog that advertises the following information:

- **Service name**: manilla
- **Service description**: OpenStack Shared File Systems
- **Type**: share
- **Region**: RegionOne
- **Public endpoint**: `http://192.168.56.56:8786/v1/`
- **Internal endpoint**: `http://192.168.56.56:8786/v1/`
- **Admin endpoint**: `http://192.168.56.56:8786/v1/`

Question 5

Create a new security group in the **trade** project called **database-sg**. It should have one rule that allows **incoming 3306** from the **default** security group.

Question 6

Boot a new instance in the **accounting** project called **instance1** with the **m1.tiny** flavor. It should use the **Cirros** image and should be attached to **tenant-network1**. Ensure that the **keypair1** public key gets injected into the instance.

Question 7

Create a new Nova flavor, accessible only by the **production** project. It should have the following properties:

- **Name**: nice-flavor
- **RAM**: 512 MB
- **VCPU**: 1
- **Disk**: 1 GB
- **Ephemeral**: 0
- **Swap**: 0

Question 8

In the **accounting** project, create a new **1 GB** empty volume called **volume1**. Attach the volume to **instance1**. After you have successfully attached the volume, use the novnc console to log in to the instance [username: cirros, password: cubswin:)]. Format the attached volume with the ext3 filesystem and mount to the /mnt directory. Place a file on the mounted drive called myfile.txt. Unmount and detach the volume from **instance1**.

Question 9

From the **auto** project, create an empty 1 GB volume called **volume1**. The volume should be from **type: lvm**.

Question 10

Adjust the quotas in the **admin** project, allowing a total of **20 instances** and **100 volumes**.

Question 11

Change the **sallyp** user email address to sallyp@openstack.org. Disable the account.

Question 12

Create a Nova snapshot of **instance1** in the **accounting** project. The snapshot should be called **instance1-snapshot**.

Question 13

Create a router within the **accounting** project called **router1**. Add **tenant-subnet1** to the router interface. Set the router gateway to **provider-network-dashboard**.

> If you don't see **provider-network-dashboard**, please go to Chapter 6, *Neutron Networking Service* and follow the exercises to create it.

Question 14

In the **accounting** project, allocate the floating IP address **172.16.0.99**. Assign this floating IP to **instance1**.

Question 15

Attempt to get a reply by pinging **instance1** via its floating IP address (172.16.0.99) set in the previous question. If you do not receive a reply, set the specific security group rule in the default security group to permit this.

> You must attempt to ping the instance from **inside** the virtual appliance, **not** your laptop or desktop system running VirtualBox.

Question 16

Perform this specific task on the CLI only. Use wget to fetch a Cirros image from the official upstream website at https://download.cirros-cloud.net/0.3.5/cirros-0.3.5-x86_64-disk.img. Upload the **qcow2** image to the **trade** project. The image should be named **awesome-cirros**. The image description should be "**COA Exam Prep Awesome Image**". The image should have a minimum RAM of **256** and minimum disk of **1 GB**. It should be accessible only to the **trade** project.

Question 17

Create a new Swift container within the **auto** project called **stuff**.

Upload a file called `object.txt` to the **stuff** container. The container content should be **readable/downloadable** by the **public** but only **writable** by **lisaw** in the **accounting** project.

Question 18

Scoped to the **trade** project, use the CLI to download the **awesome-cirros** image to the `/tmp` directory.

Question 19

Create a Heat stack within the **accounting** project from the following template:

```
heat_template_version: 2013-05-23
description: Test Stack
parameters:
  ServerName:
    type: string
    description: A name for the server
  Image:
    type: string
    description: Image ID used to boot the server
  Flavor:
    type: string
    description: Flavor of server
  Net:
    type: string
    description: Network ID for the server
  VolumeName:
    type: string
    description: A name for the volume

resources:
  server1:
    type: OS::Nova::Server
    properties:
      name: { get_param: ServerName }
      image: { get_param: Image }
      flavor: { get_param: Flavor }
      networks:
      - network: { get_param: Net }
  volume1:
```

```
        type: OS::Cinder::Volume
        properties:
          name: { get_param: VolumeName }
          size: 1

    volumeattach1:
      type: OS::Cinder::VolumeAttachment
      properties:
        volume_id: { get_resource: volume1 }
        instance_uuid: { get_resource: server1}
```

The stack name should be called **test-accounting-stack**. Use the **Cirros** image, **m1.tiny** flavor, and attach to the **tenant-network1** network. The instance that gets created should be called **heat-instance**. The volume should be called **volume1**.

Question 20

Within the **auto** project, set the `object.txt` file in the **stuff** container to expire on **1596822650** (Friday, August 7, 2020, 5:50:50 PM).

Question 21

Create a new domain called **zevotoys**.

Question 22

Create a new user within this domain called **maryw** with the password set to **password**.

Question 23

Create a project within the **zevotoys** domain called **marketing**.

Question 24

Create a new group within the **zevotoys** domain called **students**. Add **maryw** to this group.

Question 25

Assign the _member_ role to the **students** group on the **marketing** project.

Question 26

Share the **awesome-cirros** image (in the **trade** project) with the **quality-control** project.

Question 27

Create a new provider network and subnet within the **admin** project with the following details:

- **Network Name**: provider-network-practice-test
- **Provider Network Type**: Flat
- **Physical Network**: public-test
- **External**: true
- **Subnet Name**: provider-subnet-practice-test
- **Subnet-Range:** 172.16.2.0/24
- **Gateway**: 172.16.2.1
- **DHCP**: Disabled

Question 28

Create a snapshot of **volume1** in the **auto** project. Call the snapshot **volume1-snapshot**. It should have this description: **COA Prep volume1-dasboard snapshot**.

Question 29

Within the **procurement** project, attempt to create another security group called **default**. You should receive an error with a request ID. Find any information regarding this error in the neutron log files and document the information you find.

Question 30

Adjust the allocation pool for **tenant-subnet1** in the **accounting** project to **192.168.5.55-192.168.5.60**.

Question 31

Create a bootable volume from the existing **volume1-dashboard** volume within the **human-resources** project.

Question 32

From the **accounting** project, back up the **volume1** volume to a container called **accounting-volume-backups**.

Question 33

SSH into **instance1** (inside the **accouting** project) via its floating IP, **172.16.0.99**. Open up any necessary security group rules if you can't connect to the instance. Bonus points if you can SSH into the instance without a password by using the private key generated in Question 3.

Question 34

Update the **test-accounting-stack** in the **accounting** project to use the image, **instance1-snapshot** (created in Question 12). Be sure to not destroy the existing stack and only update the image. After the image has been successfully updated, delete the entire stack.

Question 35

Within the **accounting** project, create another tenant network called **tenant-network2**. It should have a subnet called **tenant-subnet2** with the following details:

- **CIDR**: 192.168.6.0/24
- **DHCP**: Enabled
- **Allocation range**: 192.168.6.50 to 192.168.6.60

After the network and subnet have been created, boot a new instance within the **accounting** project called **instance2** with the **m1.tiny** flavor. It should use the **Cirros** image and should be attached to **tenant-network2**. Once the intance has been booted, use the Horizon dashboard console to ping **instance1** via its fixed IP address. You may need to create a router to allow traffic between **tenant-network1** and **tenant-network2**.

Index

59892598R00185